KISS ME, SATAN!

SKREEEECH!

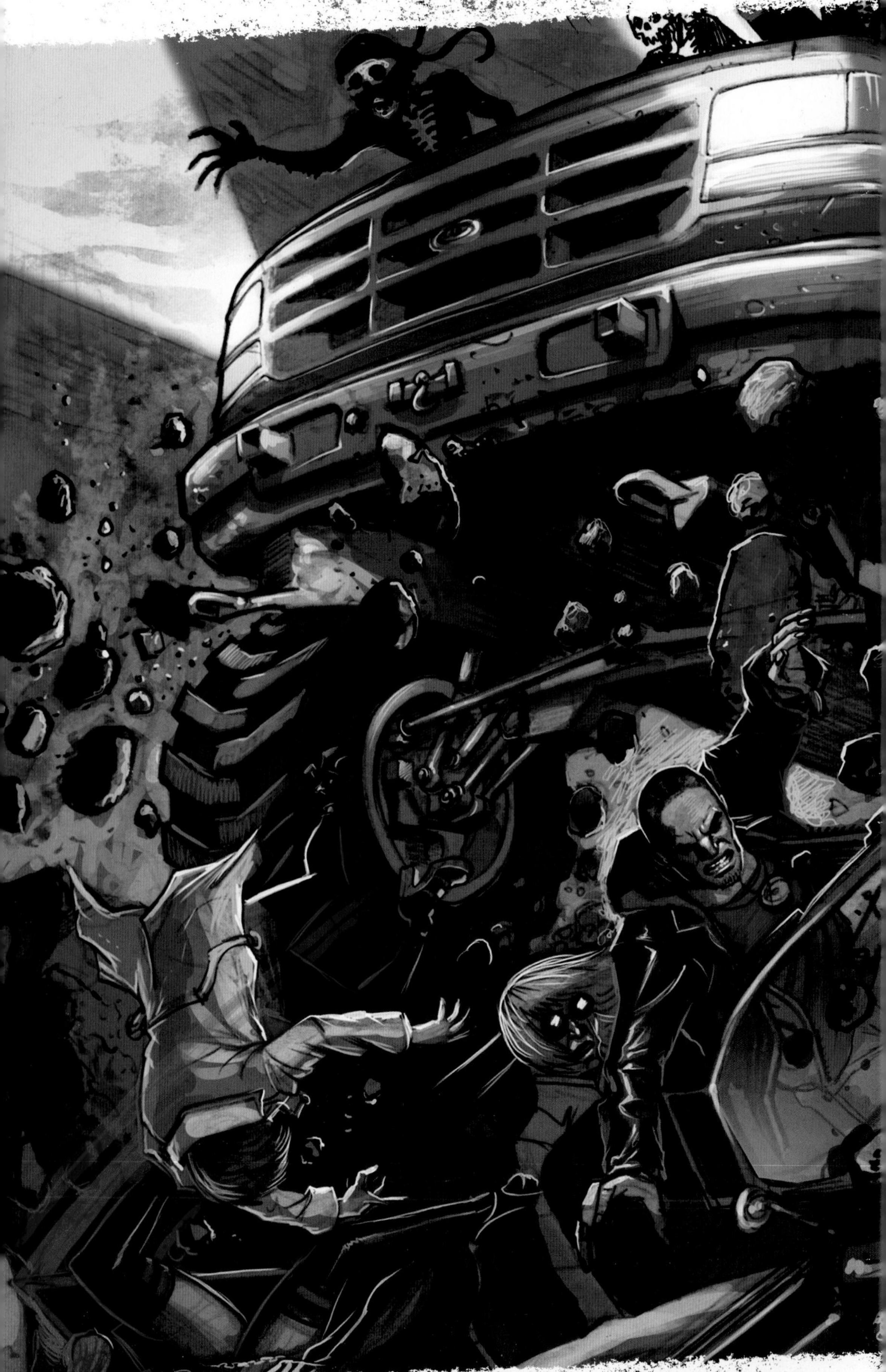

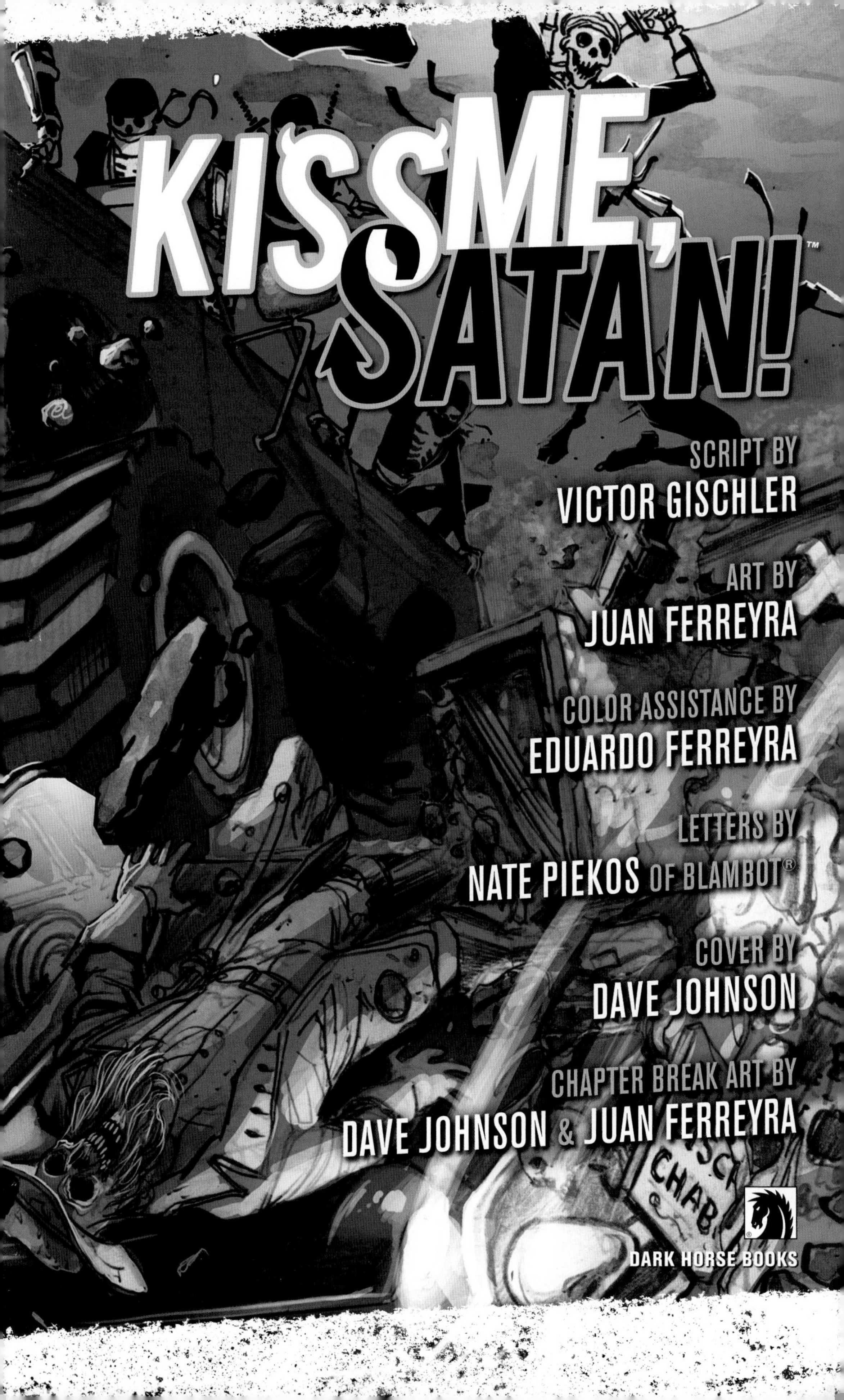

KISS ME, SATAN!™

SCRIPT BY
VICTOR GISCHLER

ART BY
JUAN FERREYRA

COLOR ASSISTANCE BY
EDUARDO FERREYRA

LETTERS BY
NATE PIEKOS OF BLAMBOT®

COVER BY
DAVE JOHNSON

CHAPTER BREAK ART BY
DAVE JOHNSON & JUAN FERREYRA

DARK HORSE BOOKS

EDITOR
DANIEL CHABON

ASSISTANT EDITORS
SHANTEL LaROCQUE & IAN TUCKER

DESIGNER
KEITH WOOD

DIGITAL PRODUCTION
RYAN JORGENSEN

PRESIDENT & PUBLISHER
MIKE RICHARDSON

NEIL HANKERSON EXECUTIVE VICE PRESIDENT • TOM WEDDLE CHIEF FINANCIAL OFFICER • RANDY STRADLEY VICE PRESIDENT OF PUBLISHING
MICHAEL MARTENS VICE PRESIDENT OF BOOK TRADE SALES • ANITA NELSON VICE PRESIDENT OF BUSINESS AFFAIRS
SCOTT ALLIE EDITOR IN CHIEF • MATT PARKINSON VICE PRESIDENT OF MARKETING • DAVID SCROGGY VICE PRESIDENT OF PRODUCT DEVELOPMENT
DALE LaFOUNTAIN VICE PRESIDENT OF INFORMATION TECHNOLOGY • DARLENE VOGEL SENIOR DIRECTOR OF PRINT, DESIGN, AND PRODUCTION
KEN LIZZI GENERAL COUNSEL • DAVEY ESTRADA EDITORIAL DIRECTOR • CHRIS WARNER SENIOR BOOKS EDITOR
DIANA SCHUTZ EXECUTIVE EDITOR • CARY GRAZZINI DIRECTOR OF PRINT AND DEVELOPMENT • LIA RIBACCHI ART DIRECTOR
CARA NIECE DIRECTOR OF SCHEDULING • TIM WIESCH DIRECTOR OF INTERNATIONAL LICENSING • MARK BERNARDI DIRECTOR OF DIGITAL PUBLISHING

THIS VOLUME COLLECTS KISS ME, SATAN! #1–#5.

PUBLISHED BY DARK HORSE BOOKS
A DIVISION OF DARK HORSE COMICS, INC.
10956 SE MAIN STREET
MILWAUKIE, OR 97222

FIRST EDITION: JULY 2014
ISBN 978-1-61655-436-1

10 9 8 7 6 5 4 3 2 1

PRINTED IN CHINA

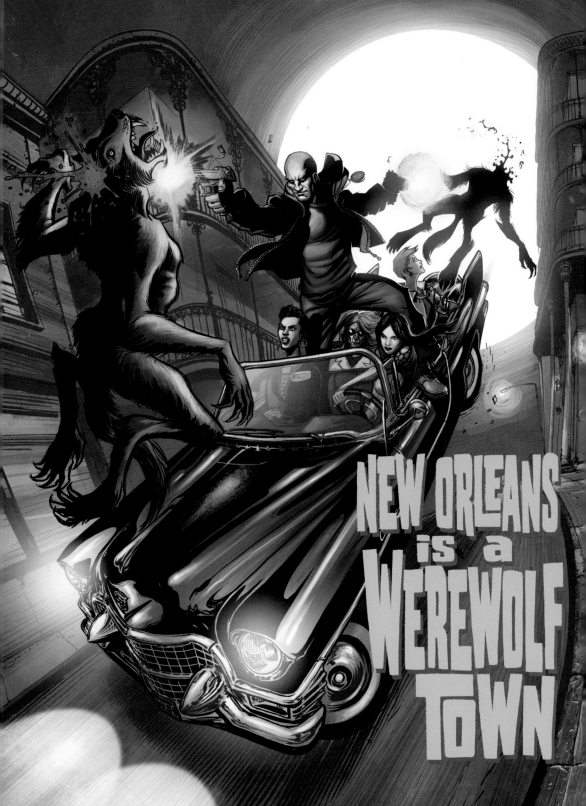

CHAPTER I

NEW ORLEANS is a WEREWOLF TOWN

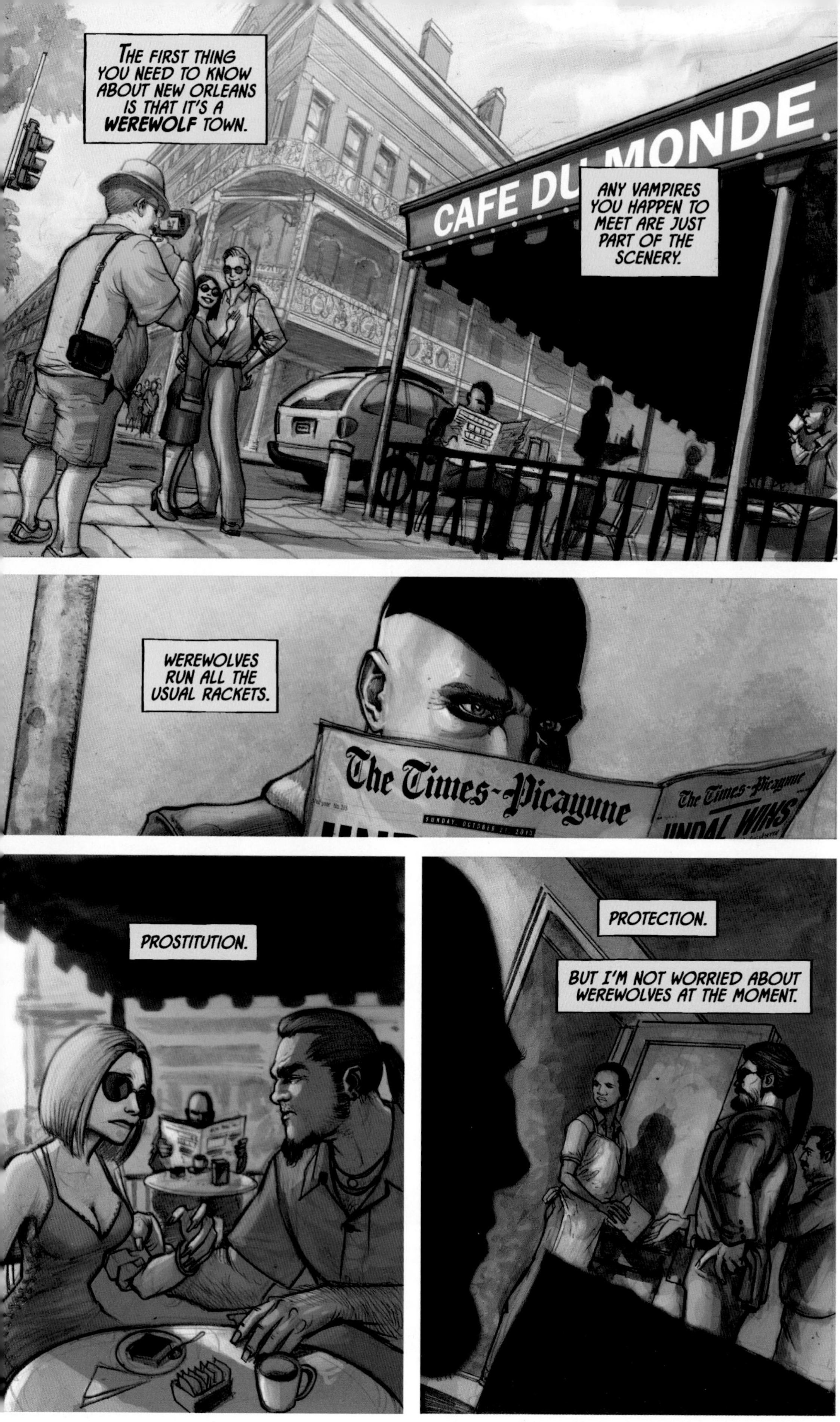
THE FIRST THING YOU NEED TO KNOW ABOUT NEW ORLEANS IS THAT IT'S A WEREWOLF TOWN.
CAFE DU MONDE
ANY VAMPIRES YOU HAPPEN TO MEET ARE JUST PART OF THE SCENERY.
WEREWOLVES RUN ALL THE USUAL RACKETS.
The Times-Picayune
The Times-Picayune
PROSTITUTION.
PROTECTION.
BUT I'M NOT WORRIED ABOUT WEREWOLVES AT THE MOMENT.

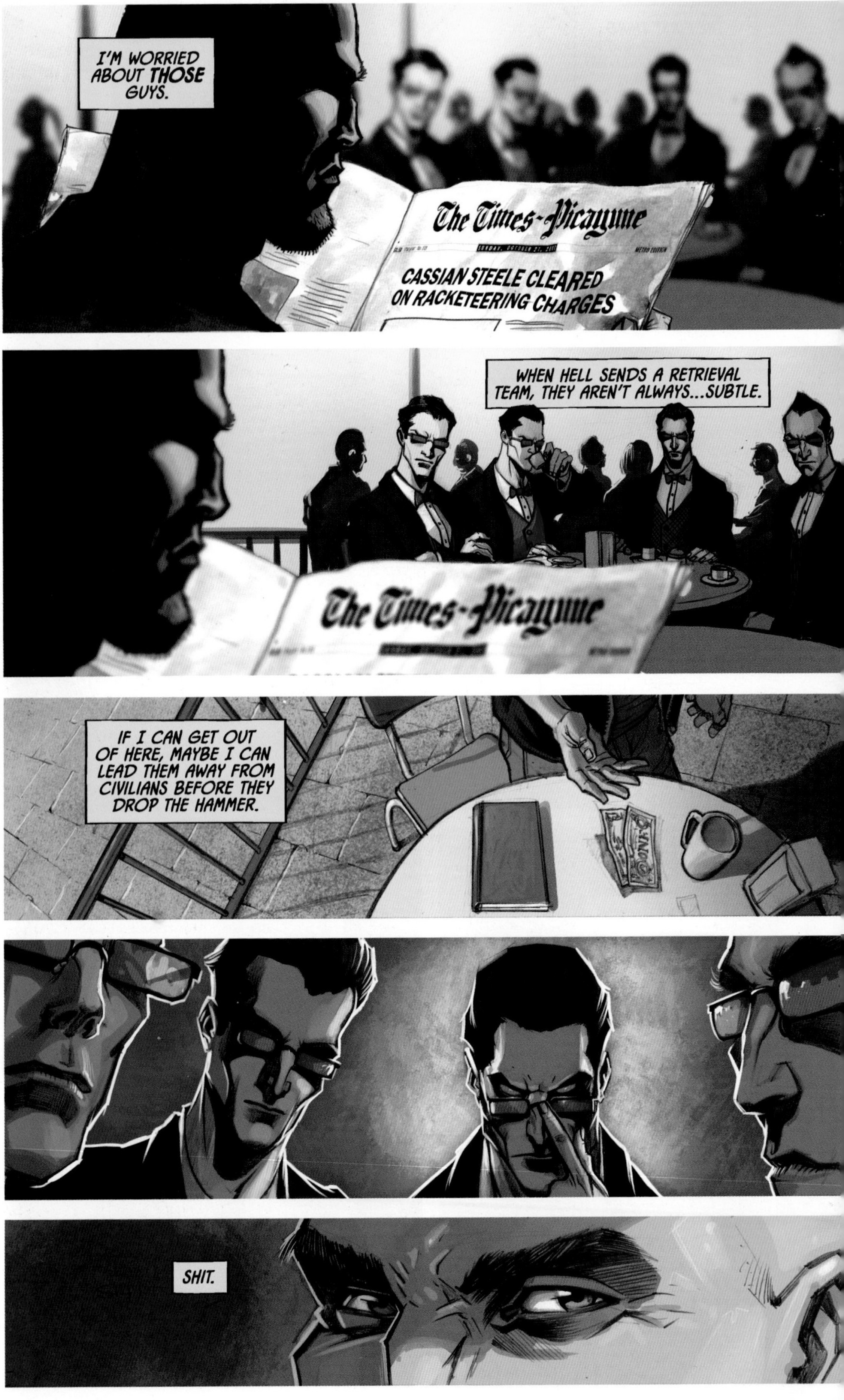
I'M WORRIED ABOUT THOSE GUYS.
The Times-Picayune
CASSIAN STEELE CLEARED ON RACKETEERING CHARGES
WHEN HELL SENDS A RETRIEVAL TEAM, THEY AREN'T ALWAYS...SUBTLE.
The Times-Picayune
IF I CAN GET OUT OF HERE, MAYBE I CAN LEAD THEM AWAY FROM CIVILIANS BEFORE THEY DROP THE HAMMER.
SHIT.

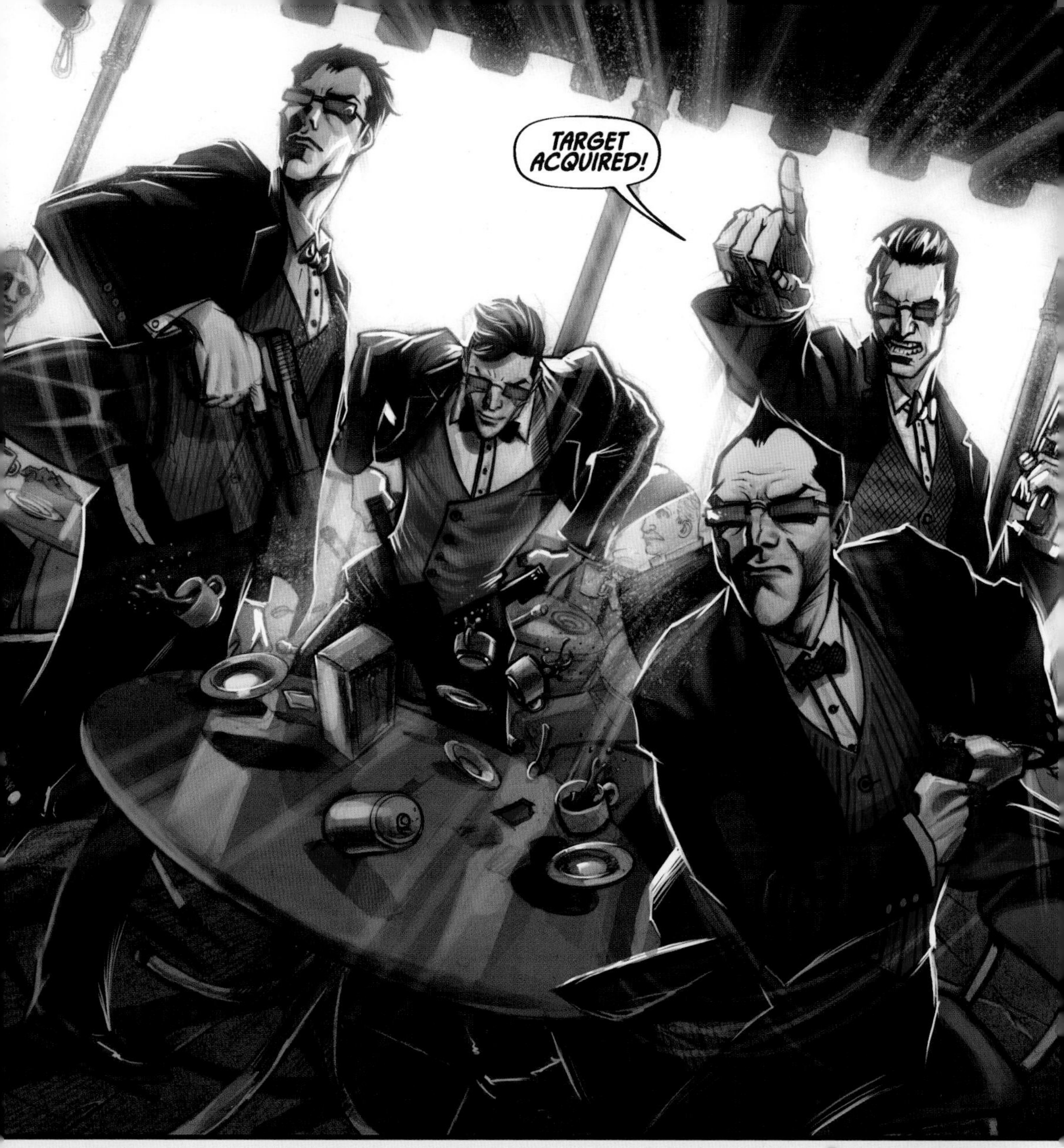
TARGET ACQUIRED!

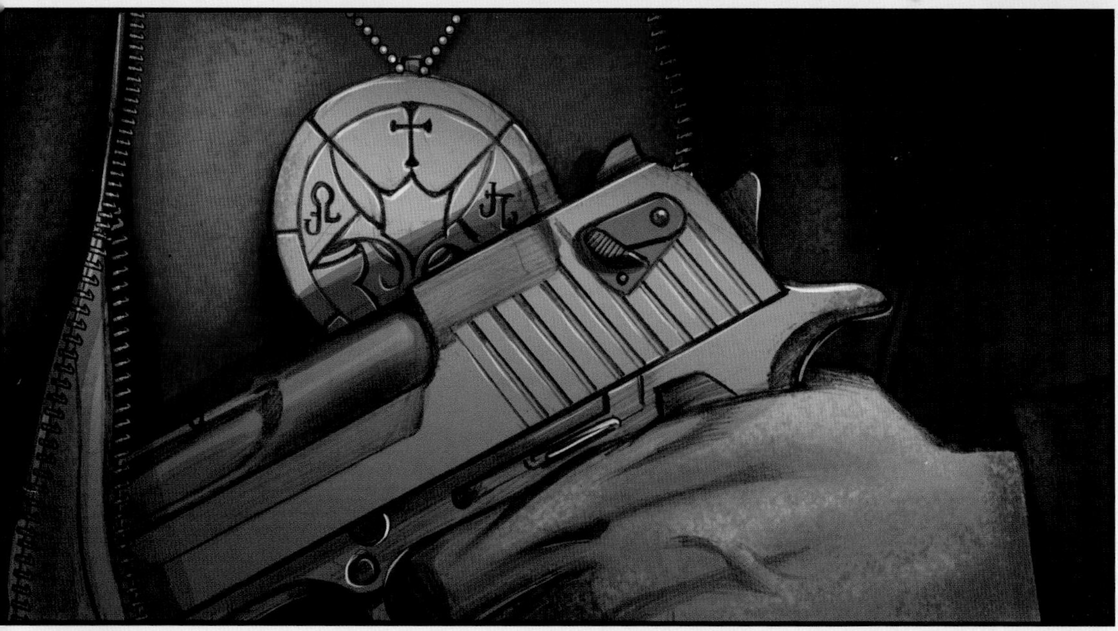

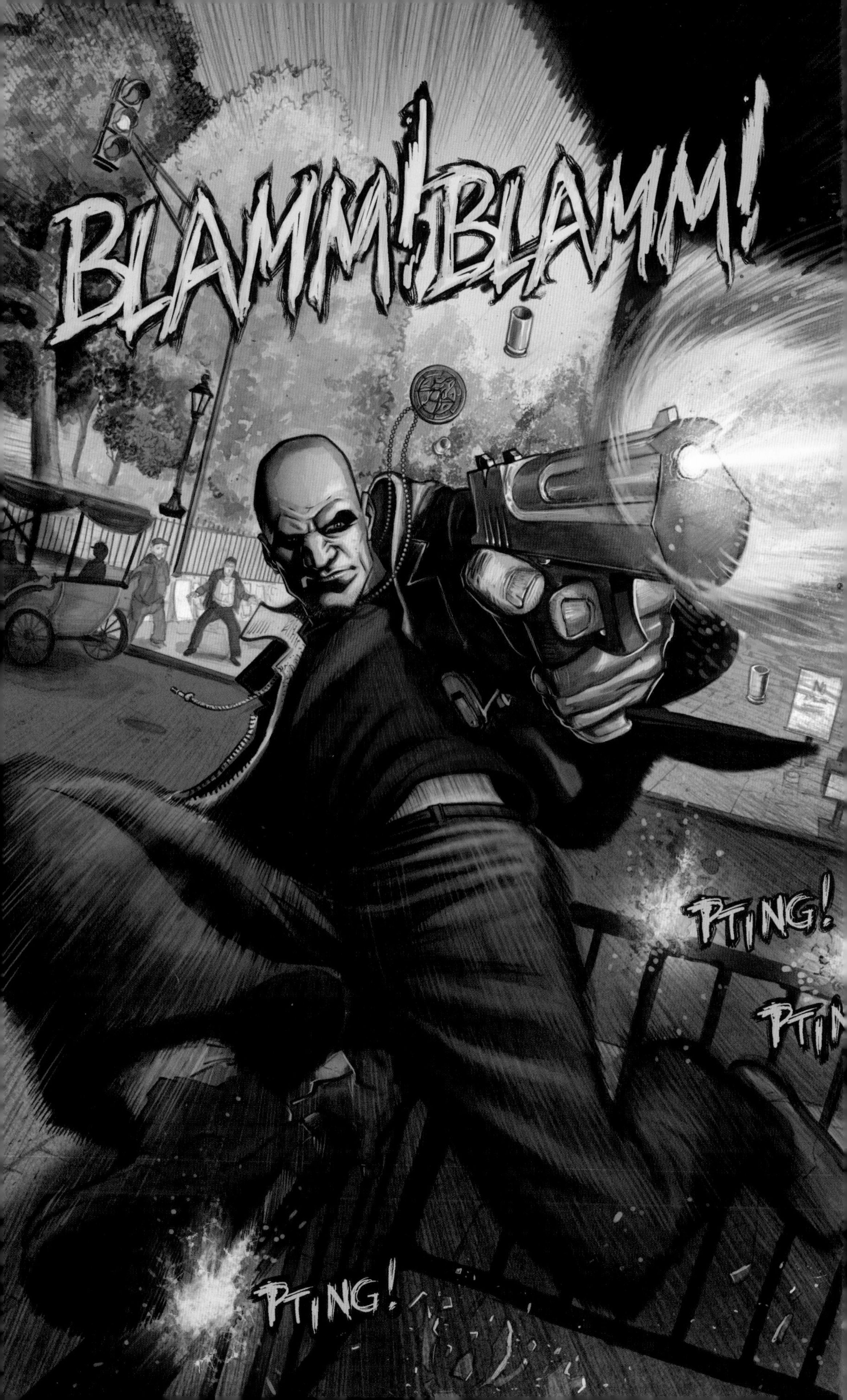
BLAMM! BLAMM!
PTING!
PTING!

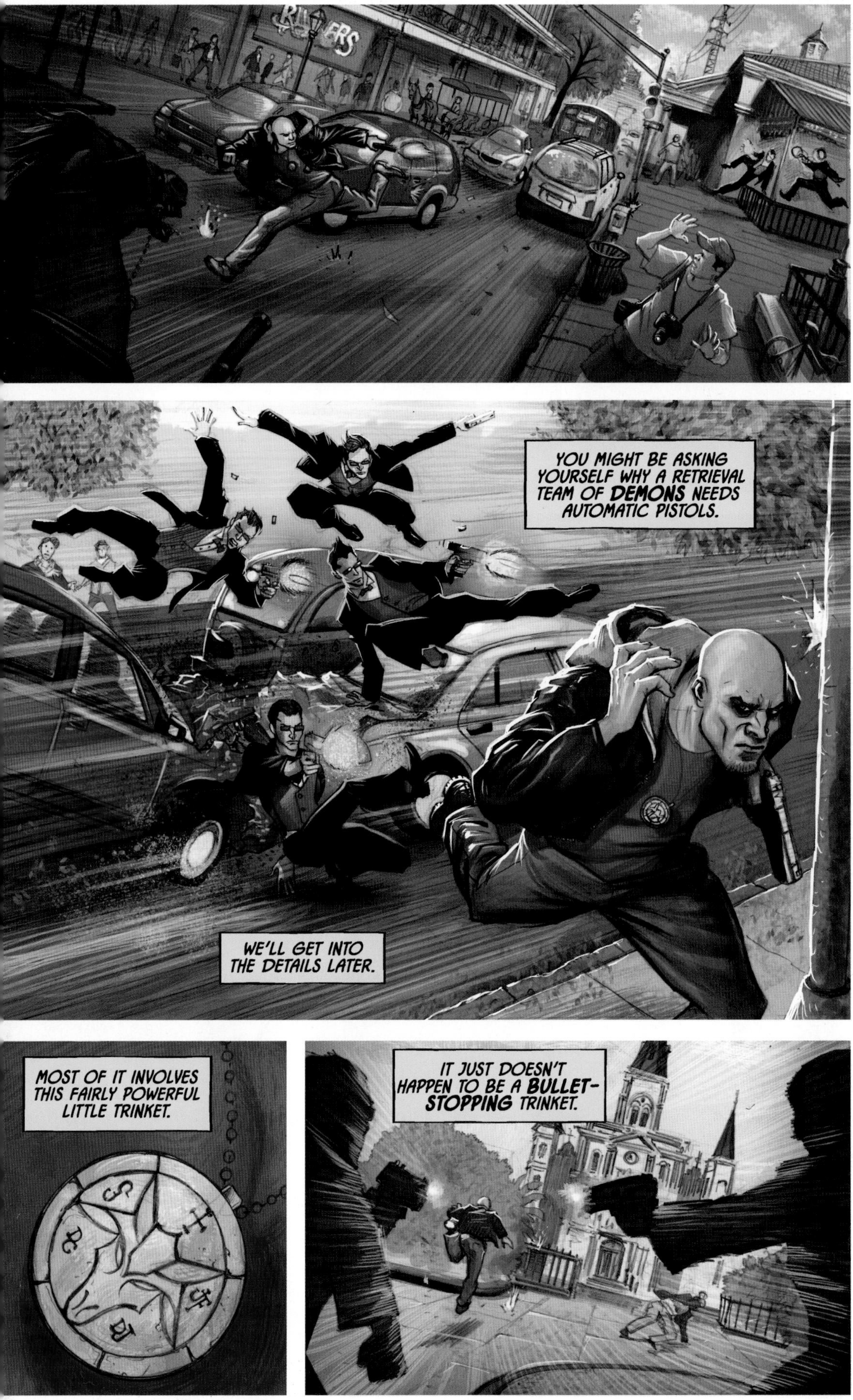
YOU MIGHT BE ASKING YOURSELF WHY A RETRIEVAL TEAM OF DEMONS NEEDS AUTOMATIC PISTOLS.
WE'LL GET INTO THE DETAILS LATER.
MOST OF IT INVOLVES THIS FAIRLY POWERFUL LITTLE TRINKET.
IT JUST DOESN'T HAPPEN TO BE A BULLET-STOPPING TRINKET.

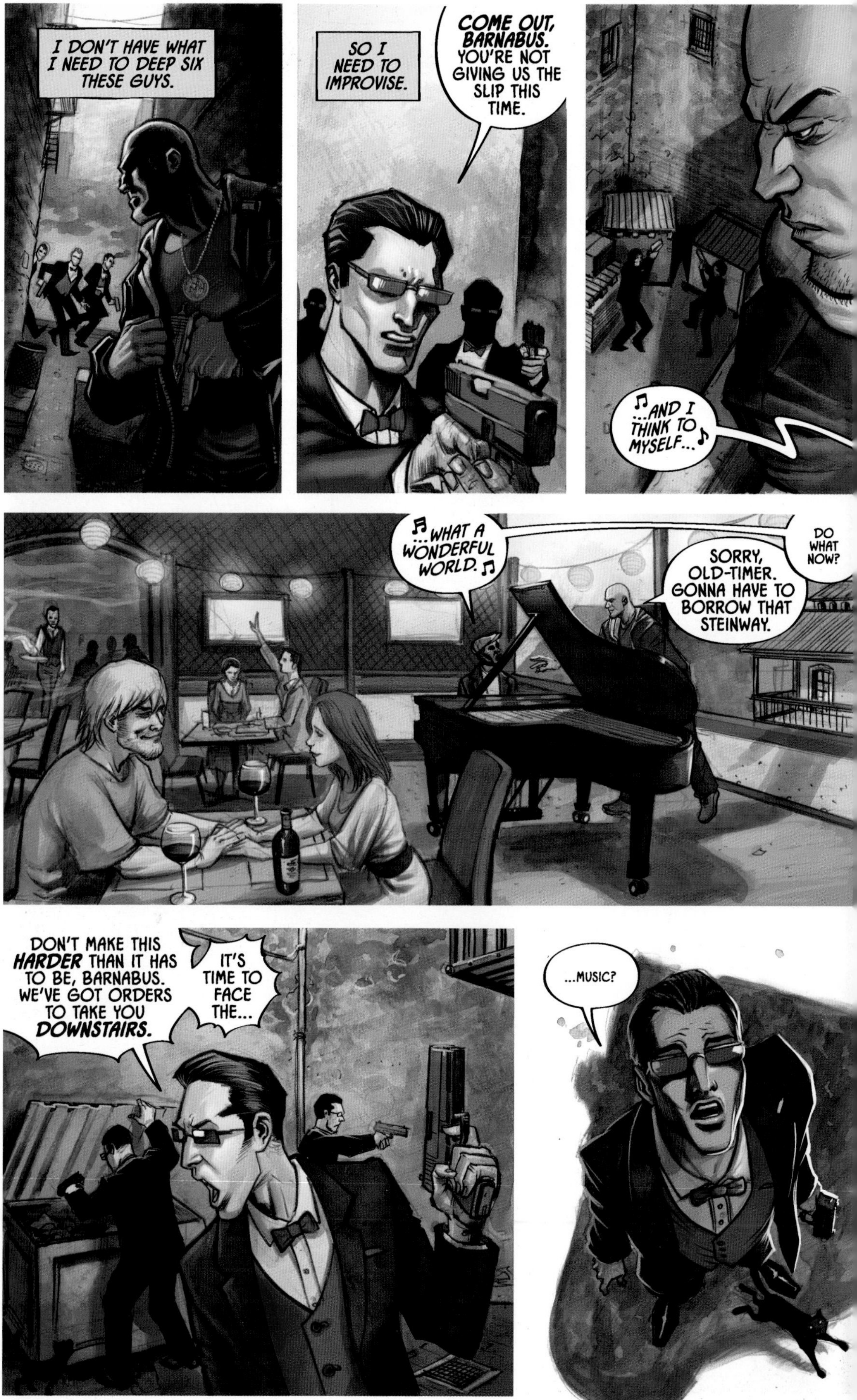
I DON'T HAVE WHAT I NEED TO DEEP SIX THESE GUYS.
SO I NEED TO IMPROVISE.
COME OUT, BARNABUS. YOU'RE NOT GIVING US THE SLIP THIS TIME.
...AND I THINK TO MYSELF...
...WHAT A WONDERFUL WORLD.
SORRY, OLD-TIMER. GONNA HAVE TO BORROW THAT STEINWAY.
DO WHAT NOW?
DON'T MAKE THIS HARDER THAN IT HAS TO BE, BARNABUS. WE'VE GOT ORDERS TO TAKE YOU DOWNSTAIRS.
IT'S TIME TO FACE THE...
...MUSIC?

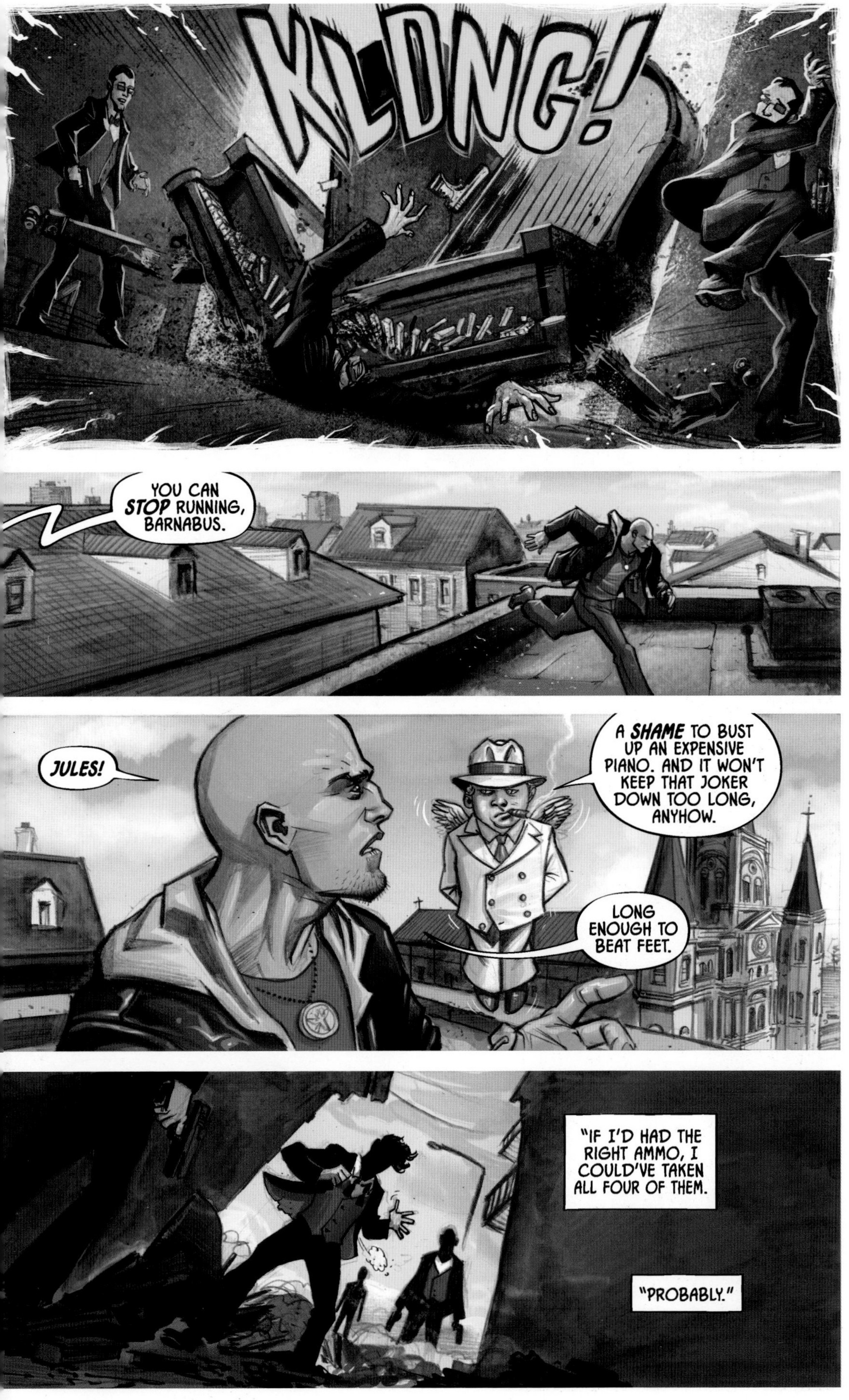

KLONG!
YOU CAN STOP RUNNING, BARNABUS.
JULES!
A SHAME TO BUST UP AN EXPENSIVE PIANO. AND IT WON'T KEEP THAT JOKER DOWN TOO LONG, ANYHOW.
LONG ENOUGH TO BEAT FEET.
"IF I'D HAD THE RIGHT AMMO, I COULD'VE TAKEN ALL FOUR OF THEM.
"PROBABLY."

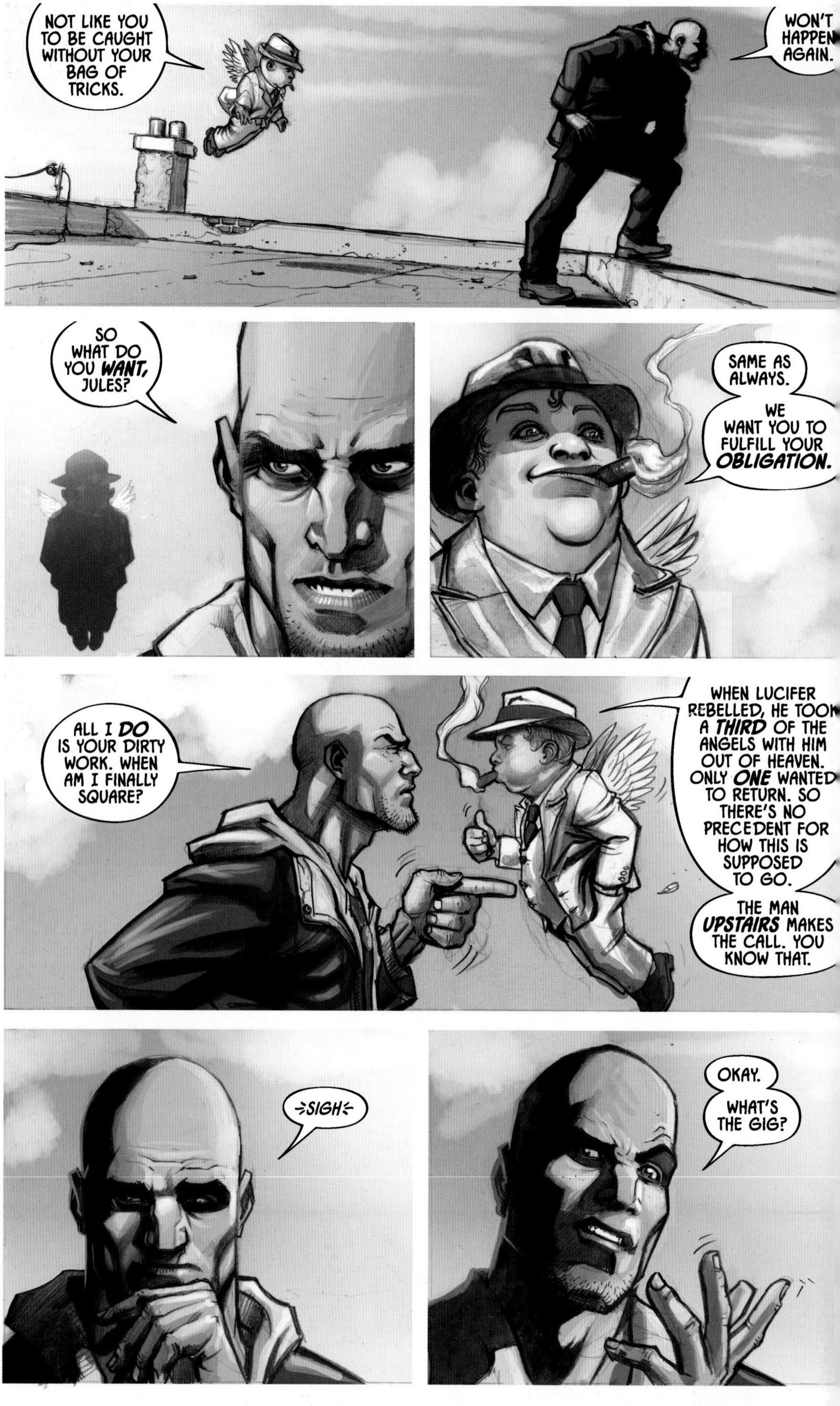
NOT LIKE YOU TO BE CAUGHT WITHOUT YOUR BAG OF TRICKS.
WON'T HAPPEN AGAIN.
SO WHAT DO YOU WANT, JULES?
SAME AS ALWAYS.
WE WANT YOU TO FULFILL YOUR OBLIGATION.
ALL I DO IS YOUR DIRTY WORK. WHEN AM I FINALLY SQUARE?
WHEN LUCIFER REBELLED, HE TOOK A THIRD OF THE ANGELS WITH HIM OUT OF HEAVEN. ONLY ONE WANTED TO RETURN. SO THERE'S NO PRECEDENT FOR HOW THIS IS SUPPOSED TO GO.
THE MAN UPSTAIRS MAKES THE CALL. YOU KNOW THAT.
SIGH
OKAY.
WHAT'S THE GIG?

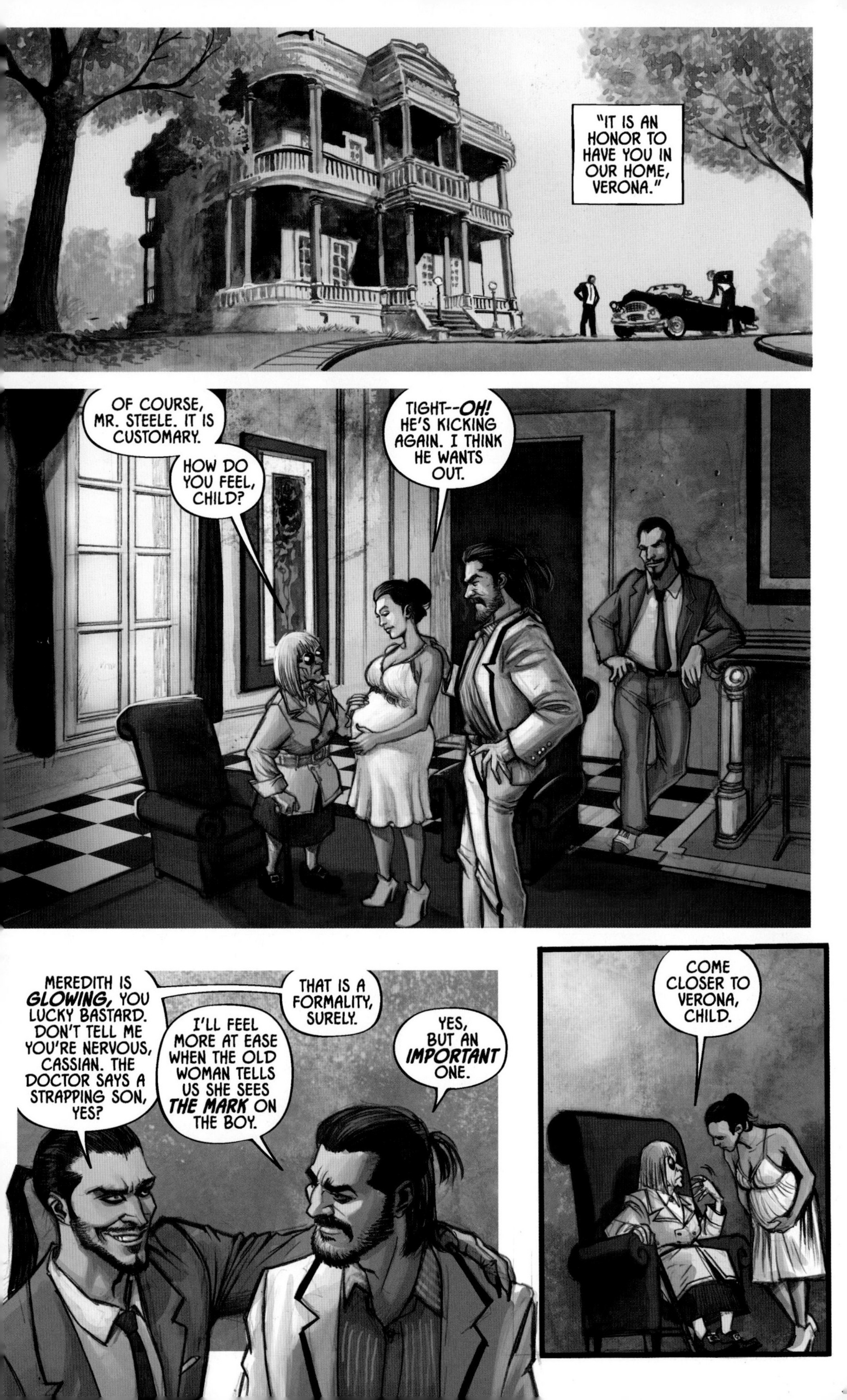
"IT IS AN HONOR TO HAVE YOU IN OUR HOME, VERONA."
OF COURSE, MR. STEELE. IT IS CUSTOMARY.
HOW DO YOU FEEL, CHILD?
TIGHT--OH! HE'S KICKING AGAIN. I THINK HE WANTS OUT.
MEREDITH IS GLOWING, YOU LUCKY BASTARD. DON'T TELL ME YOU'RE NERVOUS, CASSIAN. THE DOCTOR SAYS A STRAPPING SON, YES?
I'LL FEEL MORE AT EASE WHEN THE OLD WOMAN TELLS US SHE SEES THE MARK ON THE BOY.
THAT IS A FORMALITY, SURELY.
YES, BUT AN IMPORTANT ONE.
COME CLOSER TO VERONA, CHILD.

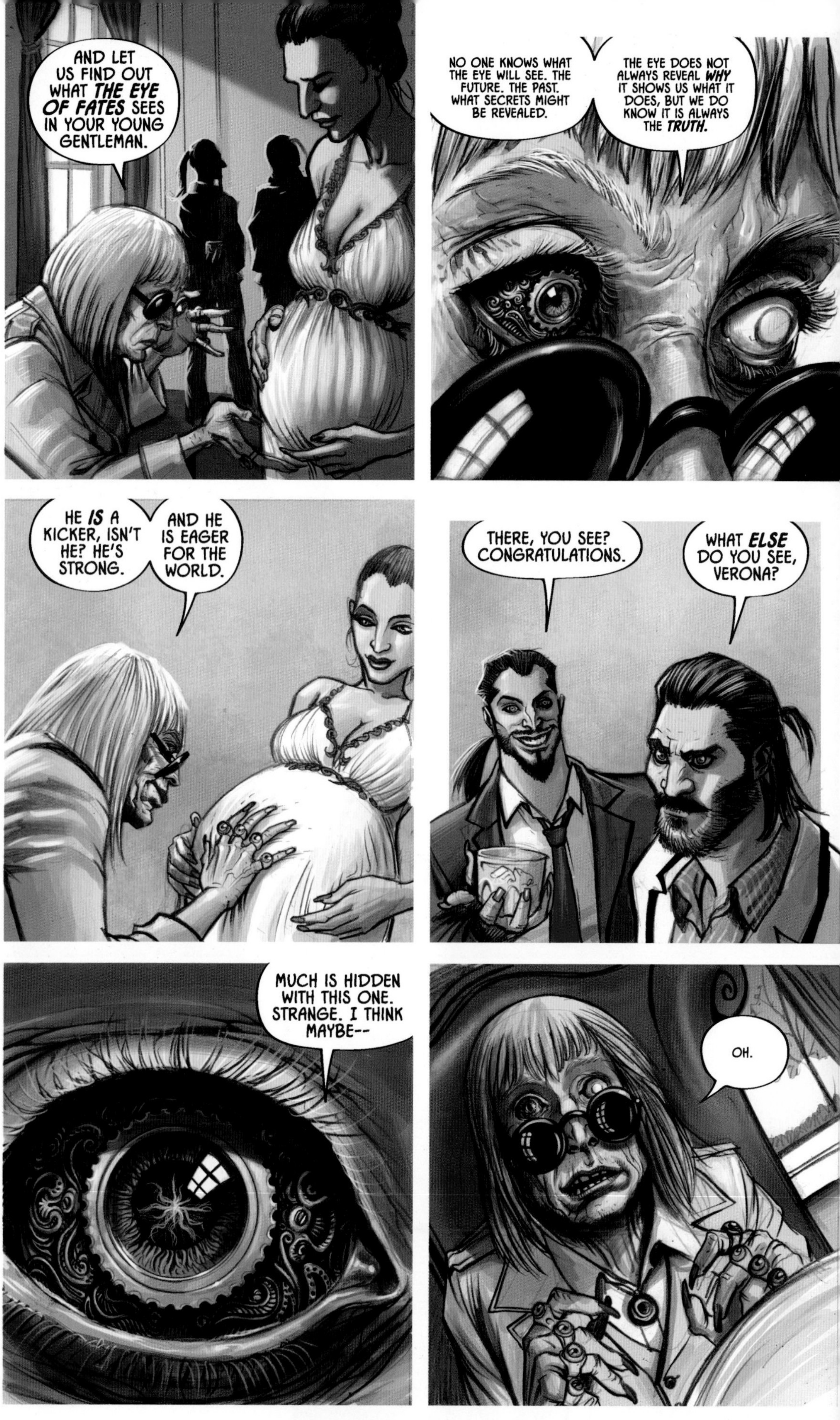
AND LET US FIND OUT WHAT THE EYE OF FATES SEES IN YOUR YOUNG GENTLEMAN.
NO ONE KNOWS WHAT THE EYE WILL SEE. THE FUTURE. THE PAST. WHAT SECRETS MIGHT BE REVEALED.
THE EYE DOES NOT ALWAYS REVEAL WHY IT SHOWS US WHAT IT DOES, BUT WE DO KNOW IT IS ALWAYS THE TRUTH.
HE IS A KICKER, ISN'T HE? HE'S STRONG.
AND HE IS EAGER FOR THE WORLD.
THERE, YOU SEE? CONGRATULATIONS.
WHAT ELSE DO YOU SEE, VERONA?
MUCH IS HIDDEN WITH THIS ONE. STRANGE. I THINK MAYBE--
OH.

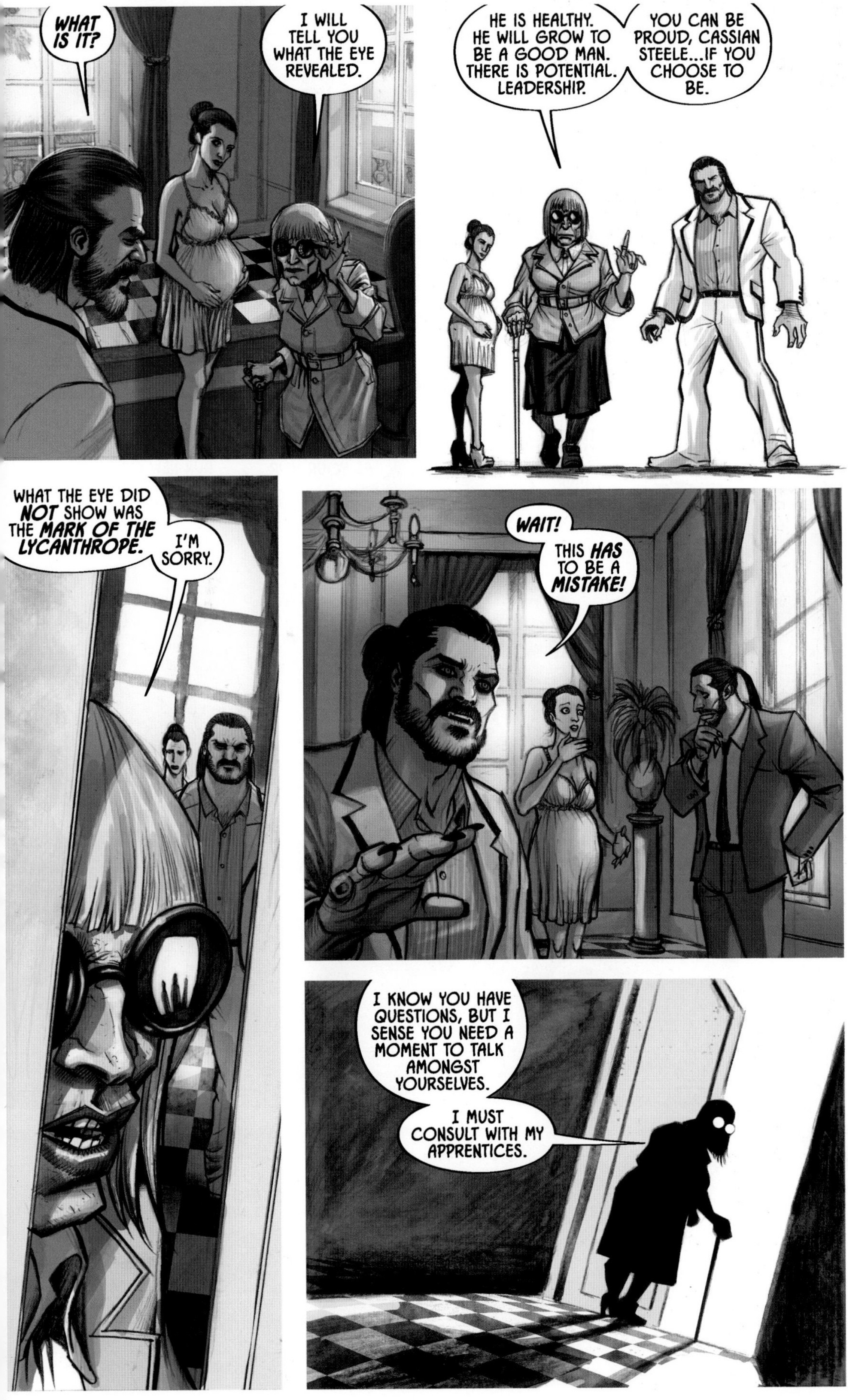
WHAT IS IT?
I WILL TELL YOU WHAT THE EYE REVEALED.
HE IS HEALTHY. HE WILL GROW TO BE A GOOD MAN. THERE IS POTENTIAL. LEADERSHIP.
YOU CAN BE PROUD, CASSIAN STEELE...IF YOU CHOOSE TO BE.
WHAT THE EYE DID NOT SHOW WAS THE MARK OF THE LYCANTHROPE.
I'M SORRY.
WAIT!
THIS HAS TO BE A MISTAKE!
I KNOW YOU HAVE QUESTIONS, BUT I SENSE YOU NEED A MOMENT TO TALK AMONGST YOURSELVES.
I MUST CONSULT WITH MY APPRENTICES.

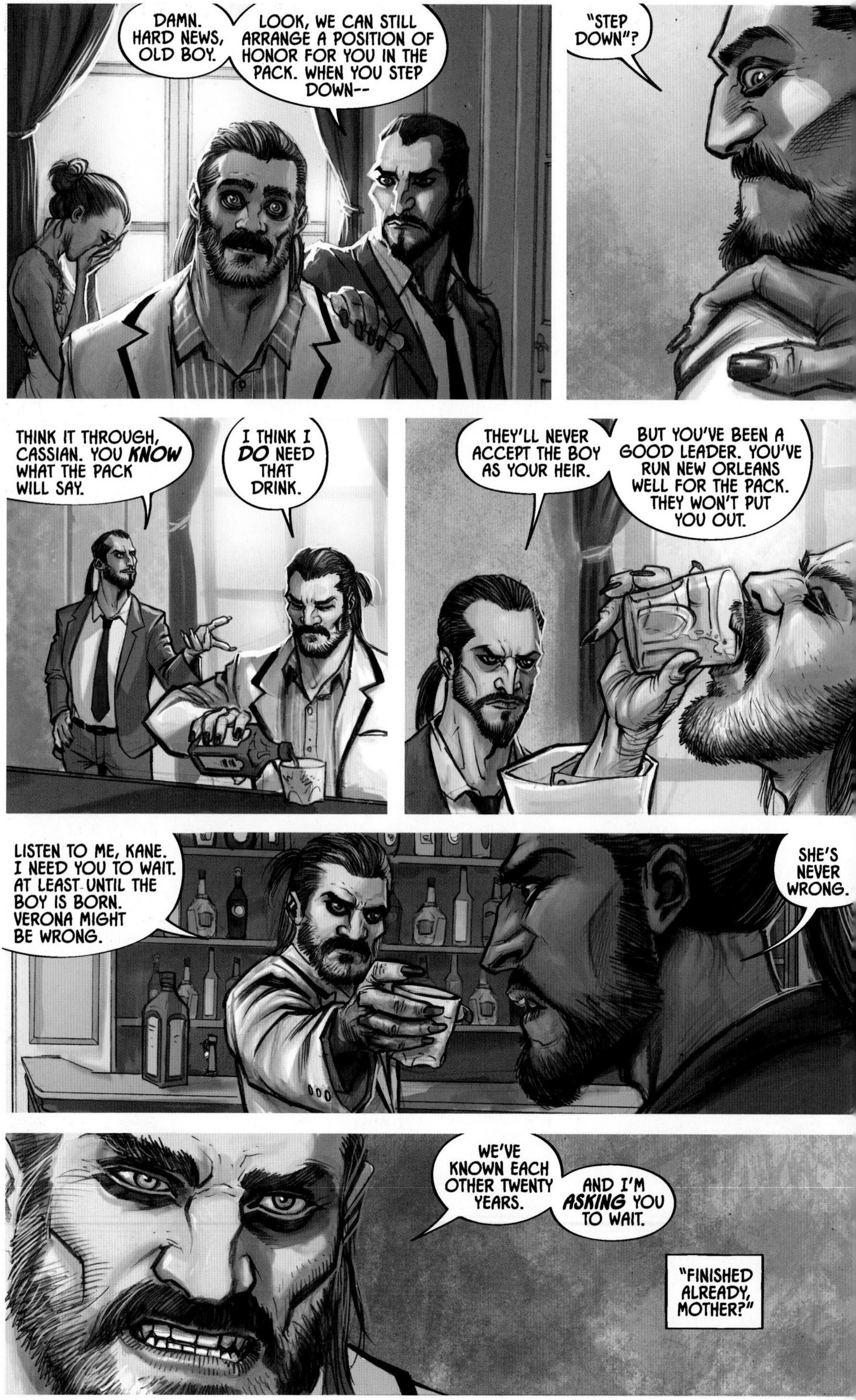
DAMN. HARD NEWS, OLD BOY.
LOOK, WE CAN STILL ARRANGE A POSITION OF HONOR FOR YOU IN THE PACK. WHEN YOU STEP DOWN--
"STEP DOWN"?
THINK IT THROUGH, CASSIAN. YOU KNOW WHAT THE PACK WILL SAY.
I THINK I DO NEED THAT DRINK.
THEY'LL NEVER ACCEPT THE BOY AS YOUR HEIR.
BUT YOU'VE BEEN A GOOD LEADER. YOU'VE RUN NEW ORLEANS WELL FOR THE PACK. THEY WON'T PUT YOU OUT.
LISTEN TO ME, KANE. I NEED YOU TO WAIT. AT LEAST UNTIL THE BOY IS BORN. VERONA MIGHT BE WRONG.
SHE'S NEVER WRONG.
WE'VE KNOWN EACH OTHER TWENTY YEARS.
AND I'M ASKING YOU TO WAIT.
"FINISHED ALREADY, MOTHER?"

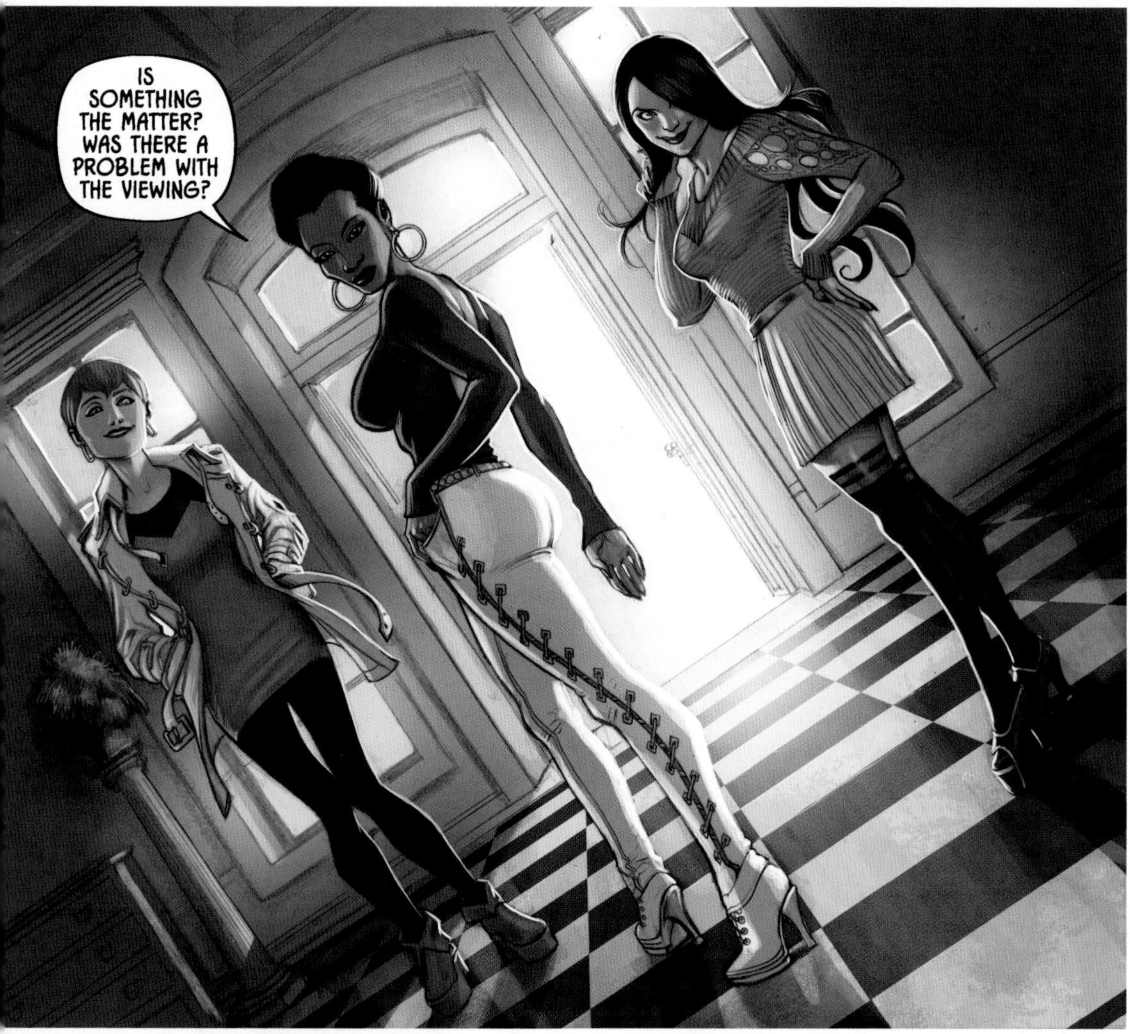
IS SOMETHING THE MATTER? WAS THERE A PROBLEM WITH THE VIEWING?

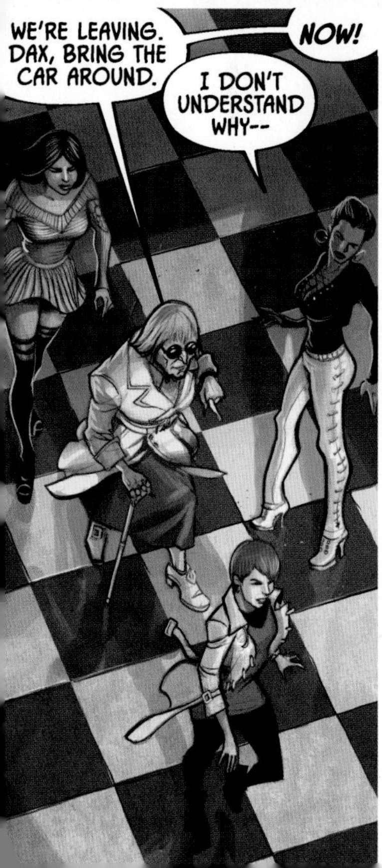
WE'RE LEAVING. DAX, BRING THE CAR AROUND.
NOW!
I DON'T UNDERSTAND WHY--

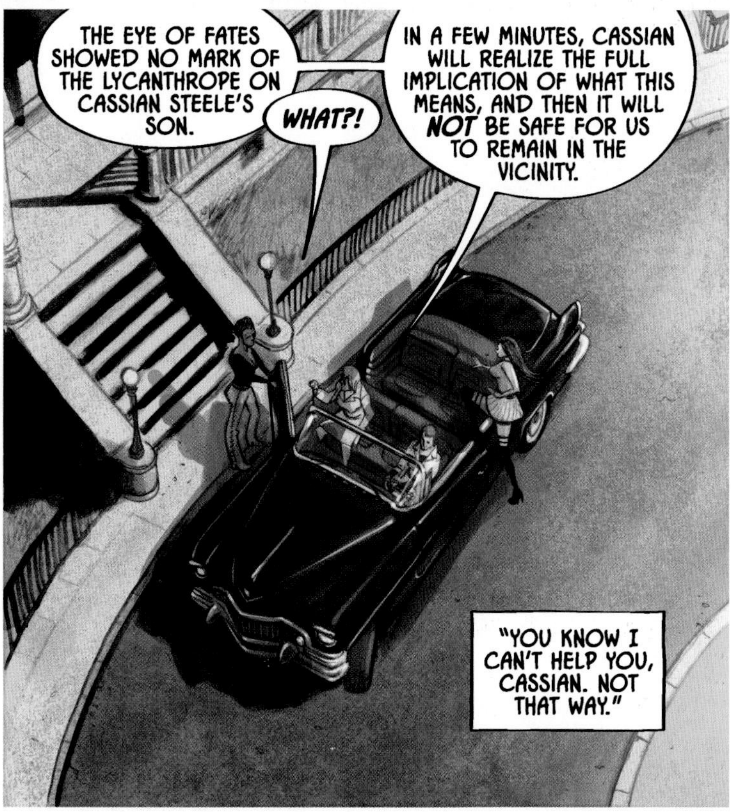
THE EYE OF FATES SHOWED NO MARK OF THE LYCANTHROPE ON CASSIAN STEELE'S SON.
WHAT?!
IN A FEW MINUTES, CASSIAN WILL REALIZE THE FULL IMPLICATION OF WHAT THIS MEANS, AND THEN IT WILL *NOT* BE SAFE FOR US TO REMAIN IN THE VICINITY.
"YOU KNOW I CAN'T HELP YOU, CASSIAN. NOT THAT WAY."

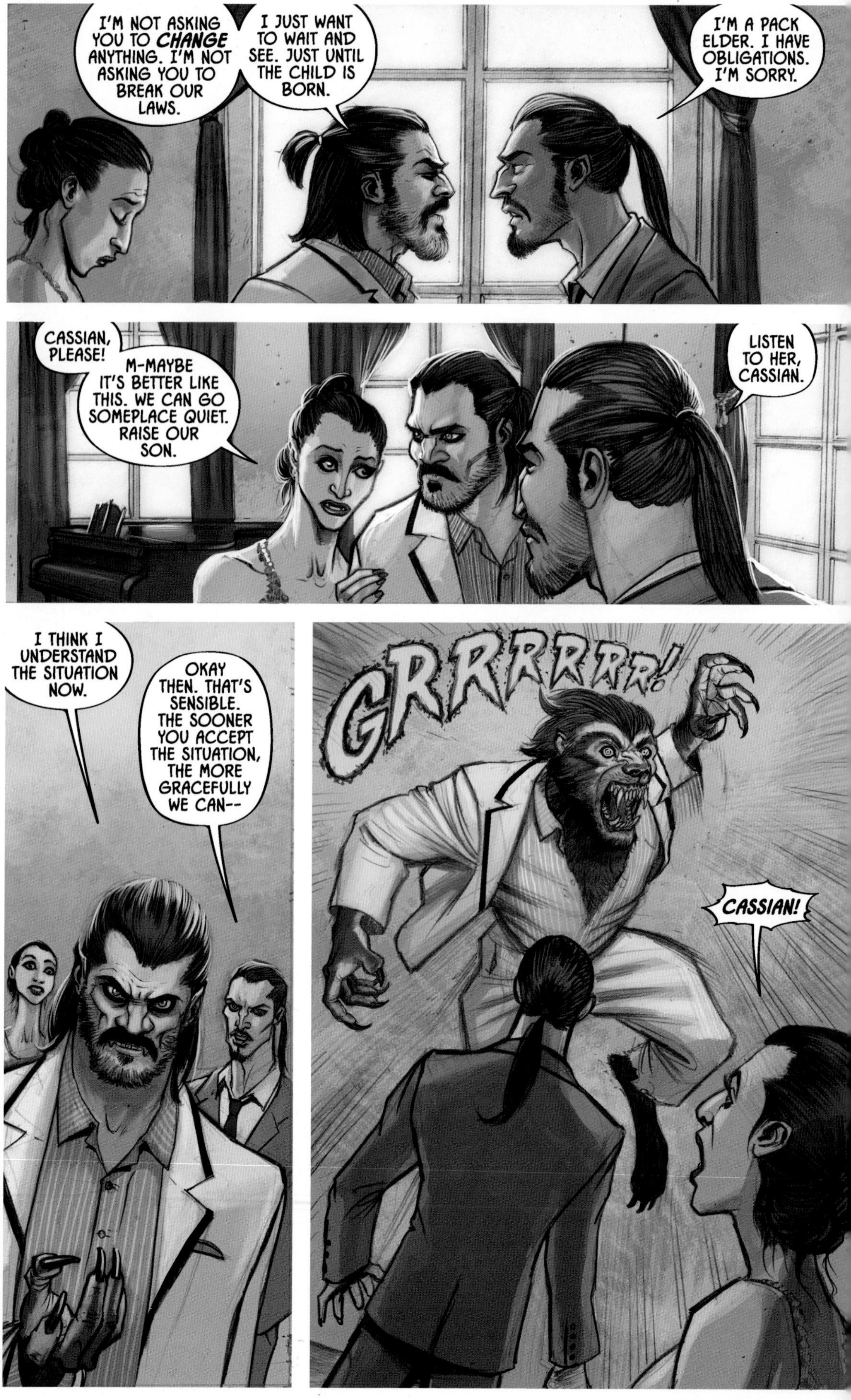
I'M NOT ASKING YOU TO *CHANGE* ANYTHING. I'M NOT ASKING YOU TO BREAK OUR LAWS.
I JUST WANT TO WAIT AND SEE. JUST UNTIL THE CHILD IS BORN.
I'M A PACK ELDER. I HAVE OBLIGATIONS. I'M SORRY.
CASSIAN, PLEASE!
M-MAYBE IT'S BETTER LIKE THIS. WE CAN GO SOMEPLACE QUIET. RAISE OUR SON.
LISTEN TO HER, CASSIAN.
I THINK I UNDERSTAND THE SITUATION NOW.
OKAY THEN. THAT'S SENSIBLE. THE SOONER YOU ACCEPT THE SITUATION, THE MORE GRACEFULLY WE CAN--
GRRRRRR!
CASSIAN!

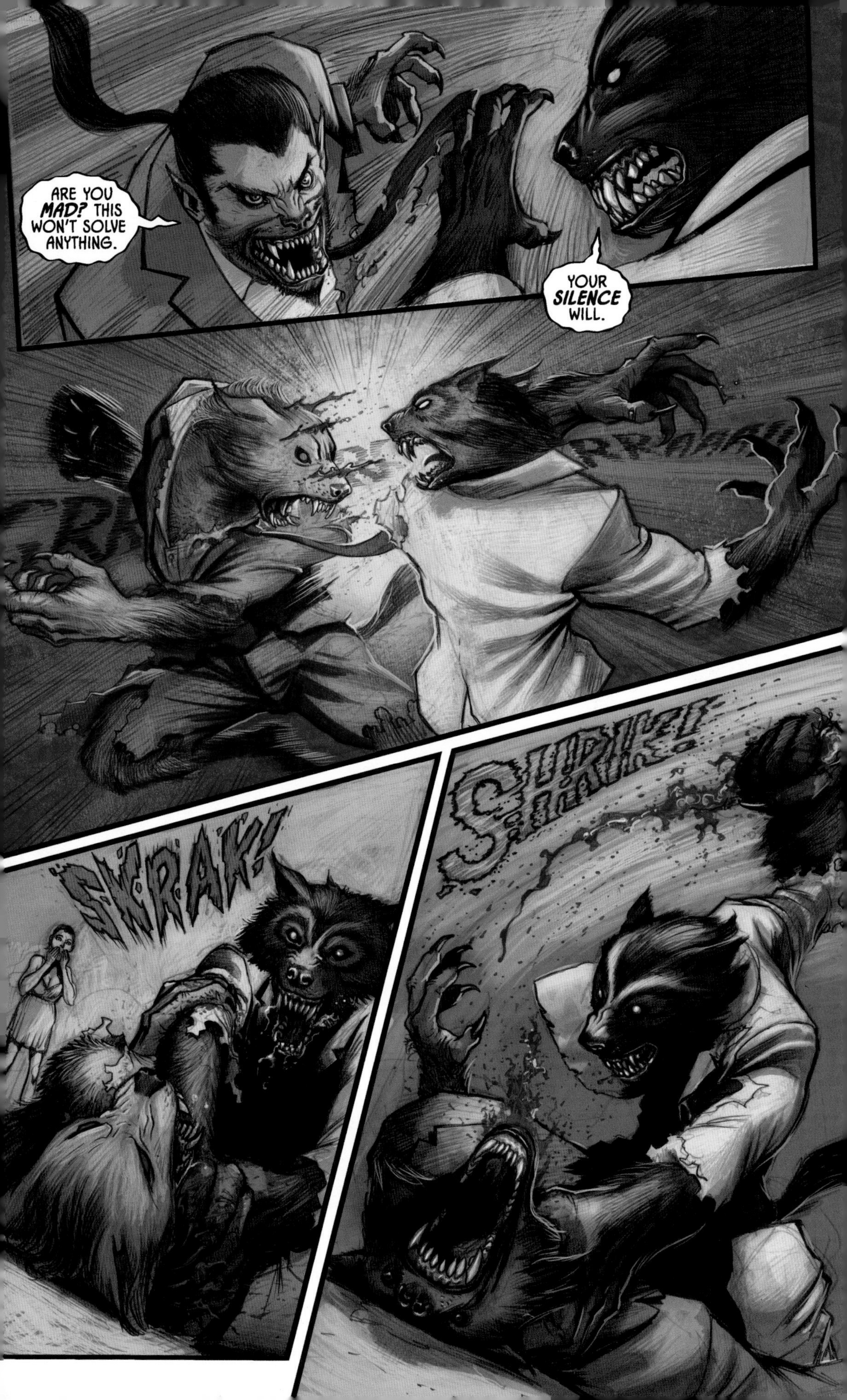
ARE YOU *MAD?* THIS WON'T SOLVE ANYTHING.
YOUR *SILENCE* WILL.
SHRAK!
SHRIK!

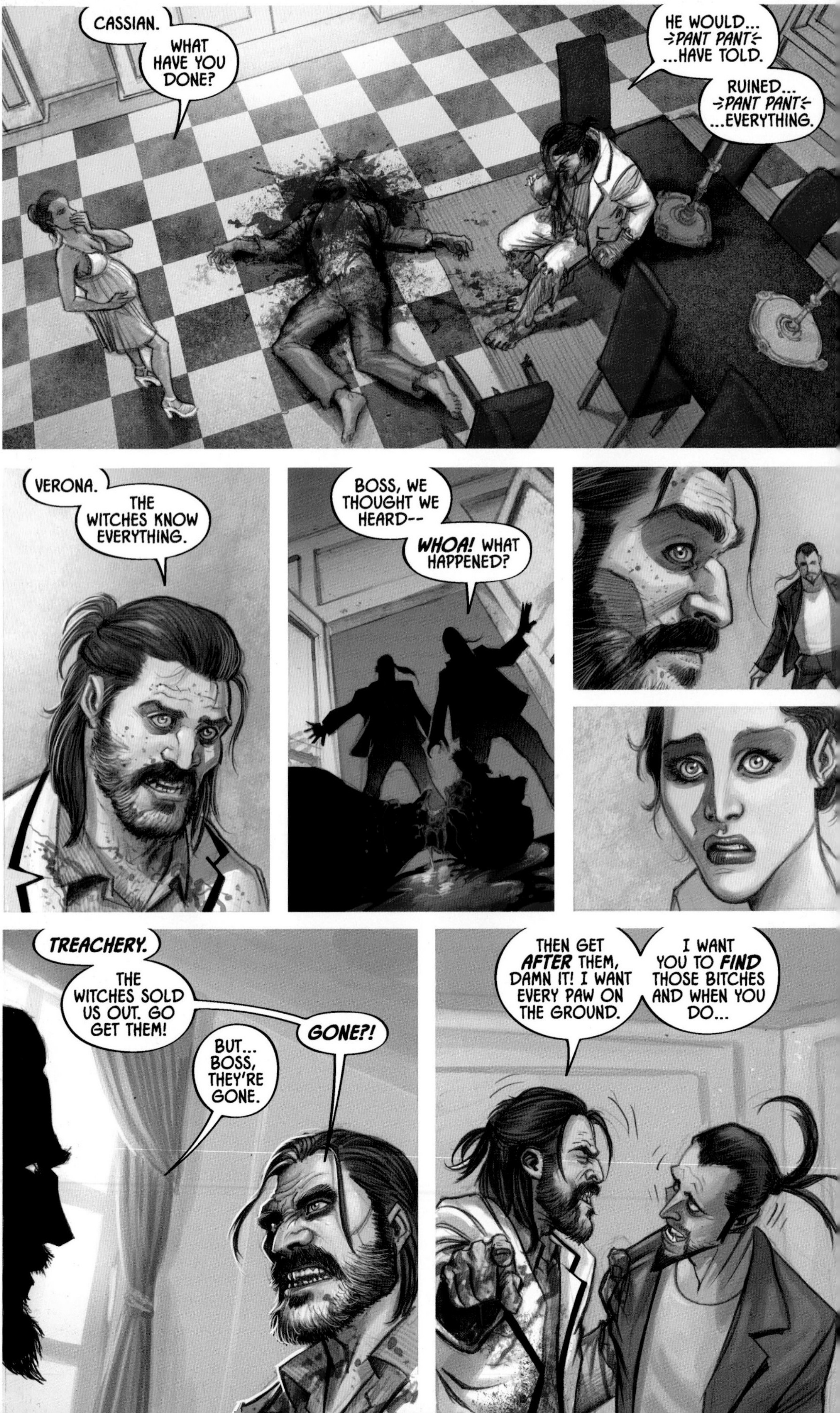
CASSIAN.
WHAT HAVE YOU DONE?
HE WOULD... ⇒PANT PANT⇐ ...HAVE TOLD.
RUINED... ⇒PANT PANT⇐ ...EVERYTHING.
VERONA.
THE WITCHES KNOW EVERYTHING.
BOSS, WE THOUGHT WE HEARD--
WHOA! WHAT HAPPENED?
TREACHERY.
THE WITCHES SOLD US OUT. GO GET THEM!
BUT... BOSS, THEY'RE GONE.
GONE?!
THEN GET AFTER THEM, DAMN IT! I WANT EVERY PAW ON THE GROUND.
I WANT YOU TO FIND THOSE BITCHES AND WHEN YOU DO...

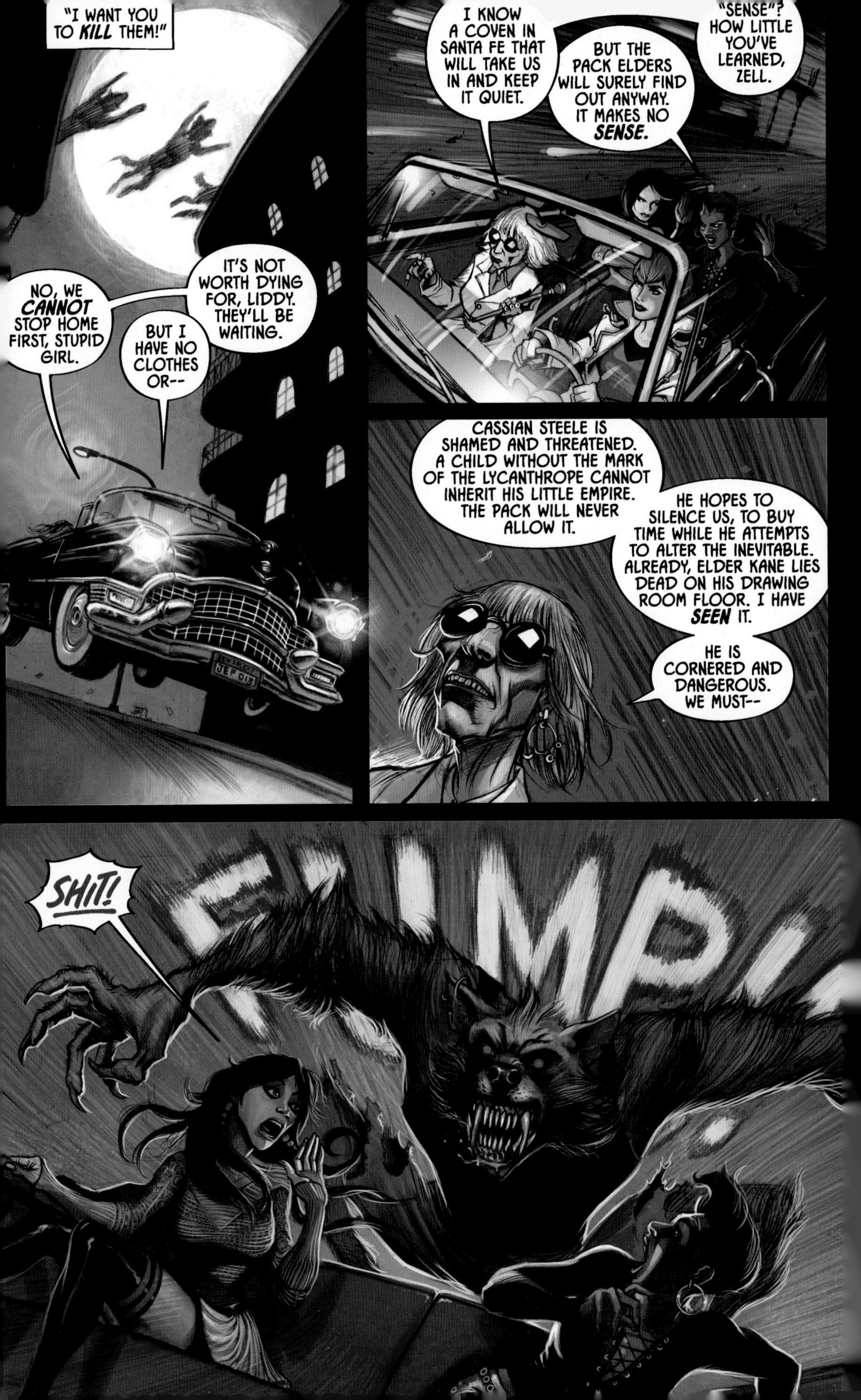
"I WANT YOU TO KILL THEM!"
I KNOW A COVEN IN SANTA FE THAT WILL TAKE US IN AND KEEP IT QUIET.
BUT THE PACK ELDERS WILL SURELY FIND OUT ANYWAY. IT MAKES NO SENSE.
"SENSE"? HOW LITTLE YOU'VE LEARNED, ZELL.
NO, WE CANNOT STOP HOME FIRST, STUPID GIRL.
IT'S NOT WORTH DYING FOR, LIDDY. THEY'LL BE WAITING.
BUT I HAVE NO CLOTHES OR--
CASSIAN STEELE IS SHAMED AND THREATENED. A CHILD WITHOUT THE MARK OF THE LYCANTHROPE CANNOT INHERIT HIS LITTLE EMPIRE. THE PACK WILL NEVER ALLOW IT.
HE HOPES TO SILENCE US, TO BUY TIME WHILE HE ATTEMPTS TO ALTER THE INEVITABLE. ALREADY, ELDER KANE LIES DEAD ON HIS DRAWING ROOM FLOOR. I HAVE SEEN IT.
HE IS CORNERED AND DANGEROUS. WE MUST--
SHIT!
FUMP

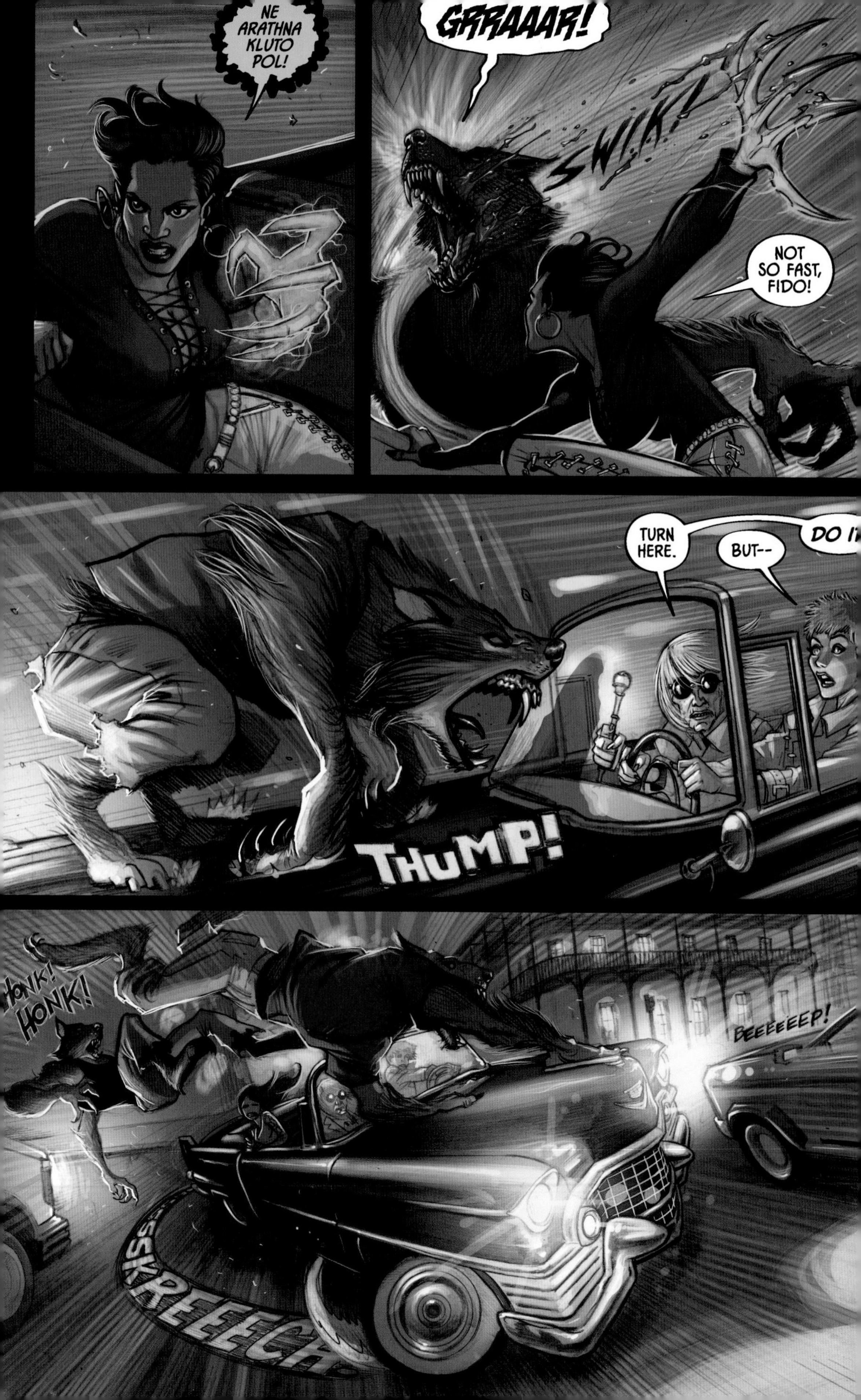
NE ARATHNA KLUTO POL!
GRRAAAR!
SWIK!
NOT SO FAST, FIDO!
TURN HERE.
BUT--
DO IT
THUMP!
HONK! HONK!
BEEEEEEP!
SSKREEEECH

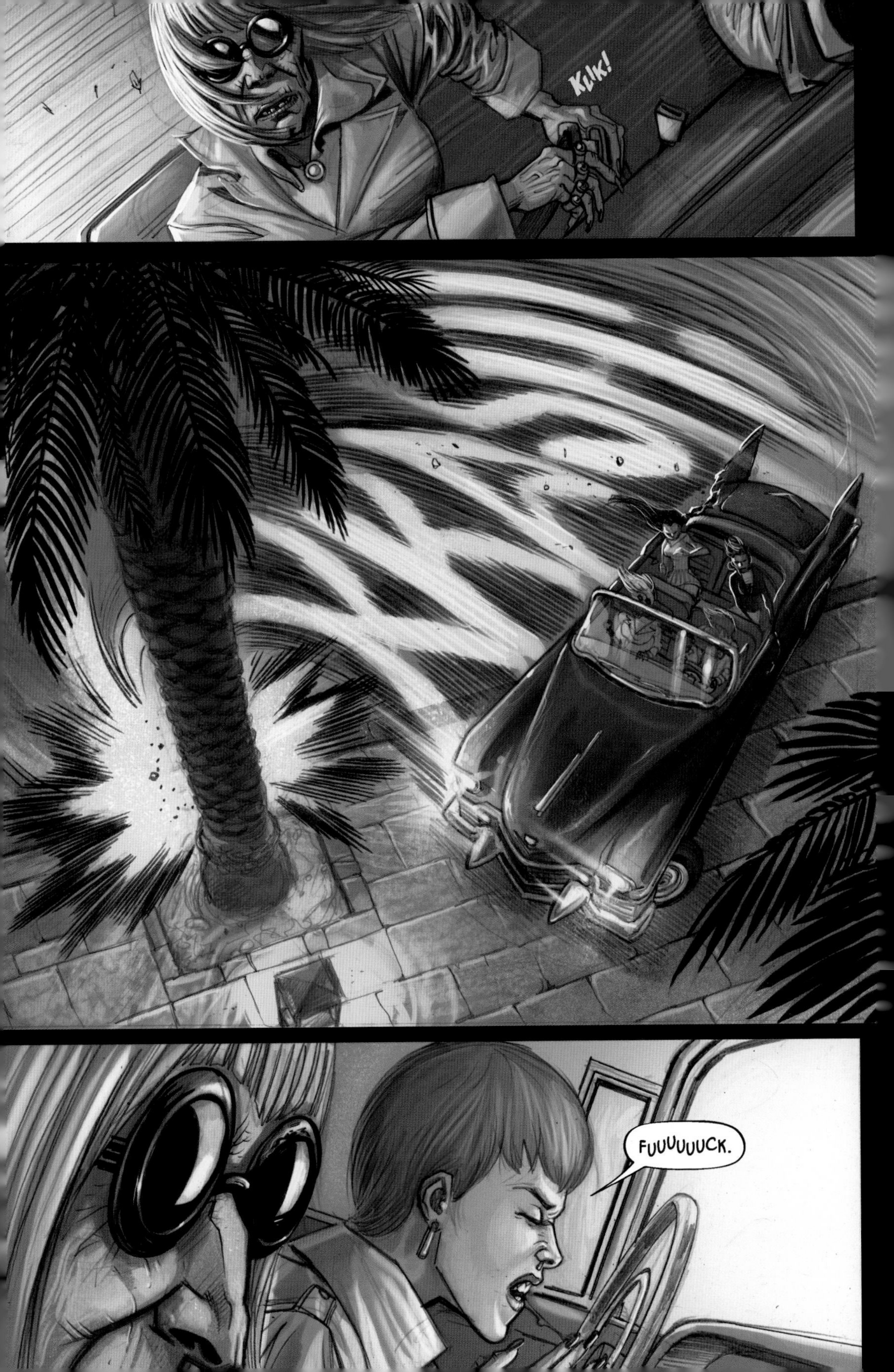
KLIK!
FUUUUUUCK.

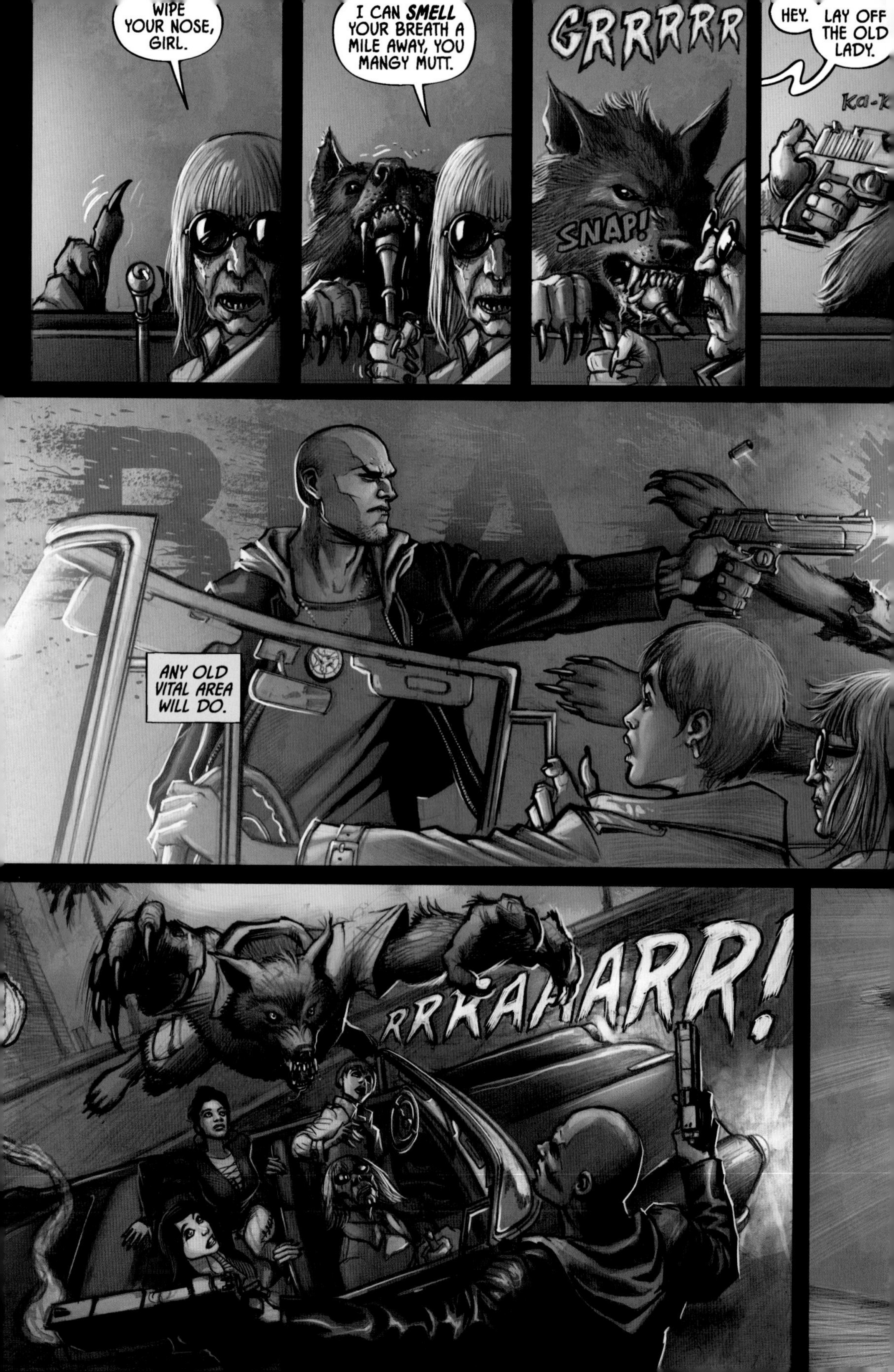
WIPE YOUR NOSE, GIRL.
I CAN SMELL YOUR BREATH A MILE AWAY, YOU MANGY MUTT.
GRRRRR
SNAP!
HEY. LAY OFF THE OLD LADY.
ANY OLD VITAL AREA WILL DO.
RRKAHARR!

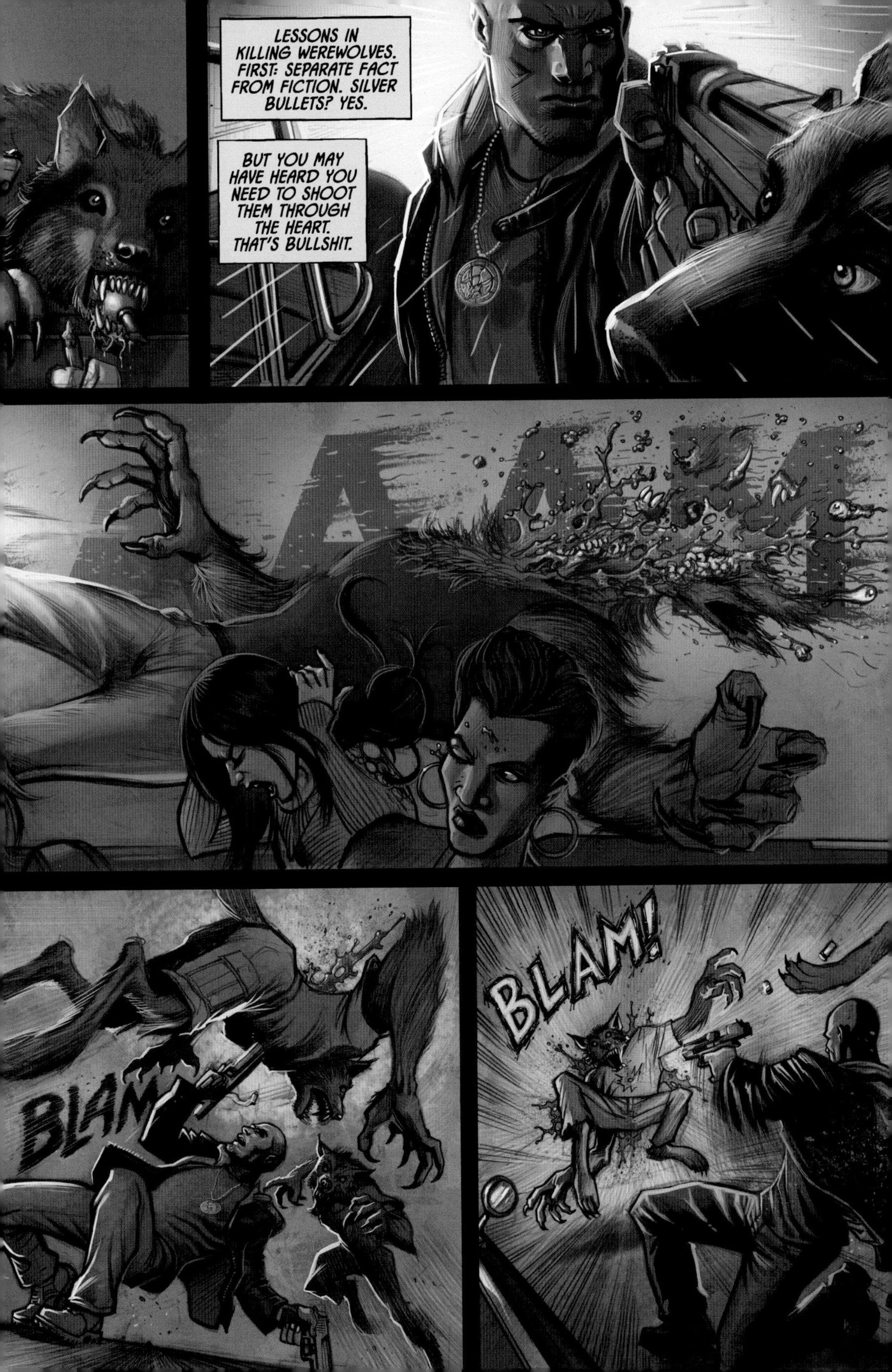
LESSONS IN KILLING WEREWOLVES. FIRST: SEPARATE FACT FROM FICTION. SILVER BULLETS? YES.
BUT YOU MAY HAVE HEARD YOU NEED TO SHOOT THEM THROUGH THE HEART. THAT'S BULLSHIT.
BLAM
BLAM!

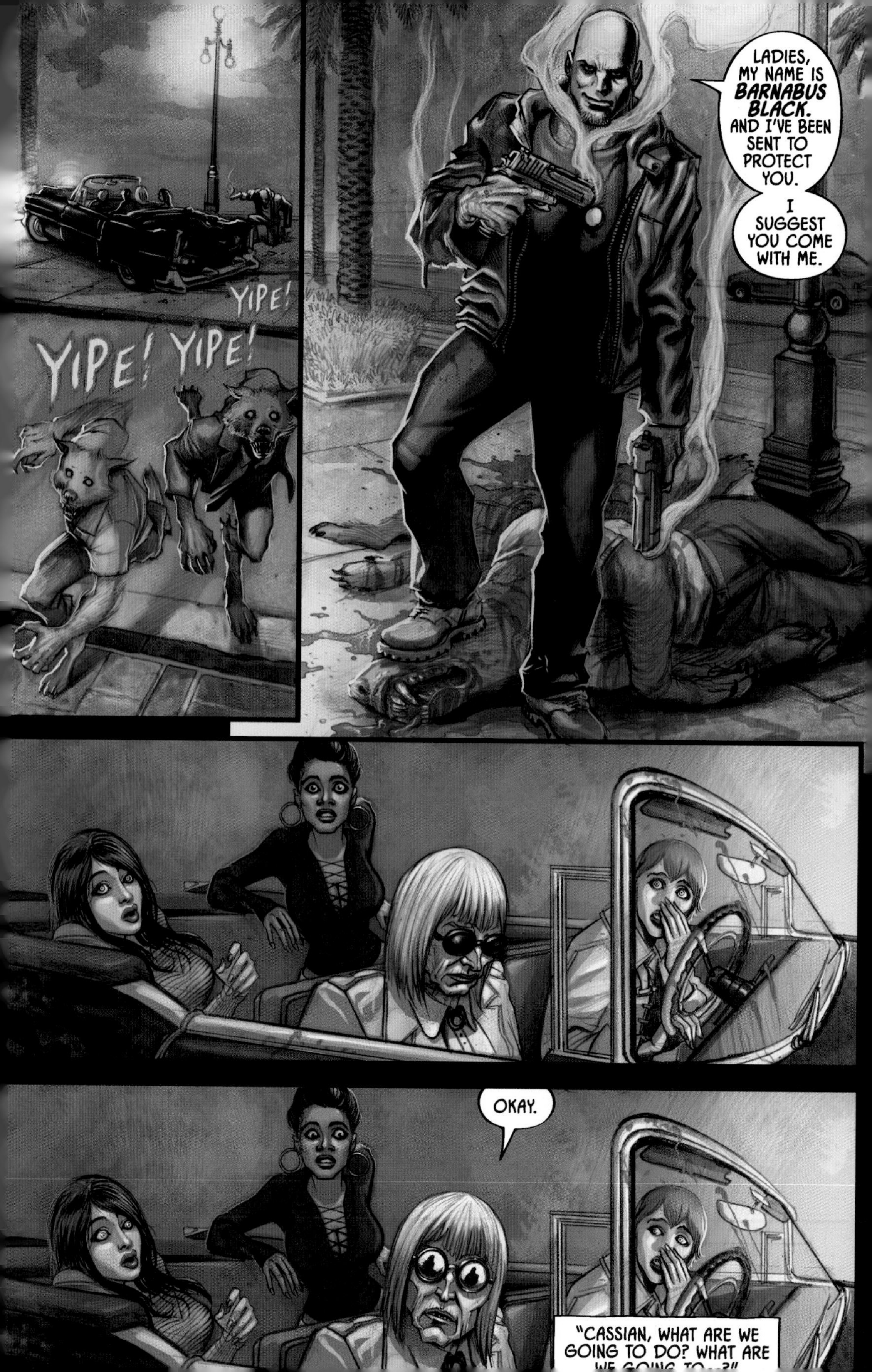
YIPE!
YIPE! YIPE!
LADIES, MY NAME IS **BARNABUS BLACK.** AND I'VE BEEN SENT TO PROTECT YOU.
I SUGGEST YOU COME WITH ME.
OKAY.
"CASSIAN, WHAT ARE WE GOING TO DO? WHAT ARE

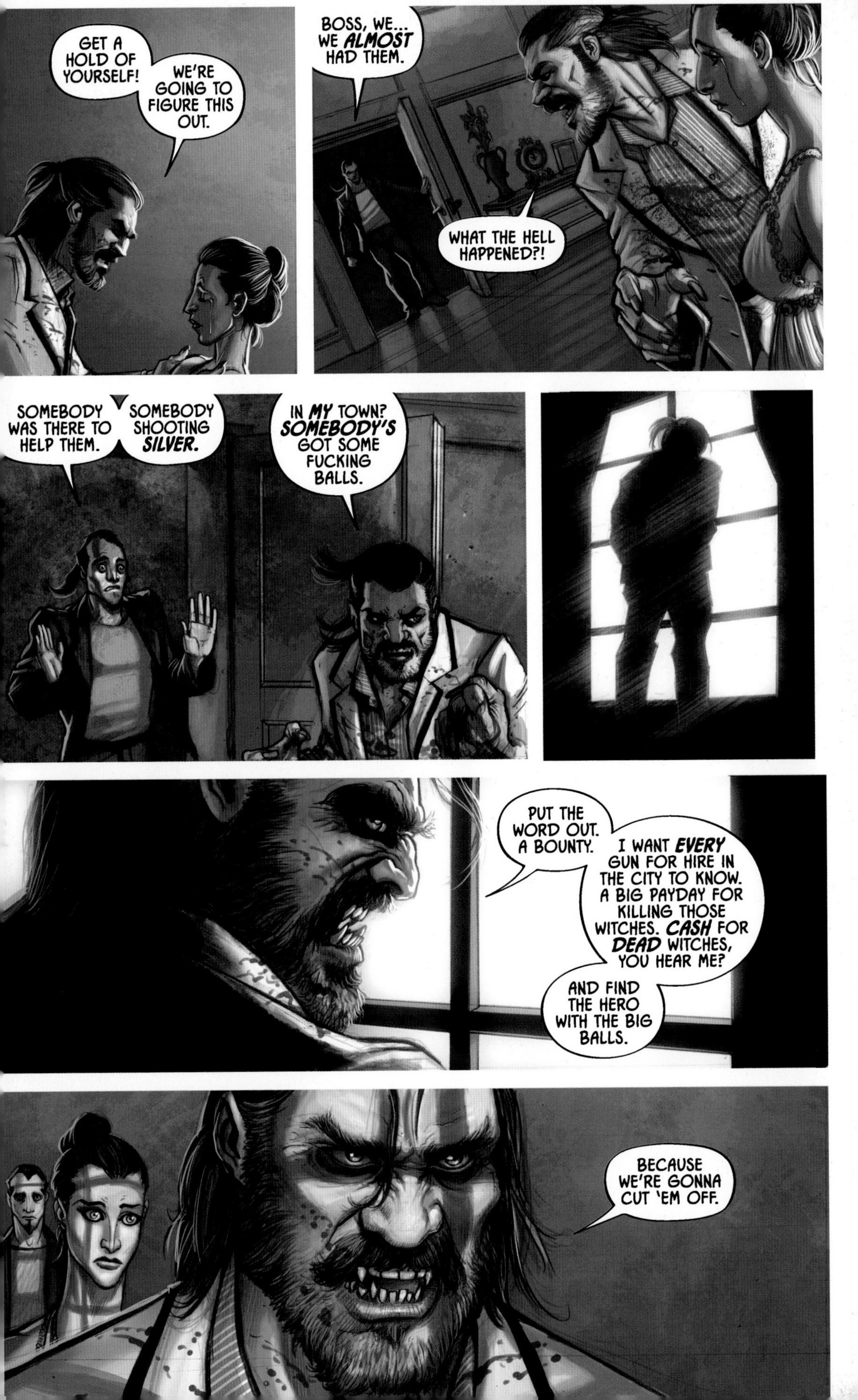
GET A HOLD OF YOURSELF!
WE'RE GOING TO FIGURE THIS OUT.
BOSS, WE... WE ALMOST HAD THEM.
WHAT THE HELL HAPPENED?!
SOMEBODY WAS THERE TO HELP THEM.
SOMEBODY SHOOTING SILVER.
IN MY TOWN? SOMEBODY'S GOT SOME FUCKING BALLS.
PUT THE WORD OUT. A BOUNTY.
I WANT EVERY GUN FOR HIRE IN THE CITY TO KNOW. A BIG PAYDAY FOR KILLING THOSE WITCHES. CASH FOR DEAD WITCHES, YOU HEAR ME?
AND FIND THE HERO WITH THE BIG BALLS.
BECAUSE WE'RE GONNA CUT 'EM OFF.

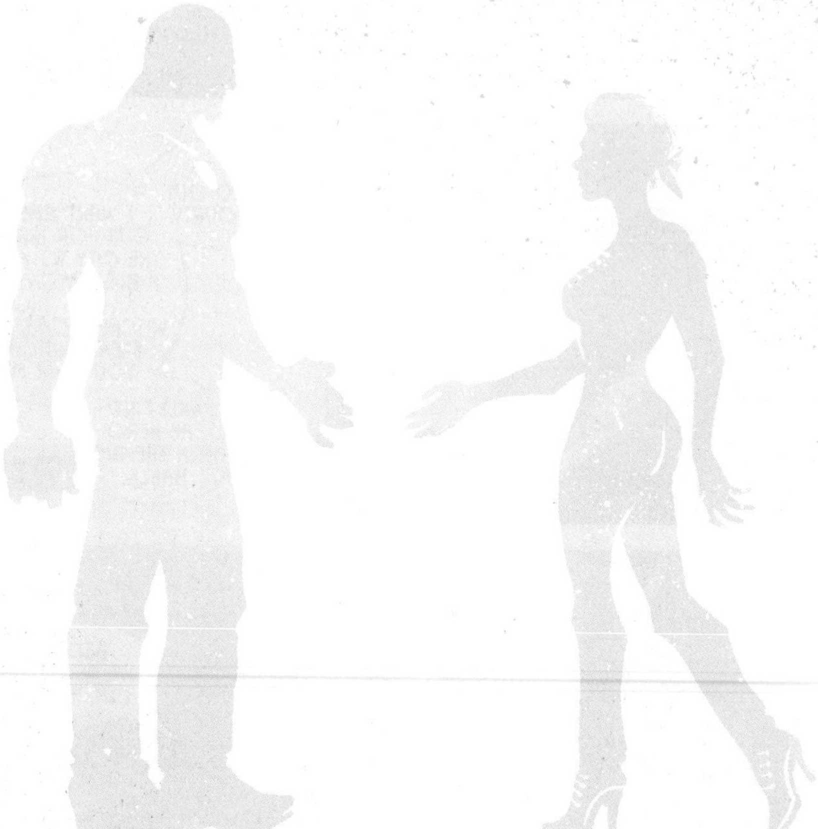

CHAPTER II

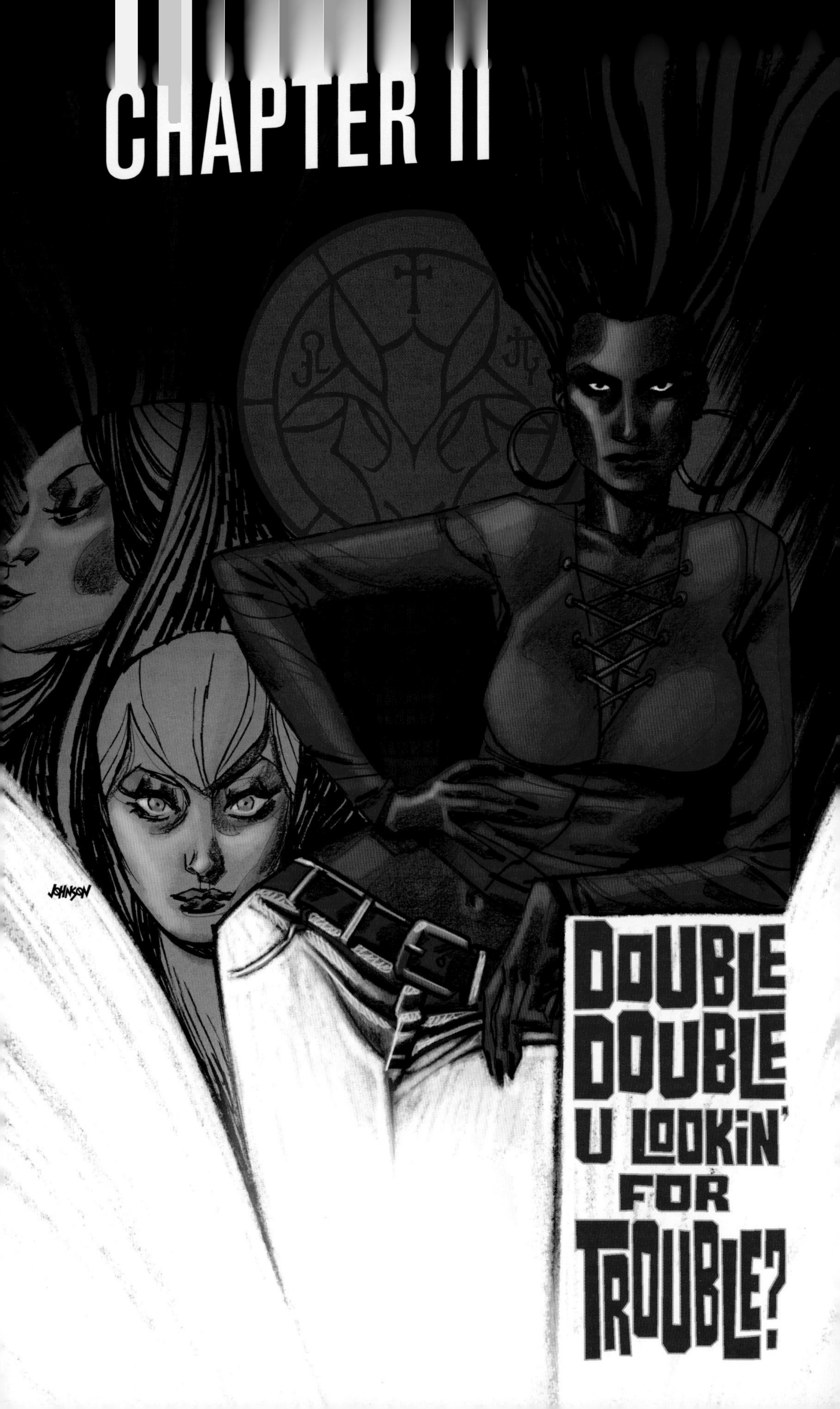
JOHNSON
DOUBLE DOUBLE U LOOKIN' FOR TROUBLE?

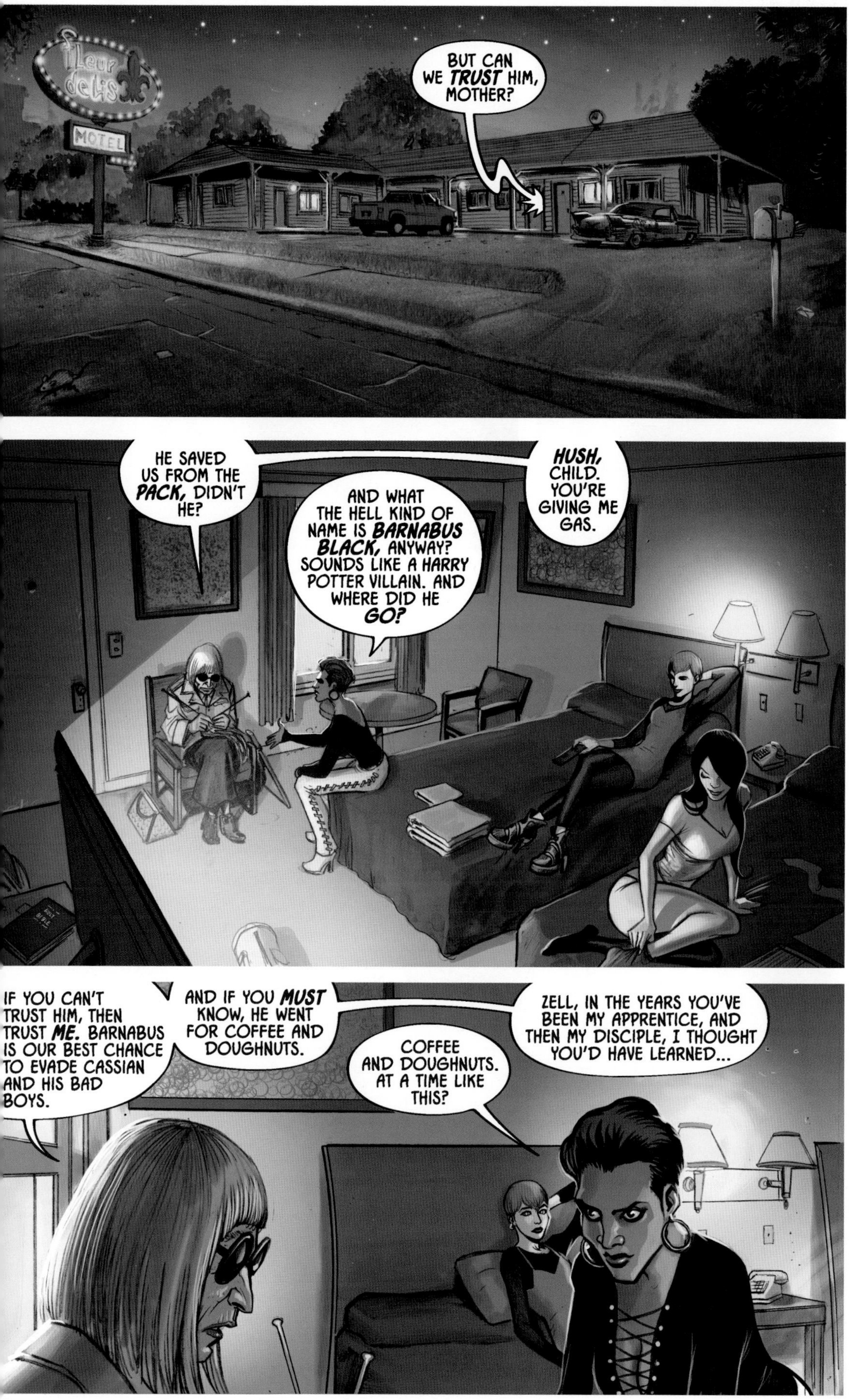
Fleur de Lis
MOTEL
BUT CAN WE TRUST HIM, MOTHER?
HE SAVED US FROM THE PACK, DIDN'T HE?
HUSH, CHILD. YOU'RE GIVING ME GAS.
AND WHAT THE HELL KIND OF NAME IS BARNABUS BLACK, ANYWAY? SOUNDS LIKE A HARRY POTTER VILLAIN. AND WHERE DID HE GO?
IF YOU CAN'T TRUST HIM, THEN TRUST ME. BARNABUS IS OUR BEST CHANCE TO EVADE CASSIAN AND HIS BAD BOYS.
AND IF YOU MUST KNOW, HE WENT FOR COFFEE AND DOUGHNUTS.
COFFEE AND DOUGHNUTS. AT A TIME LIKE THIS?
ZELL, IN THE YEARS YOU'VE BEEN MY APPRENTICE, AND THEN MY DISCIPLE, I THOUGHT YOU'D HAVE LEARNED...

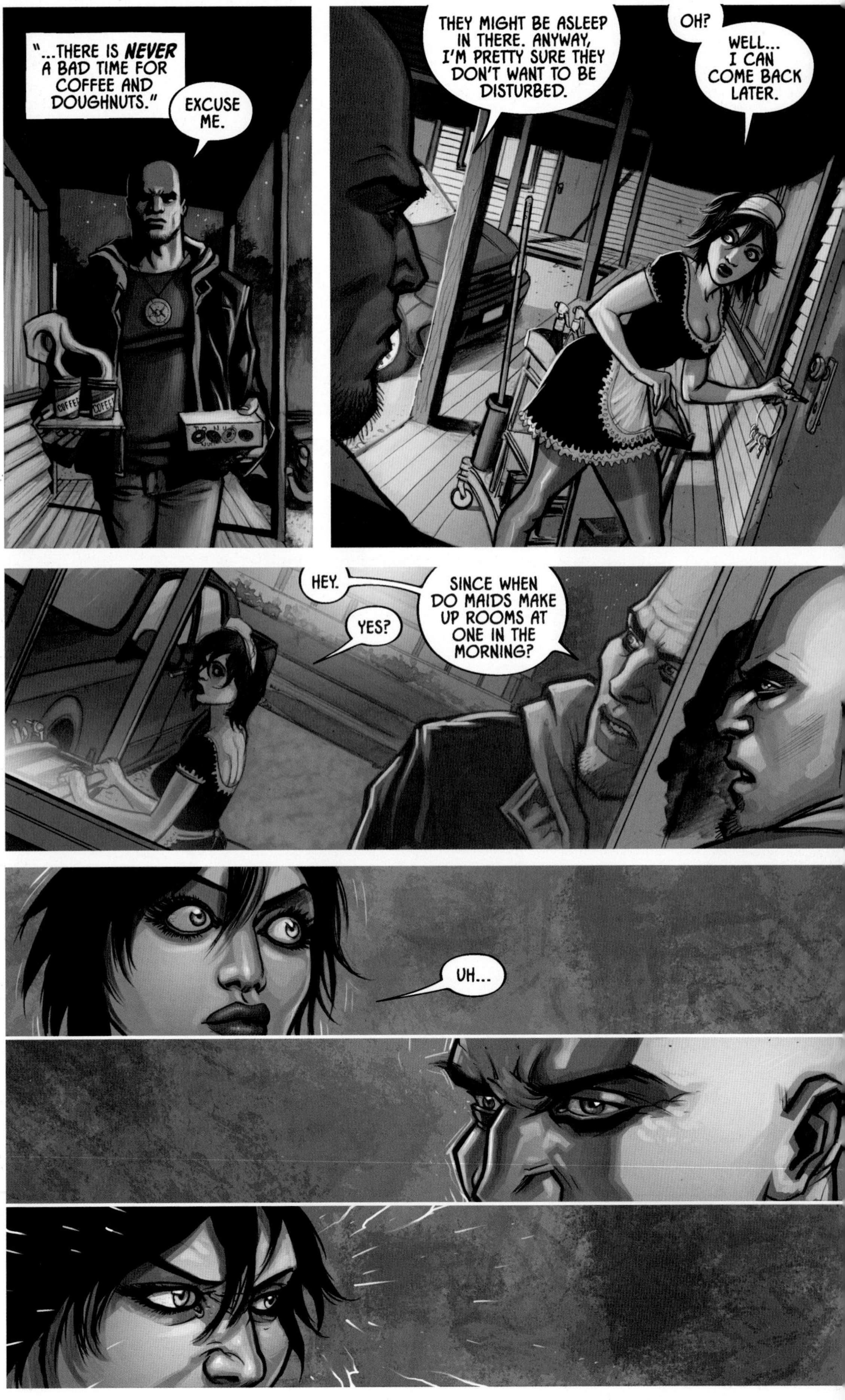
"...THERE IS NEVER A BAD TIME FOR COFFEE AND DOUGHNUTS."
EXCUSE ME.
THEY MIGHT BE ASLEEP IN THERE. ANYWAY, I'M PRETTY SURE THEY DON'T WANT TO BE DISTURBED.
OH?
WELL... I CAN COME BACK LATER.
HEY.
YES?
SINCE WHEN DO MAIDS MAKE UP ROOMS AT ONE IN THE MORNING?
UH...

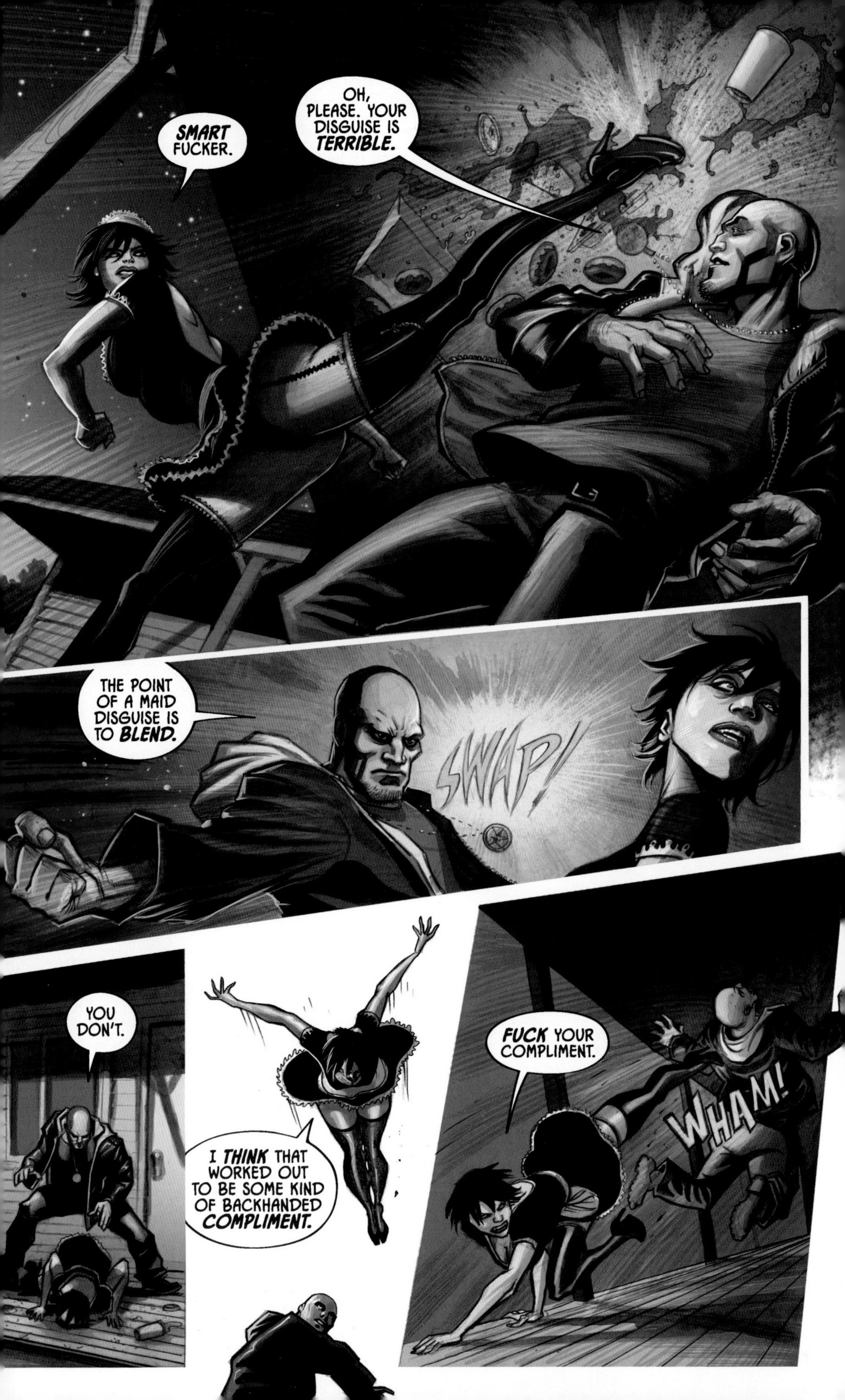
SMART FUCKER.
OH, PLEASE. YOUR DISGUISE IS TERRIBLE.
THE POINT OF A MAID DISGUISE IS TO BLEND.
SWAP!
YOU DON'T.
I THINK THAT WORKED OUT TO BE SOME KIND OF BACKHANDED COMPLIMENT.
FUCK YOUR COMPLIMENT.
WHAM!

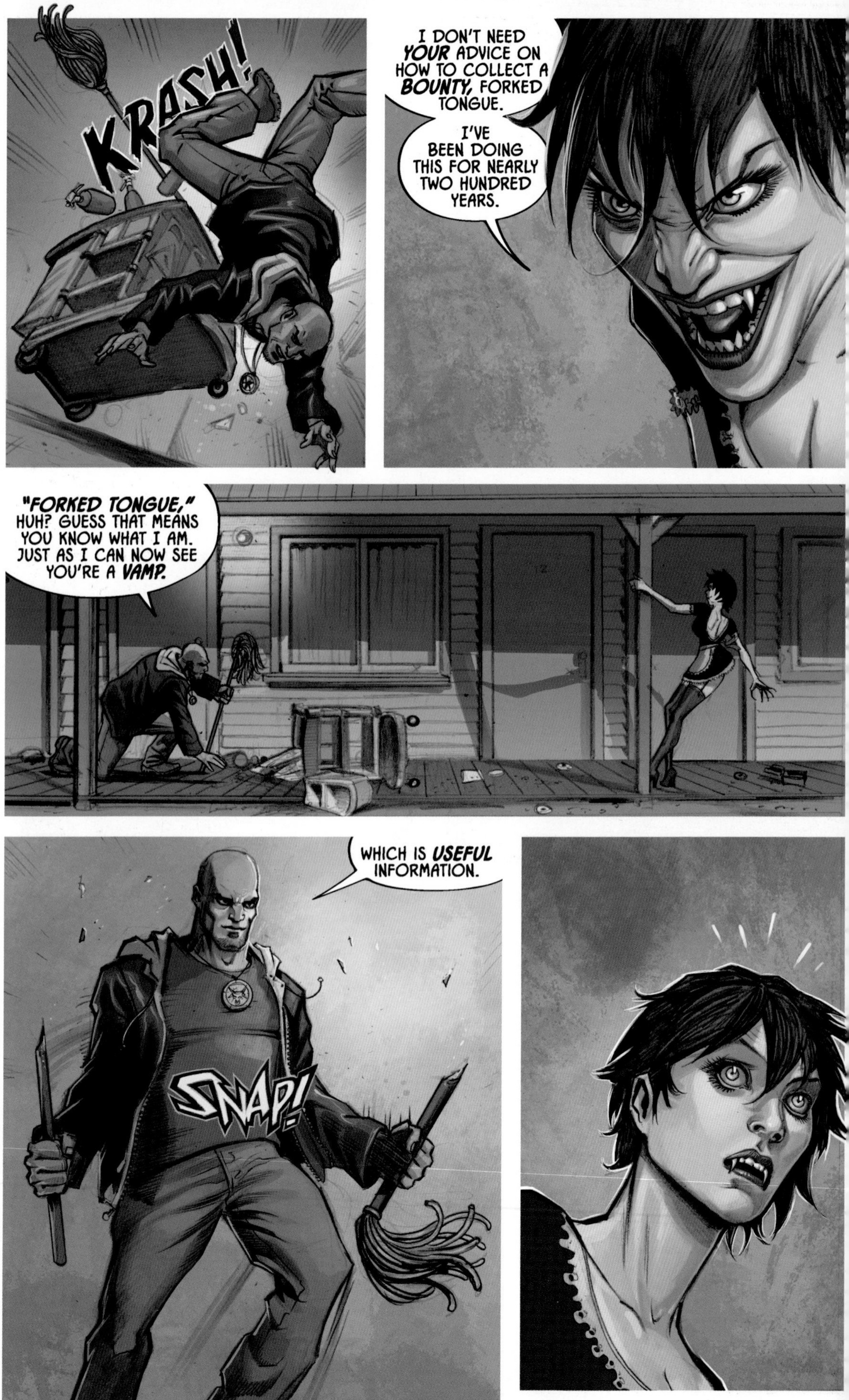
KRASH!
I DON'T NEED *YOUR* ADVICE ON HOW TO COLLECT A *BOUNTY,* FORKED TONGUE.
I'VE BEEN DOING THIS FOR NEARLY TWO HUNDRED YEARS.
"FORKED TONGUE," HUH? GUESS THAT MEANS YOU KNOW WHAT I AM. JUST AS I CAN NOW SEE YOU'RE A *VAMP.*
WHICH IS *USEFUL* INFORMATION.
SNAP!

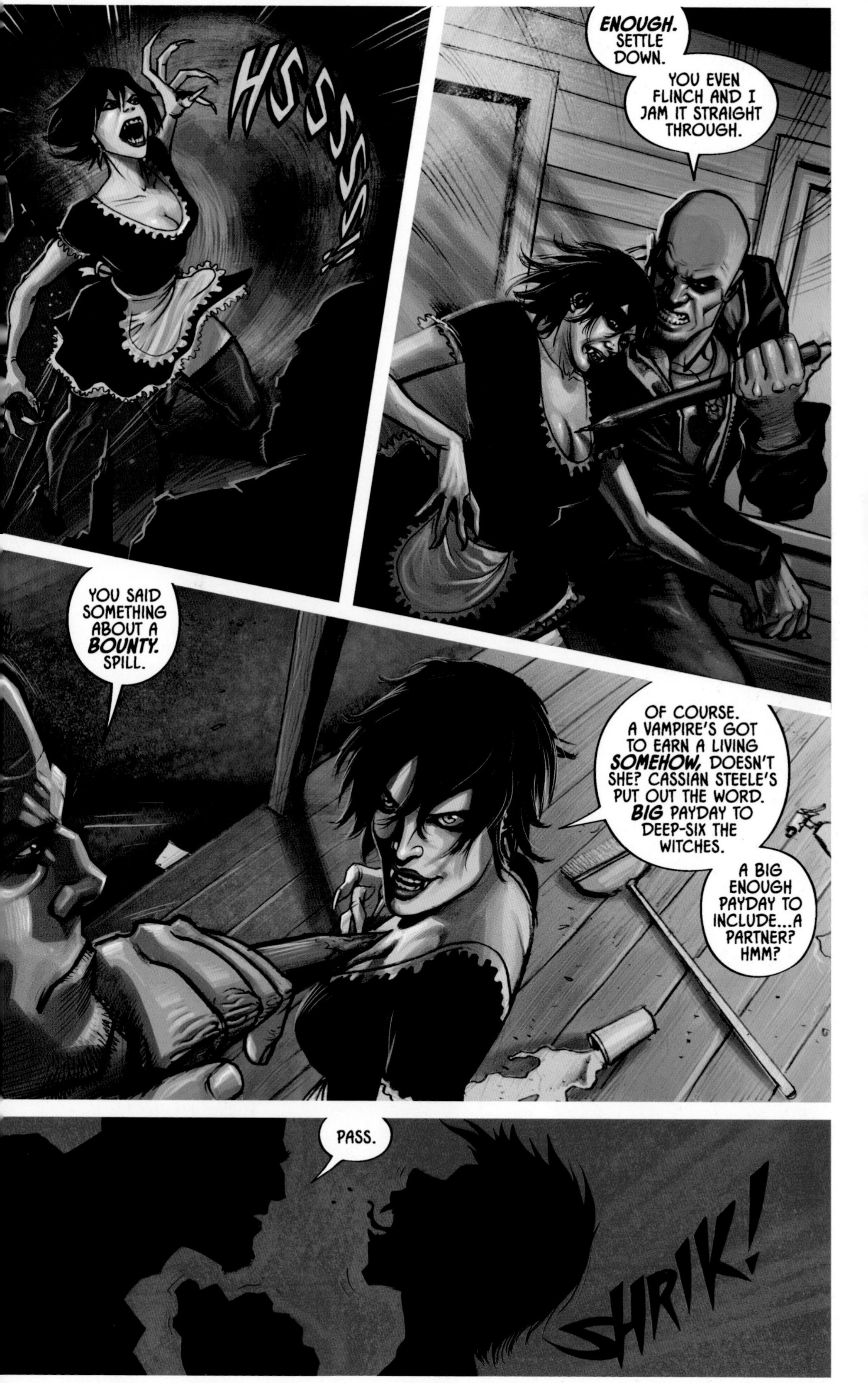
HSSSSS!!
ENOUGH. SETTLE DOWN.
YOU EVEN FLINCH AND I JAM IT STRAIGHT THROUGH.
YOU SAID SOMETHING ABOUT A BOUNTY. SPILL.
OF COURSE. A VAMPIRE'S GOT TO EARN A LIVING SOMEHOW, DOESN'T SHE? CASSIAN STEELE'S PUT OUT THE WORD. BIG PAYDAY TO DEEP-SIX THE WITCHES.
A BIG ENOUGH PAYDAY TO INCLUDE...A PARTNER? HMM?
PASS.
SHRIK!

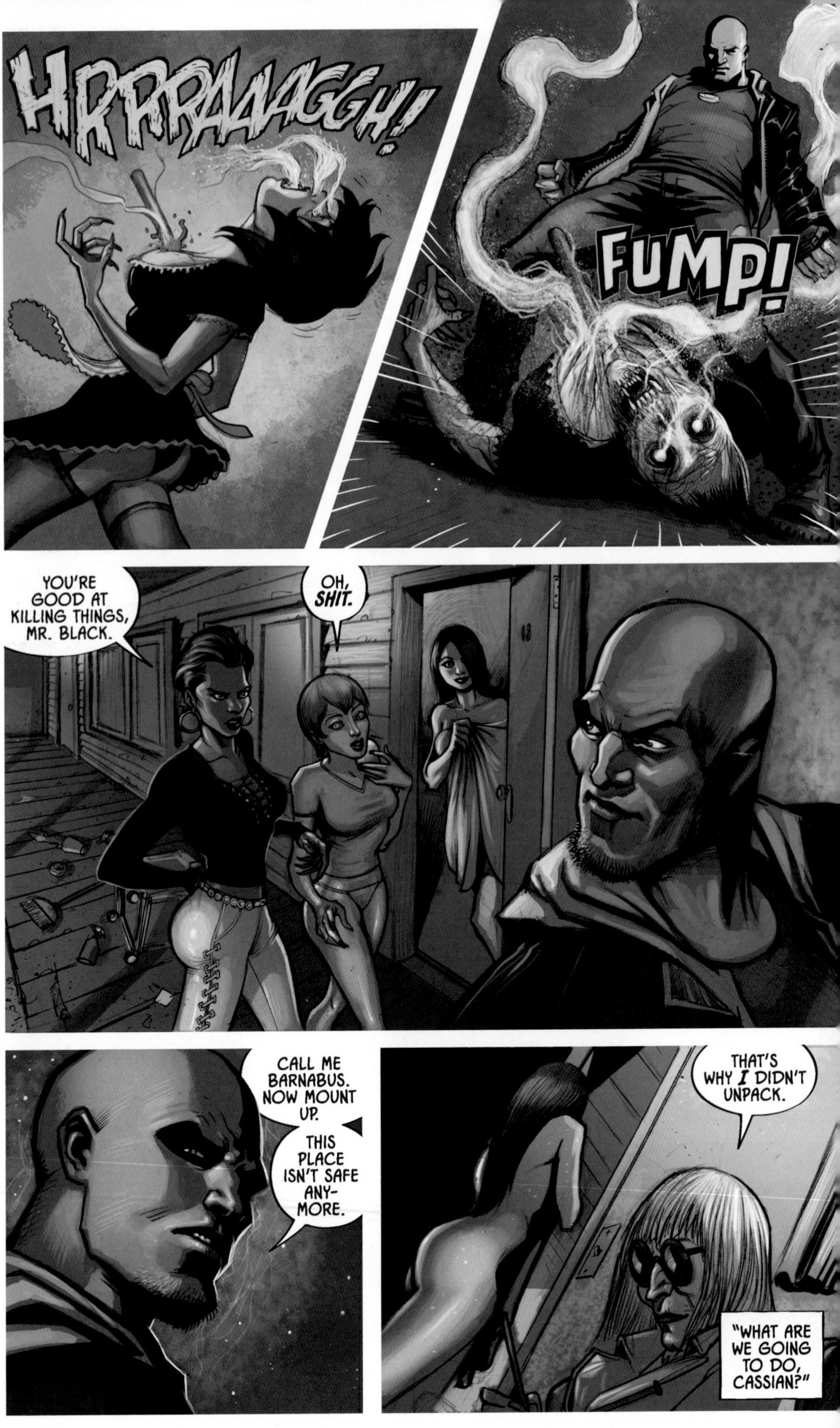
HRRRAAAGGH!
FUMP!
YOU'RE GOOD AT KILLING THINGS, MR. BLACK.
OH, SHIT.
CALL ME BARNABUS. NOW MOUNT UP.
THIS PLACE ISN'T SAFE ANY-MORE.
THAT'S WHY I DIDN'T UNPACK.
"WHAT ARE WE GOING TO DO, CASSIAN?"

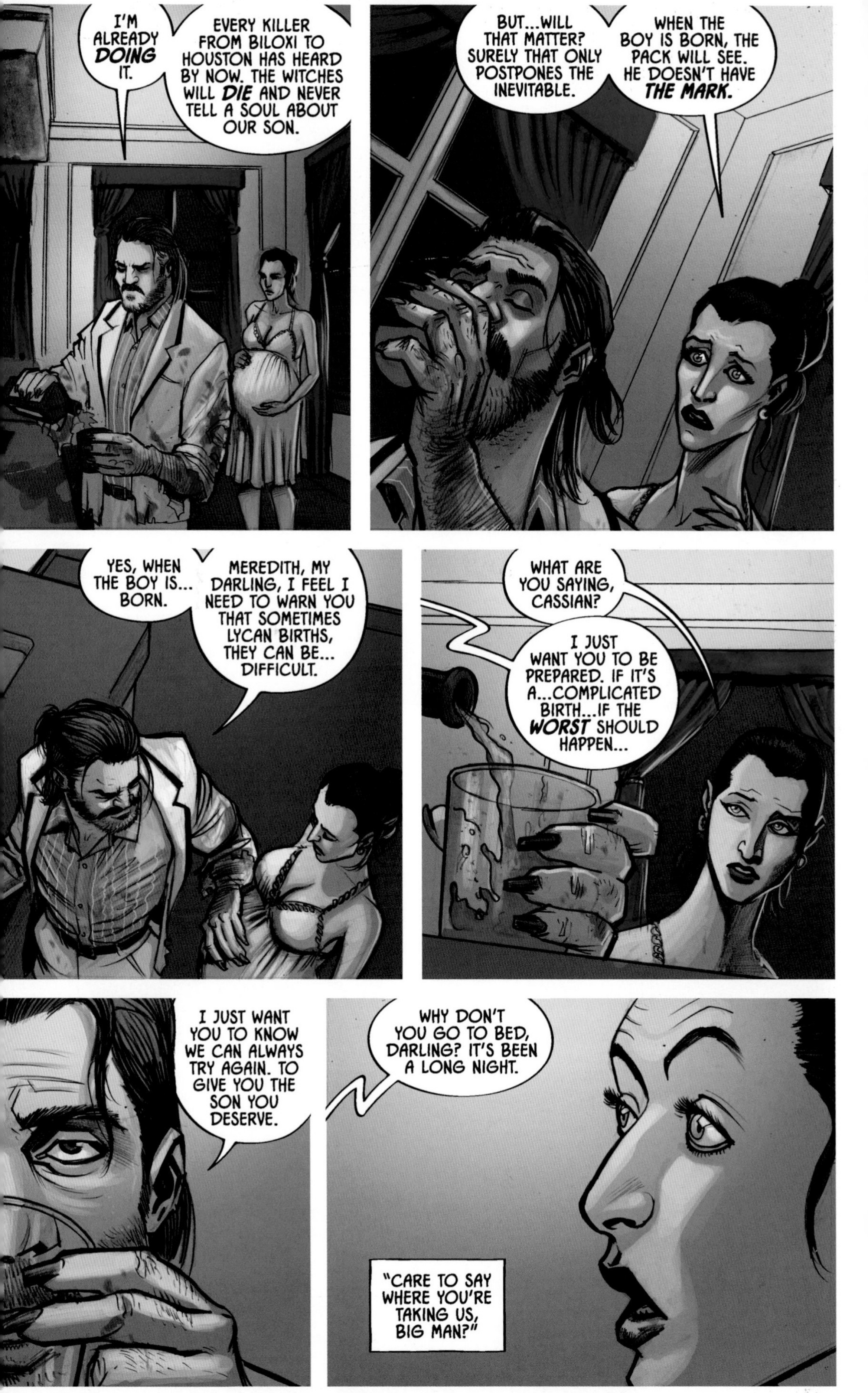
I'M ALREADY *DOING* IT.
EVERY KILLER FROM BILOXI TO HOUSTON HAS HEARD BY NOW. THE WITCHES WILL *DIE* AND NEVER TELL A SOUL ABOUT OUR SON.
BUT...WILL THAT MATTER? SURELY THAT ONLY POSTPONES THE INEVITABLE.
WHEN THE BOY IS BORN, THE PACK WILL SEE. HE DOESN'T HAVE *THE MARK.*
YES, WHEN THE BOY IS... BORN.
MEREDITH, MY DARLING, I FEEL I NEED TO WARN YOU THAT SOMETIMES LYCAN BIRTHS, THEY CAN BE... DIFFICULT.
WHAT ARE YOU SAYING, CASSIAN?
I JUST WANT YOU TO BE PREPARED. IF IT'S A...COMPLICATED BIRTH...IF THE *WORST* SHOULD HAPPEN...
I JUST WANT YOU TO KNOW WE CAN ALWAYS TRY AGAIN. TO GIVE YOU THE SON YOU DESERVE.
WHY DON'T YOU GO TO BED, DARLING? IT'S BEEN A LONG NIGHT.
"CARE TO SAY WHERE YOU'RE TAKING US, BIG MAN?"

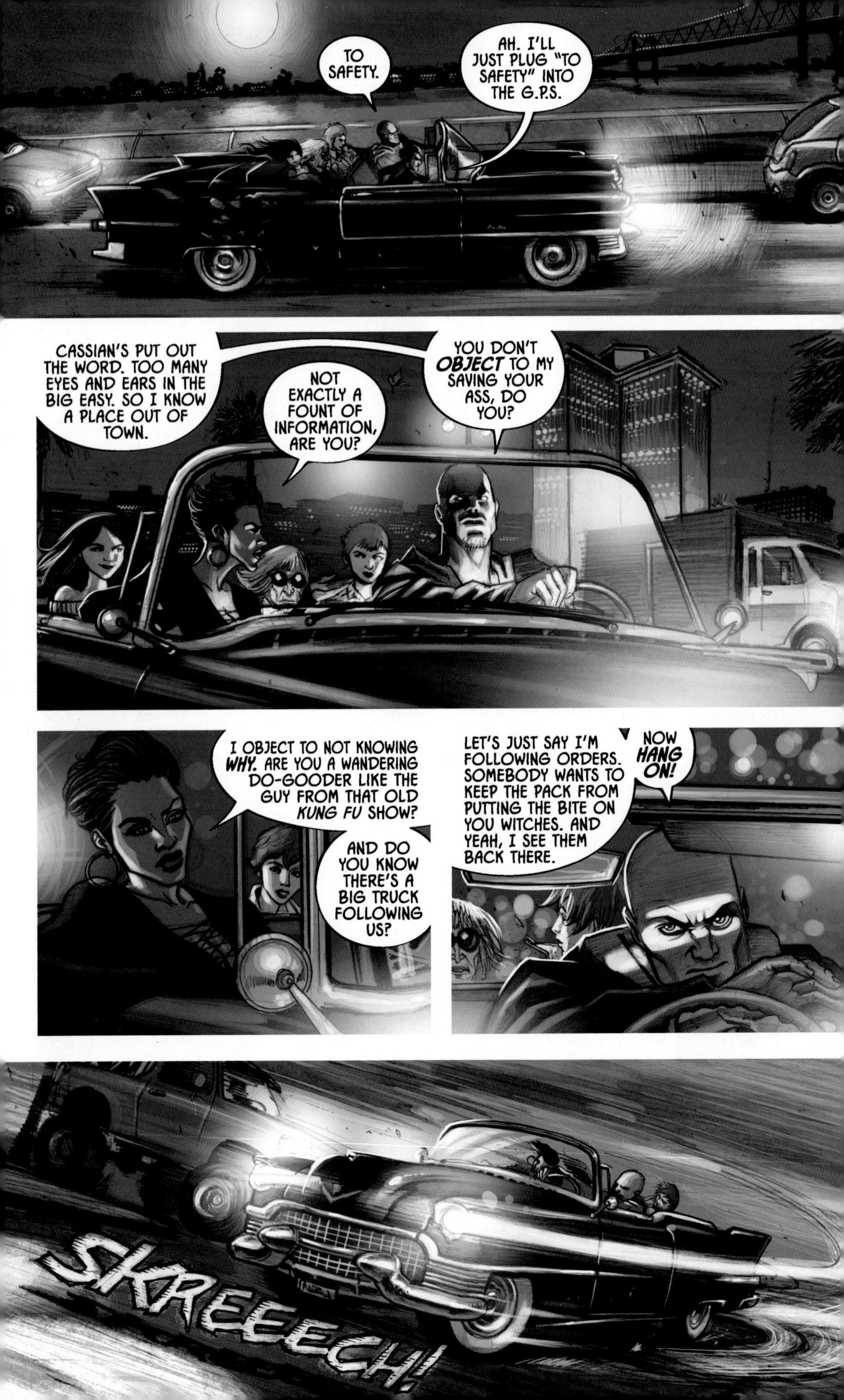
TO SAFETY.
AH. I'LL JUST PLUG "TO SAFETY" INTO THE G.P.S.
CASSIAN'S PUT OUT THE WORD. TOO MANY EYES AND EARS IN THE BIG EASY. SO I KNOW A PLACE OUT OF TOWN.
NOT EXACTLY A FOUNT OF INFORMATION, ARE YOU?
YOU DON'T OBJECT TO MY SAVING YOUR ASS, DO YOU?
I OBJECT TO NOT KNOWING WHY. ARE YOU A WANDERING DO-GOODER LIKE THE GUY FROM THAT OLD KUNG FU SHOW?
AND DO YOU KNOW THERE'S A BIG TRUCK FOLLOWING US?
LET'S JUST SAY I'M FOLLOWING ORDERS. SOMEBODY WANTS TO KEEP THE PACK FROM PUTTING THE BITE ON YOU WITCHES. AND YEAH, I SEE THEM BACK THERE.
NOW HANG ON!
SKREEEECH!

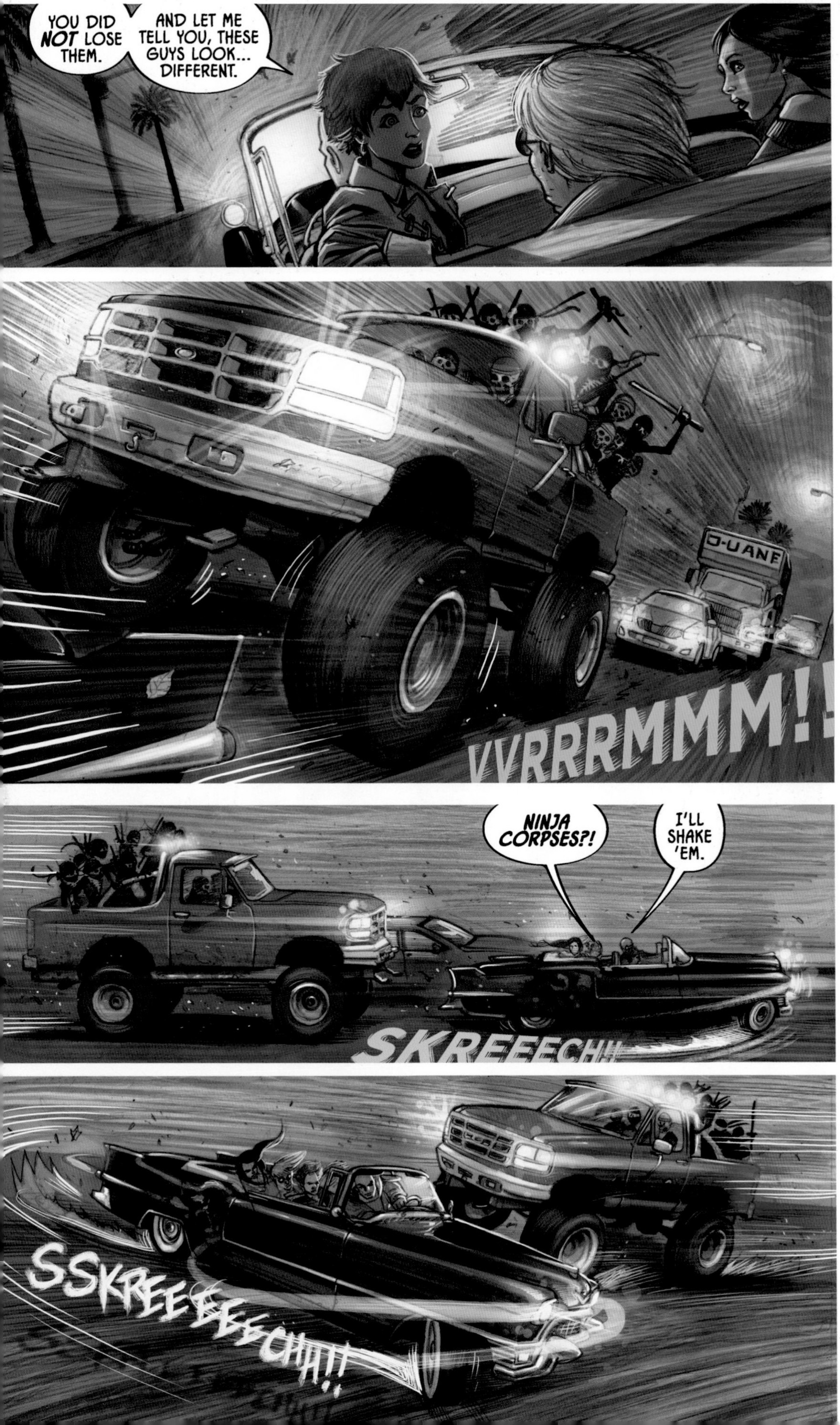
YOU DID NOT LOSE THEM.
AND LET ME TELL YOU, THESE GUYS LOOK... DIFFERENT.
U-HAUL
VVRRRMMMM!!
NINJA CORPSES?!
I'LL SHAKE 'EM.
SKREEEECH!!
SSKREEEEEEECHH!!

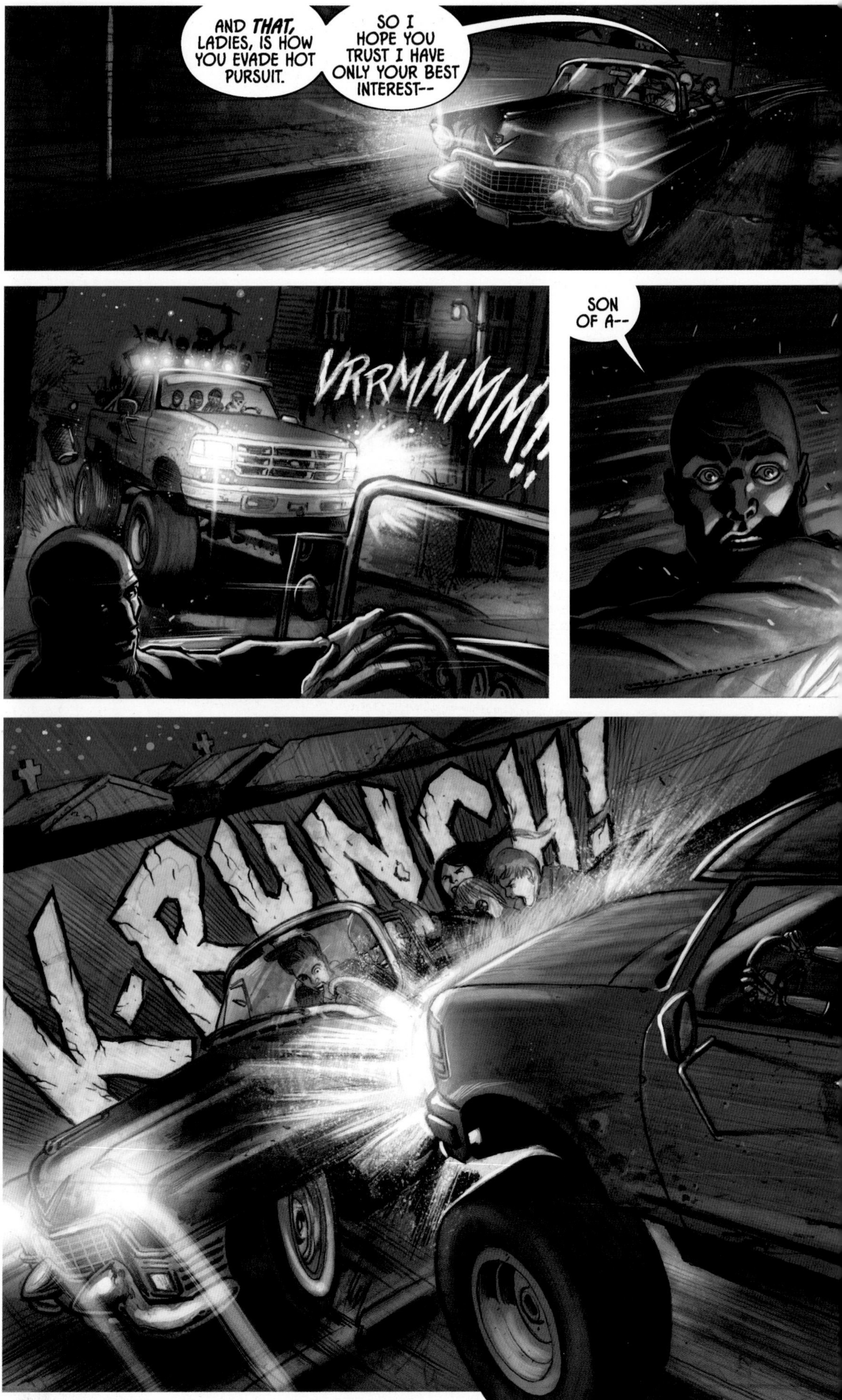
AND THAT, LADIES, IS HOW YOU EVADE HOT PURSUIT.
SO I HOPE YOU TRUST I HAVE ONLY YOUR BEST INTEREST--
VRRMMMMM!!
SON OF A--
KRUNCH!

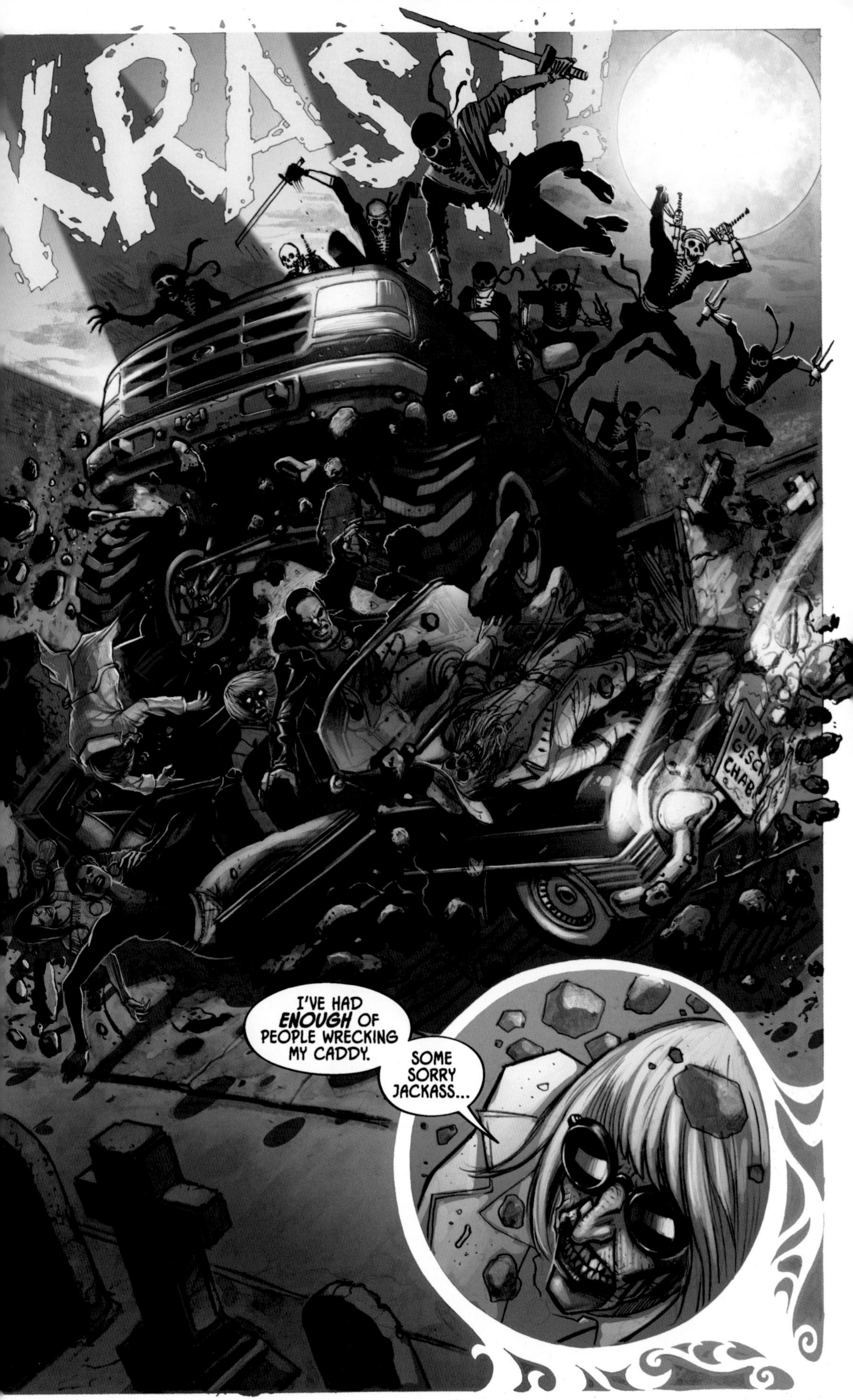
I'VE HAD ENOUGH OF PEOPLE WRECKING MY CADDY.
SOME SORRY JACKASS...

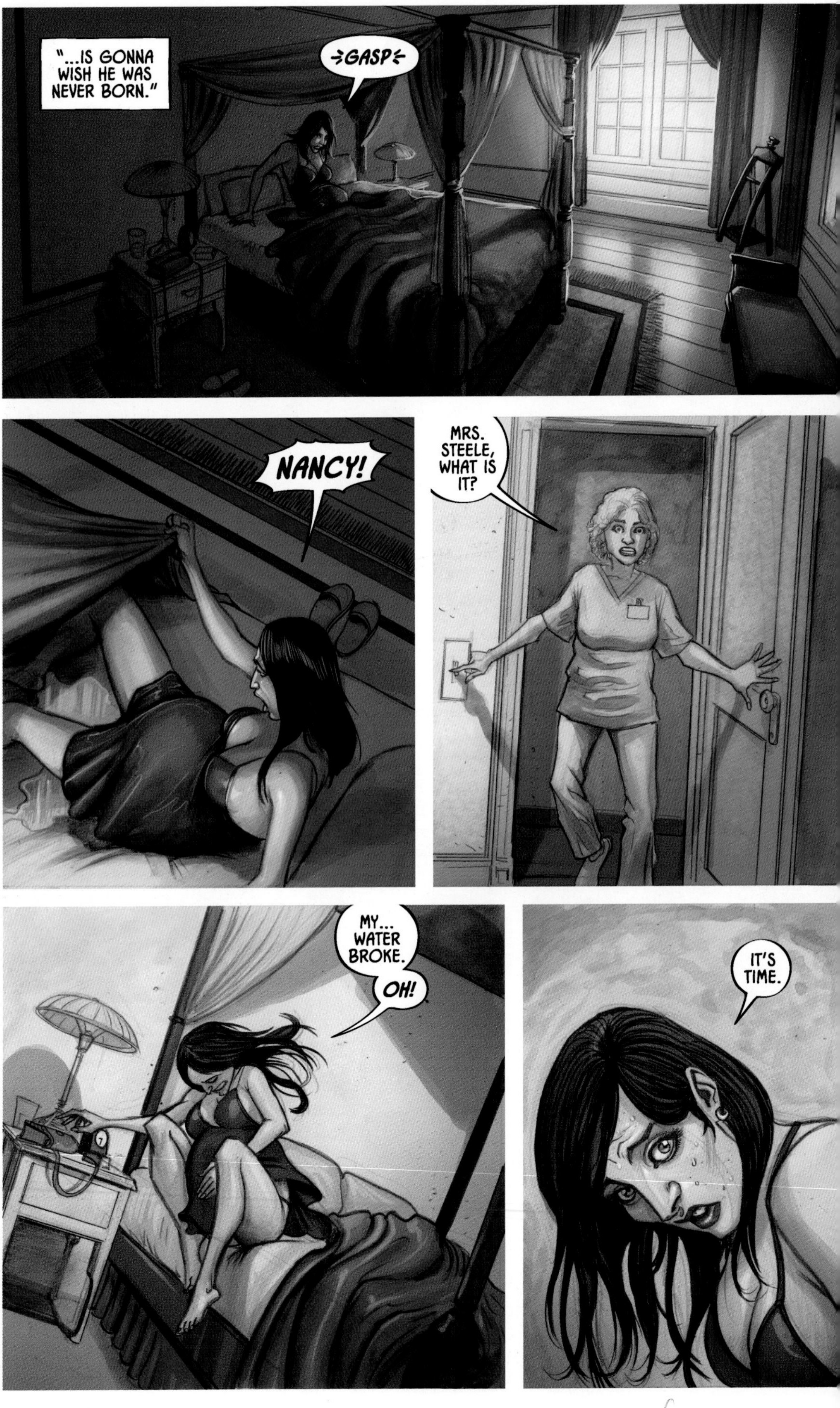
"...IS GONNA WISH HE WAS NEVER BORN."
GASP
NANCY!
MRS. STEELE, WHAT IS IT?
MY... WATER BROKE.
OH!
IT'S TIME.

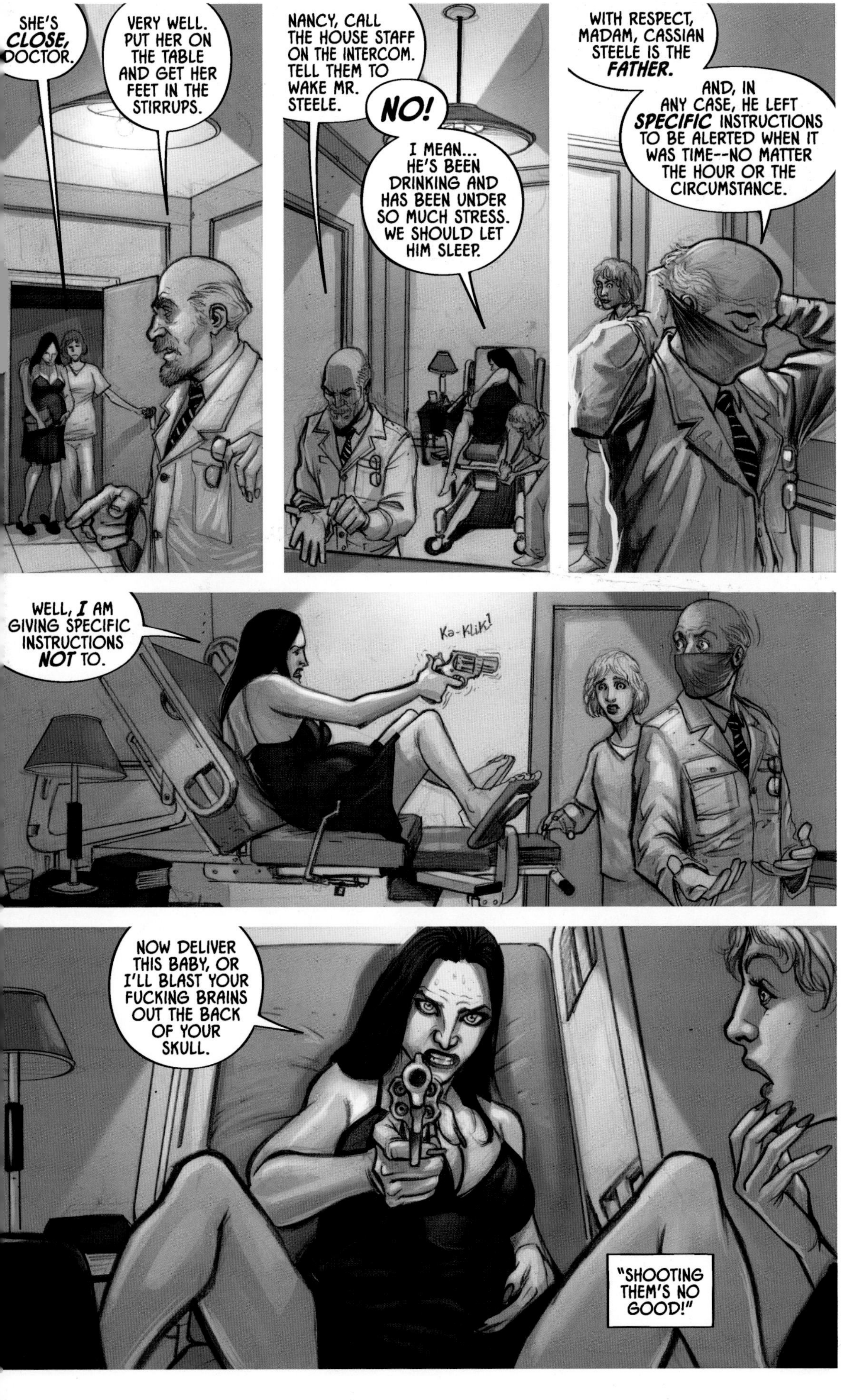
SHE'S CLOSE, DOCTOR.
VERY WELL. PUT HER ON THE TABLE AND GET HER FEET IN THE STIRRUPS.
NANCY, CALL THE HOUSE STAFF ON THE INTERCOM. TELL THEM TO WAKE MR. STEELE.
NO!
I MEAN... HE'S BEEN DRINKING AND HAS BEEN UNDER SO MUCH STRESS. WE SHOULD LET HIM SLEEP.
WITH RESPECT, MADAM, CASSIAN STEELE IS THE FATHER.
AND, IN ANY CASE, HE LEFT SPECIFIC INSTRUCTIONS TO BE ALERTED WHEN IT WAS TIME--NO MATTER THE HOUR OR THE CIRCUMSTANCE.
WELL, I AM GIVING SPECIFIC INSTRUCTIONS NOT TO.
Ka-KliK!
NOW DELIVER THIS BABY, OR I'LL BLAST YOUR FUCKING BRAINS OUT THE BACK OF YOUR SKULL.
"SHOOTING THEM'S NO GOOD!"

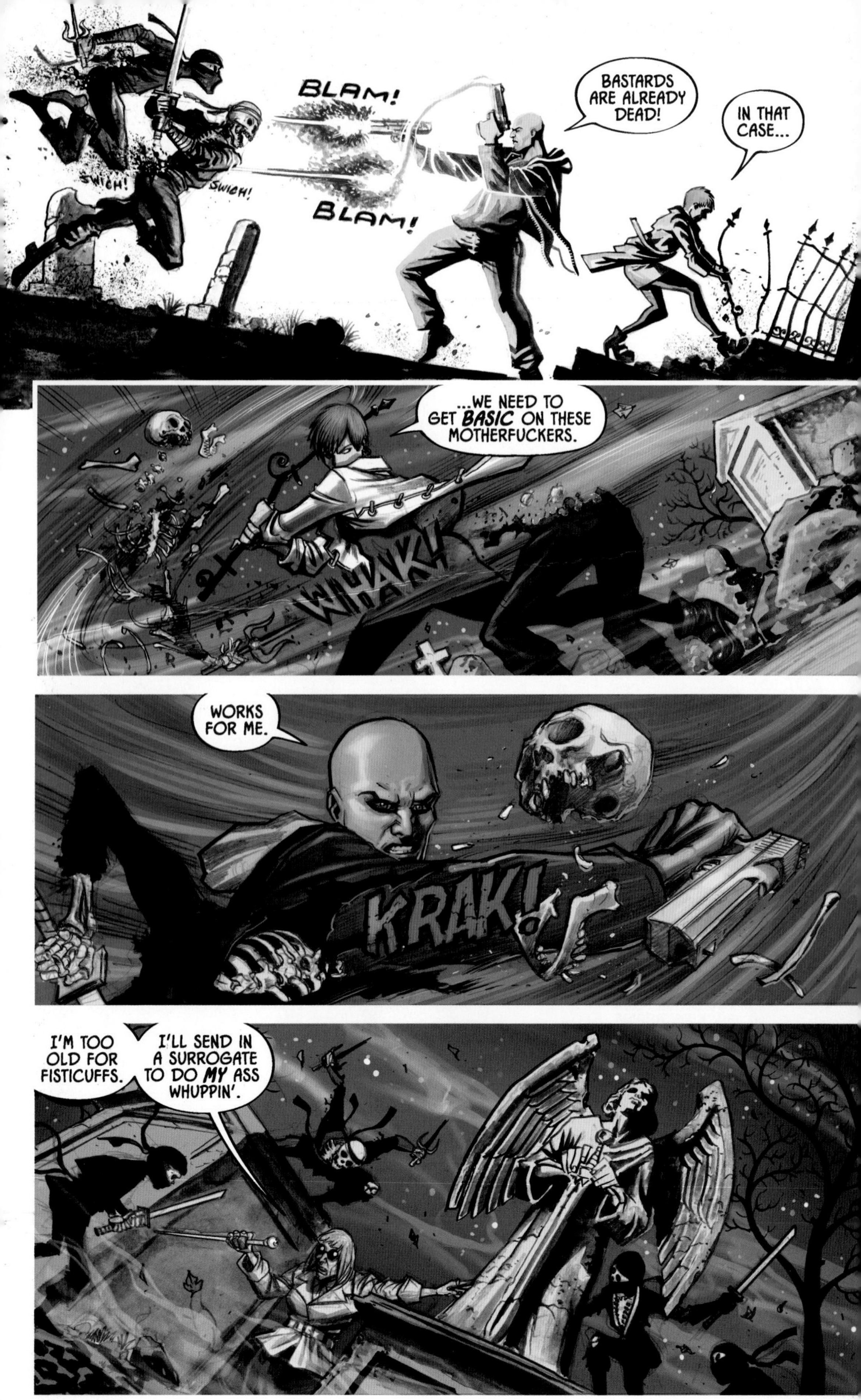
BLAM!
SWICH!
SWICH!
BLAM!
BASTARDS ARE ALREADY DEAD!
IN THAT CASE...
...WE NEED TO GET BASIC ON THESE MOTHERFUCKERS.
WHAK!
WORKS FOR ME.
KRAK!
I'M TOO OLD FOR FISTICUFFS.
I'LL SEND IN A SURROGATE TO DO MY ASS WHUPPIN'.

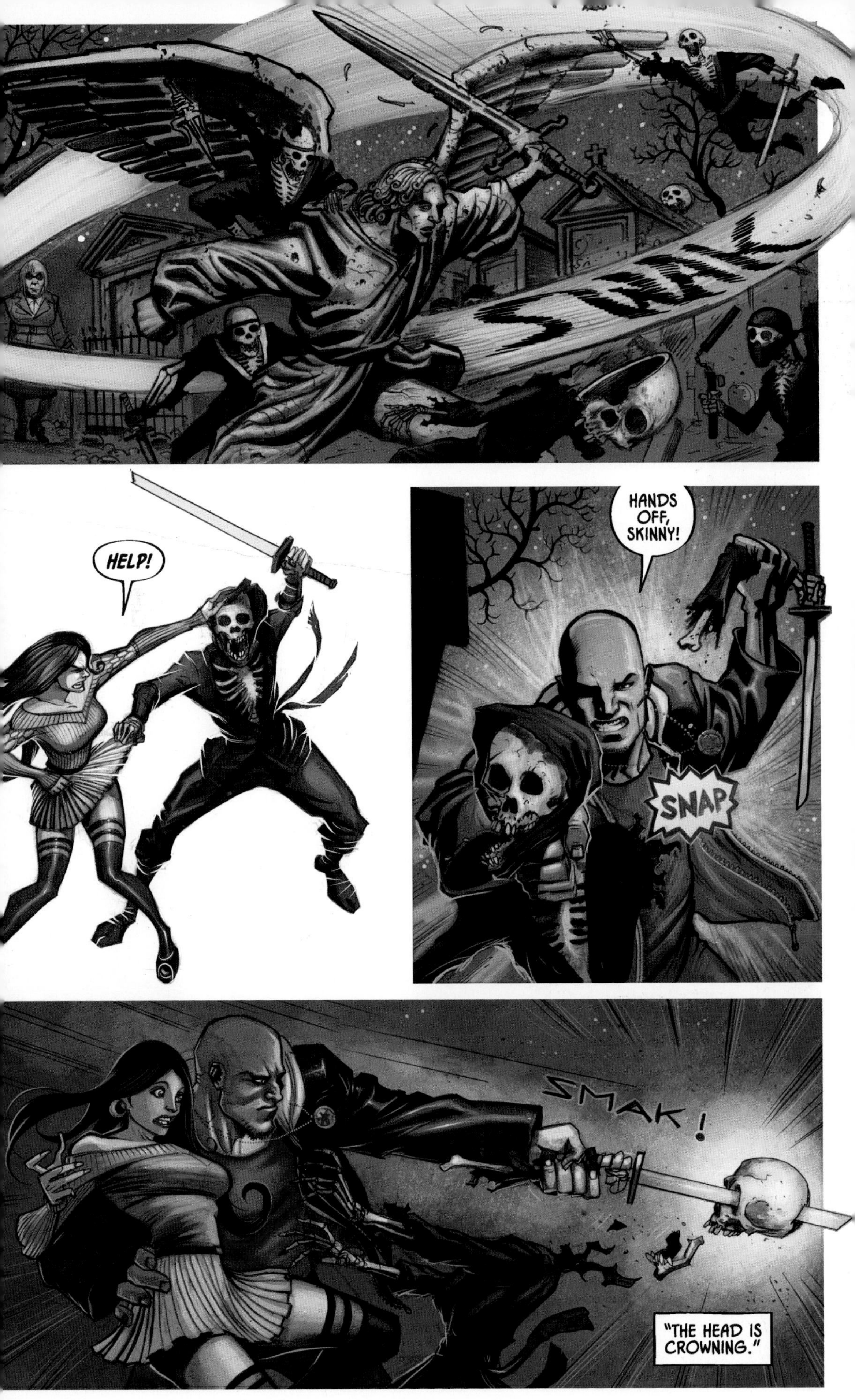
SMAK
HELP!
HANDS OFF, SKINNY!
SNAP
SMAK!
"THE HEAD IS CROWNING."

NGH!

PUSH. YOU'VE GOT TO *PUSH!*

GAH!

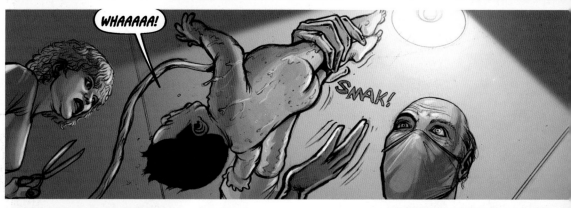

WHAAAAA!

SMAK!

G-GIVE ME...MY B-BABY.

COME NOW. I'VE *TOLERATED* THIS BEHAVIOR BECAUSE I KNOW PREGNANT WOMEN MUST CONTEND WITH VIOLENT, IRRATIONAL MOOD SWINGS.

WHAAA WHAAA!

I'VE SERVED THE PACK AS PHYSICIAN FOR OVER TWENTY YEARS. THERE IS A PROTOCOL.

NO MORE FOOLISHNESS.

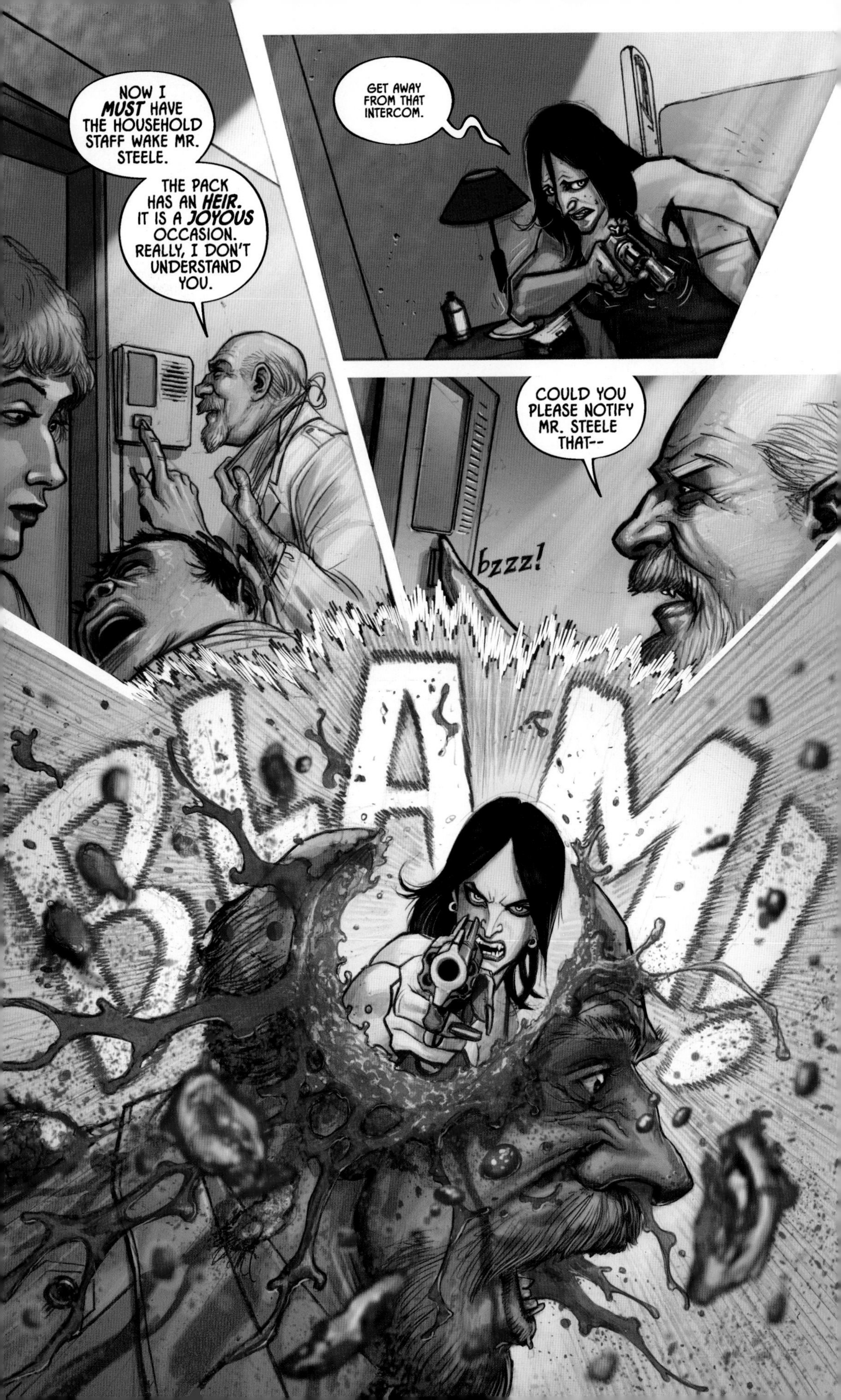
NOW I MUST HAVE THE HOUSEHOLD STAFF WAKE MR. STEELE.
THE PACK HAS AN HEIR. IT IS A JOYOUS OCCASION. REALLY, I DON'T UNDERSTAND YOU.
GET AWAY FROM THAT INTERCOM.
COULD YOU PLEASE NOTIFY MR. STEELE THAT--
bzzz!

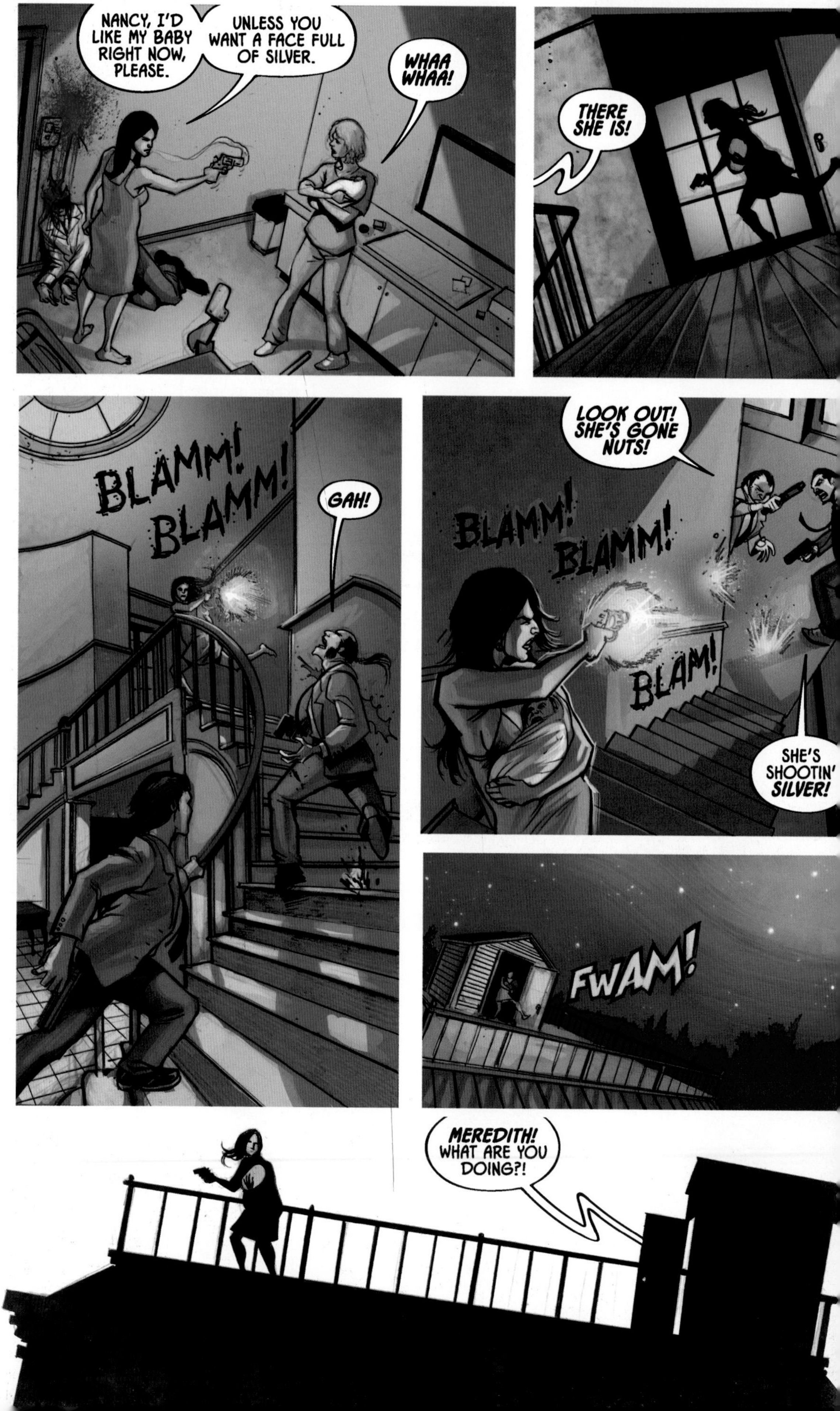
NANCY, I'D LIKE MY BABY RIGHT NOW, PLEASE.
UNLESS YOU WANT A FACE FULL OF SILVER.
WHAA WHAA!
THERE SHE IS!
BLAMM! BLAMM!
GAH!
LOOK OUT! SHE'S GONE NUTS!
BLAMM! BLAMM!
BLAM!
SHE'S SHOOTIN' SILVER!
FWAM!
MEREDITH! WHAT ARE YOU DOING?!

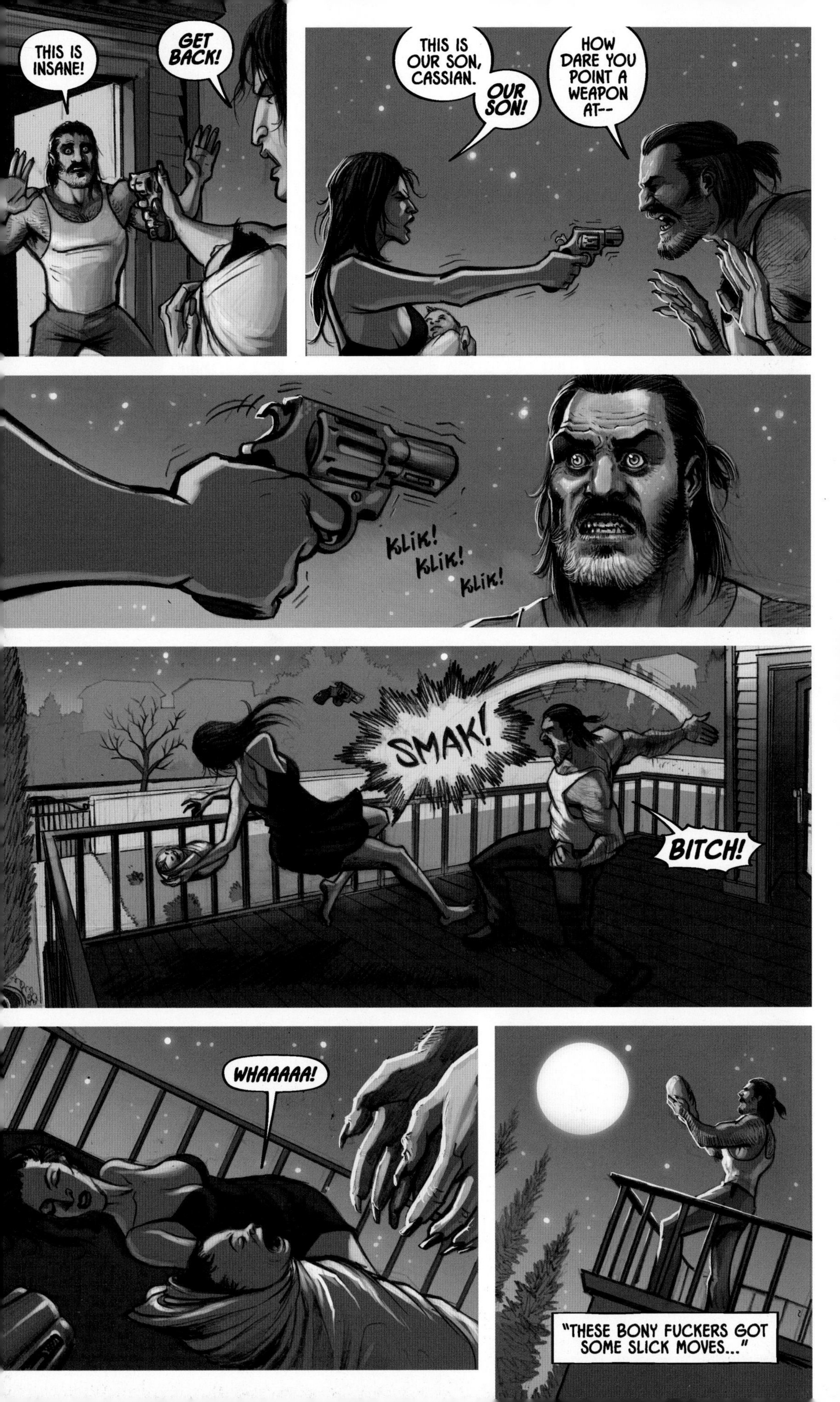
THIS IS INSANE!
GET BACK!
THIS IS OUR SON, CASSIAN.
OUR SON!
HOW DARE YOU POINT A WEAPON AT--
KLIK! KLIK! KLIK!
SMAK!
BITCH!
WHAAAAAA!
"THESE BONY FUCKERS GOT SOME SLICK MOVES..."

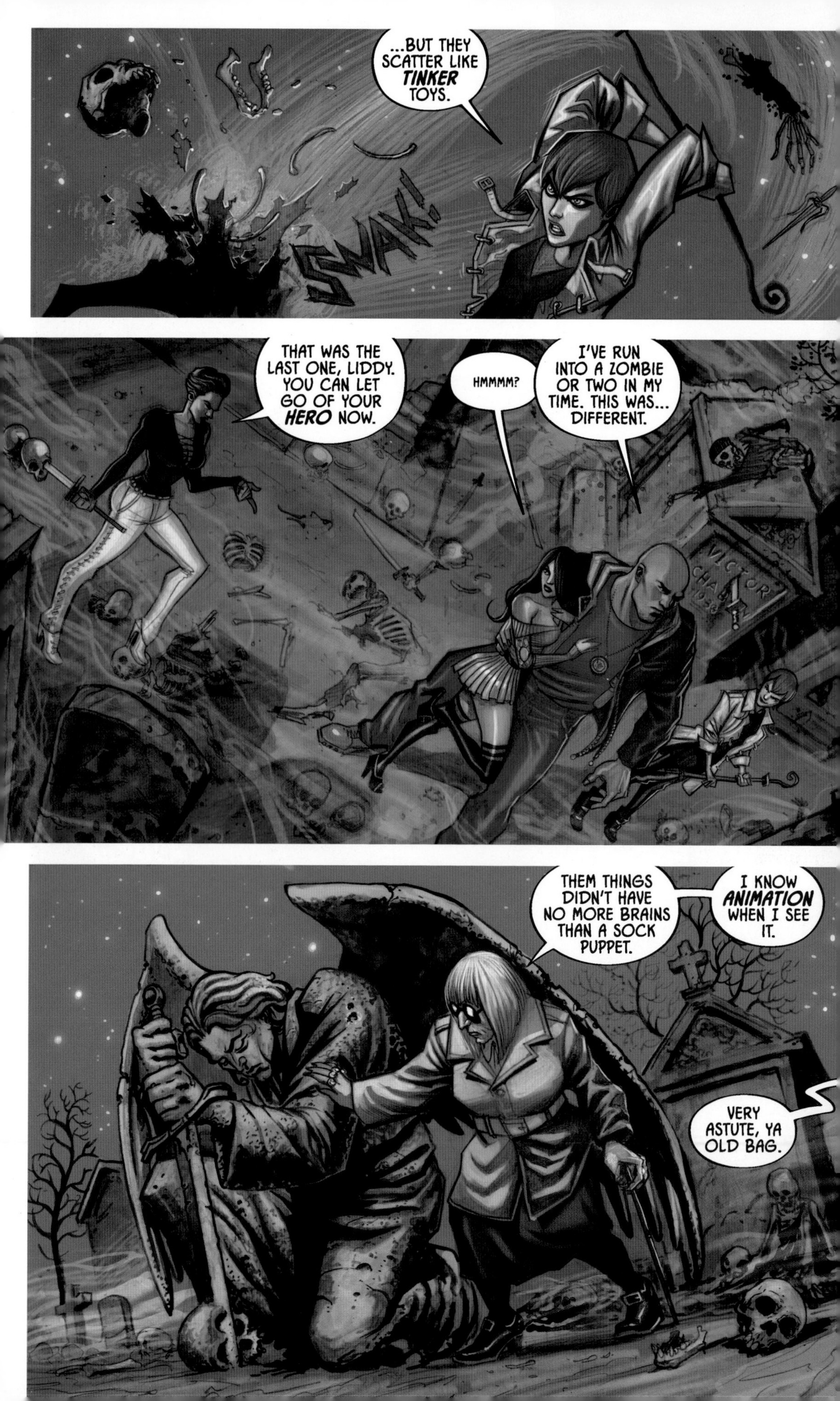
...BUT THEY SCATTER LIKE *TINKER* TOYS.
SWAK!
THAT WAS THE LAST ONE, LIDDY. YOU CAN LET GO OF YOUR *HERO* NOW.
HMMMM?
I'VE RUN INTO A ZOMBIE OR TWO IN MY TIME. THIS WAS... DIFFERENT.
THEM THINGS DIDN'T HAVE NO MORE BRAINS THAN A SOCK PUPPET.
I KNOW *ANIMATION* WHEN I SEE IT.
VERY ASTUTE, YA OLD BAG.

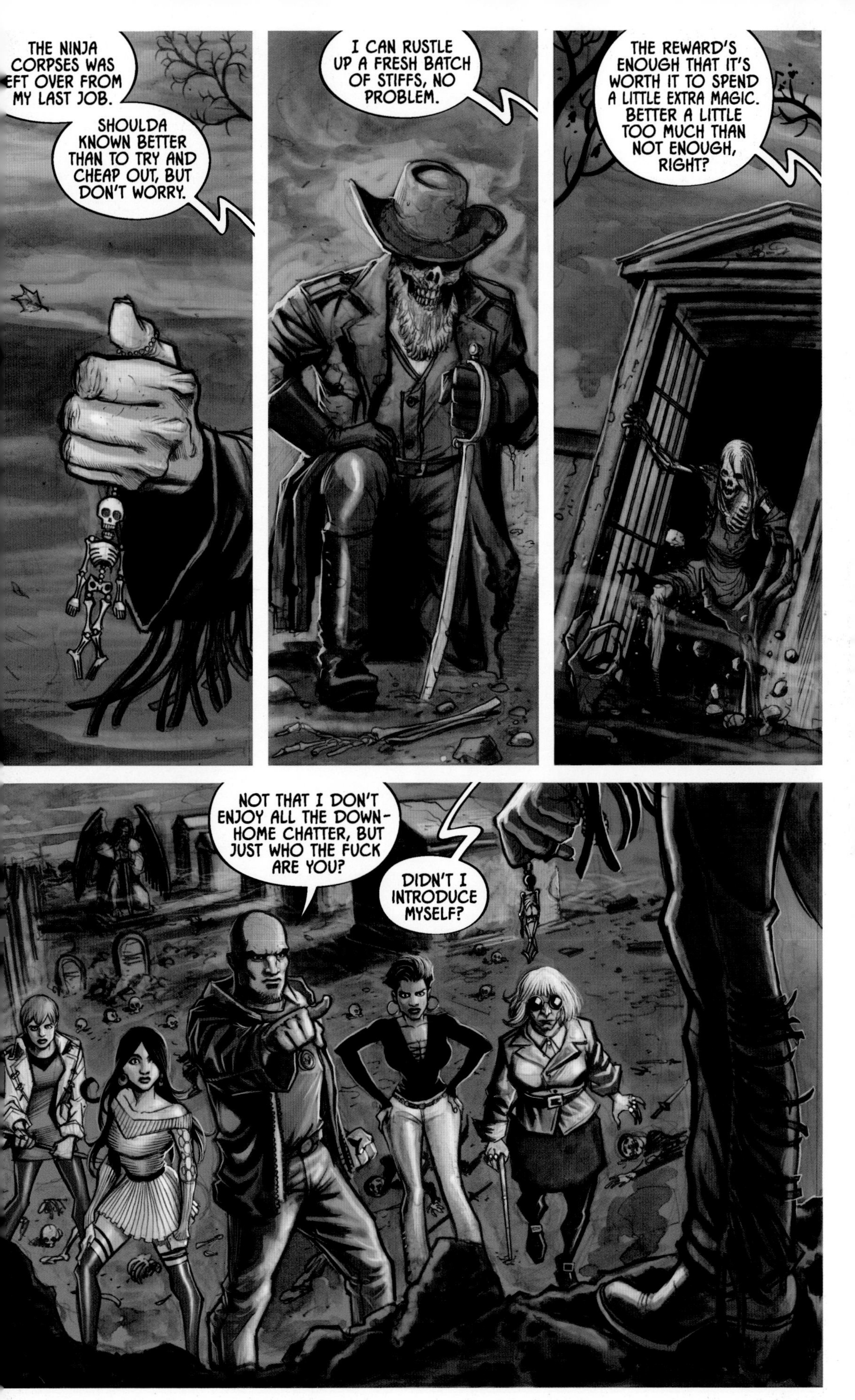
THE NINJA CORPSES WAS LEFT OVER FROM MY LAST JOB.
SHOULDA KNOWN BETTER THAN TO TRY AND CHEAP OUT, BUT DON'T WORRY.
I CAN RUSTLE UP A FRESH BATCH OF STIFFS, NO PROBLEM.
THE REWARD'S ENOUGH THAT IT'S WORTH IT TO SPEND A LITTLE EXTRA MAGIC. BETTER A LITTLE TOO MUCH THAN NOT ENOUGH, RIGHT?
NOT THAT I DON'T ENJOY ALL THE DOWN-HOME CHATTER, BUT JUST WHO THE FUCK ARE YOU?
DIDN'T I INTRODUCE MYSELF?

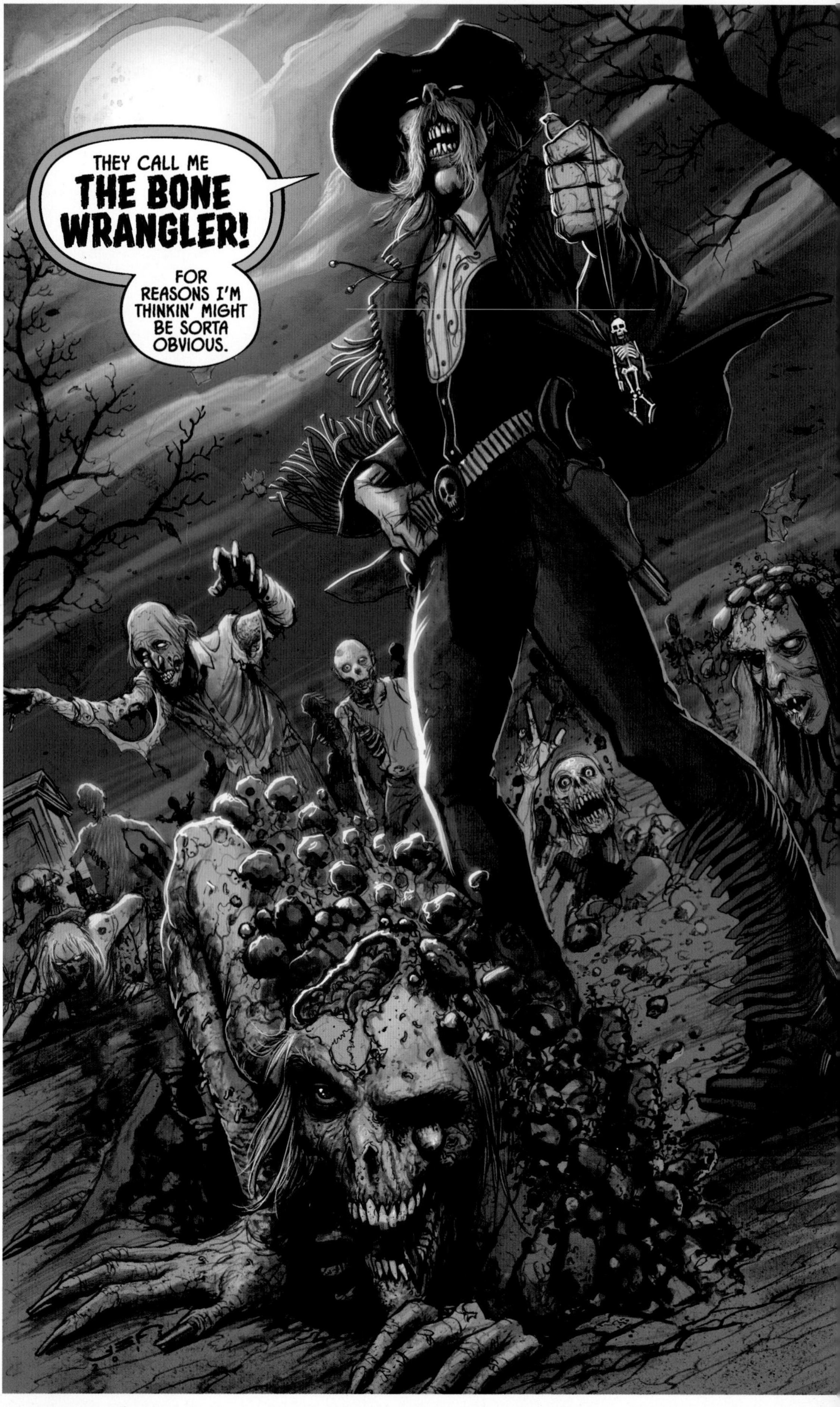
THEY CALL ME THE BONE WRANGLER!
FOR REASONS I'M THINKIN' MIGHT BE SORTA OBVIOUS.

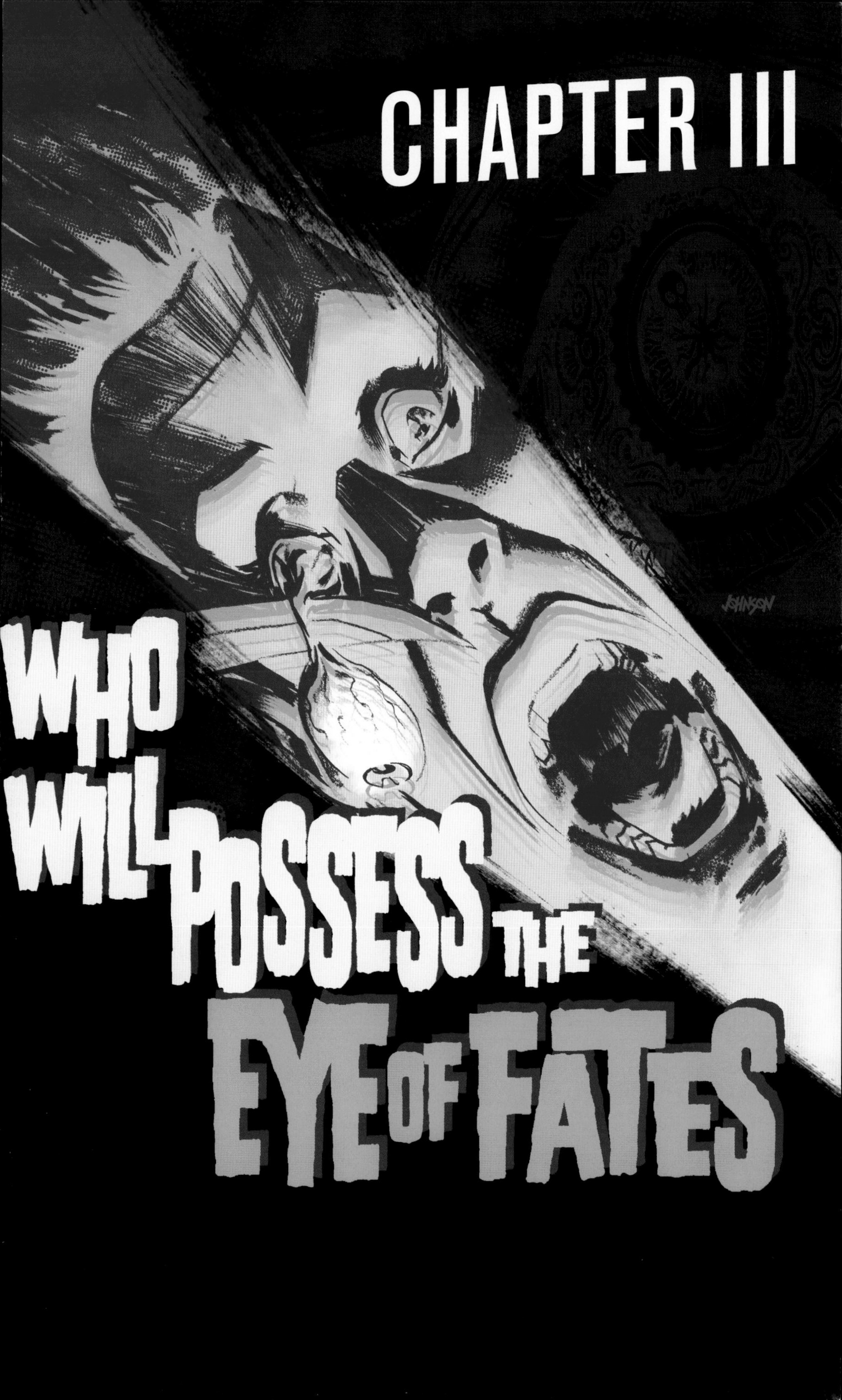
CHAPTER III
WHO WILL POSSESS THE EYE OF FATES
JOHNSON

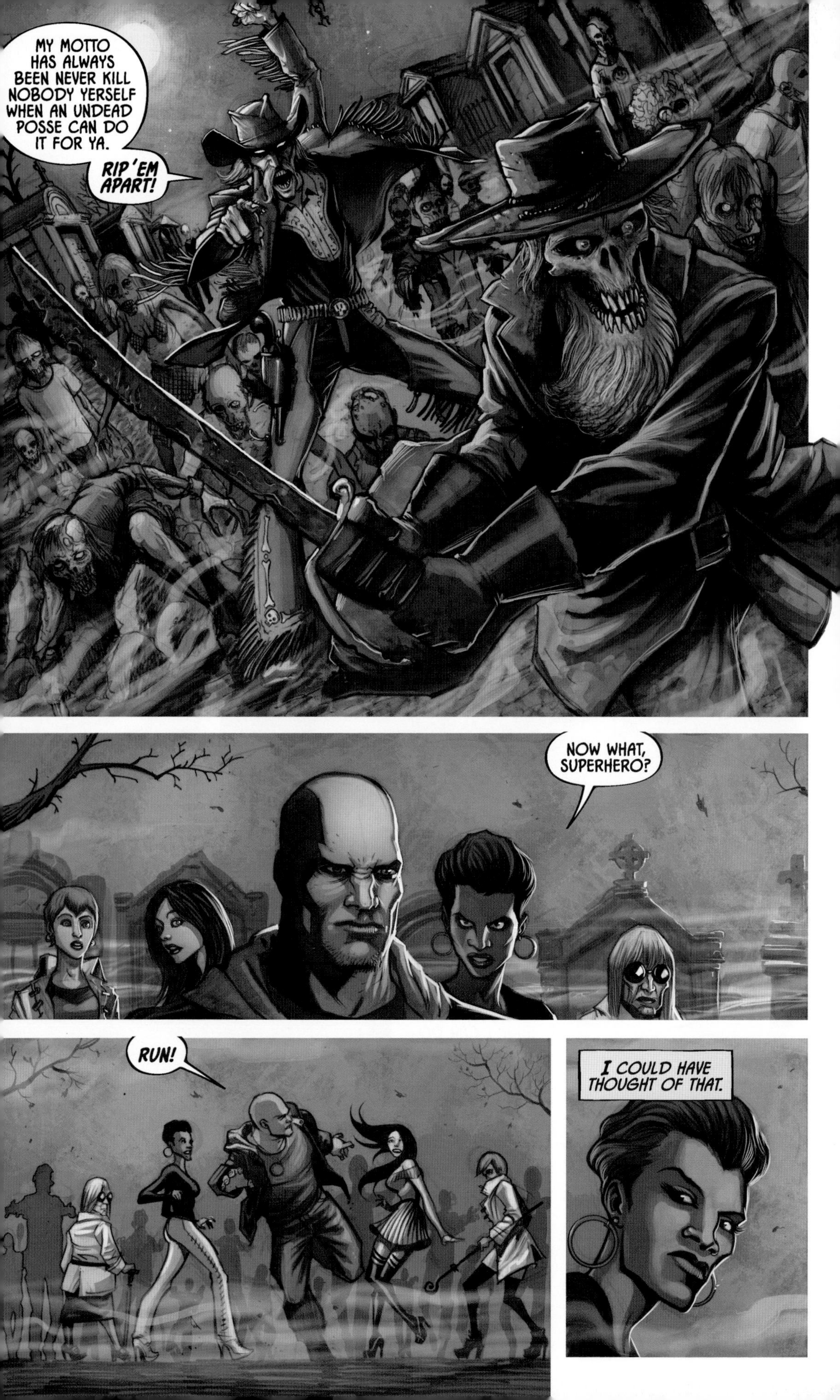
MY MOTTO HAS ALWAYS BEEN NEVER KILL NOBODY YERSELF WHEN AN UNDEAD POSSE CAN DO IT FOR YA.
RIP'EM APART!
NOW WHAT, SUPERHERO?
RUN!
I COULD HAVE THOUGHT OF THAT.

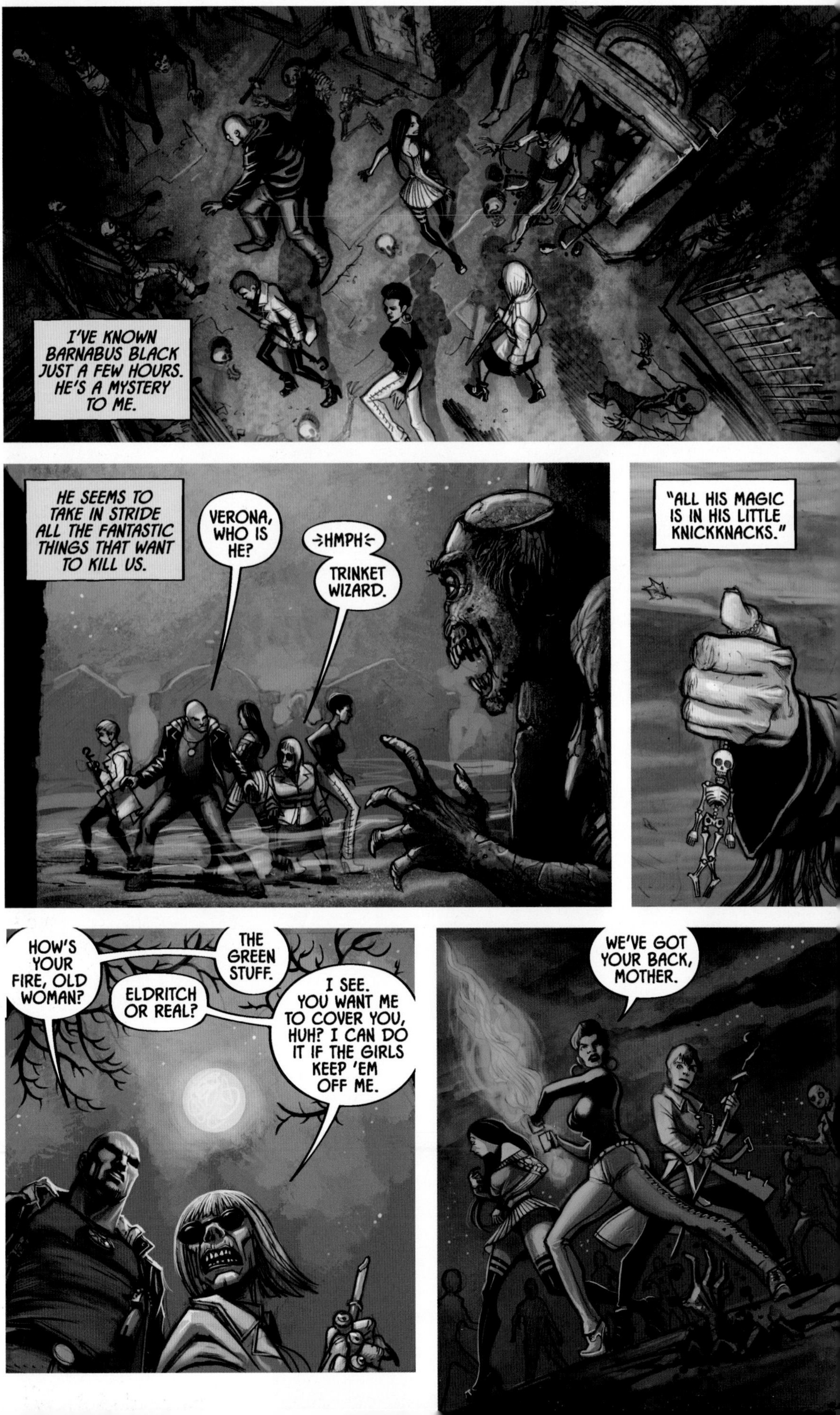
I'VE KNOWN BARNABUS BLACK JUST A FEW HOURS. HE'S A MYSTERY TO ME.
HE SEEMS TO TAKE IN STRIDE ALL THE FANTASTIC THINGS THAT WANT TO KILL US.
VERONA, WHO IS HE?
HMPH
TRINKET WIZARD.
"ALL HIS MAGIC IS IN HIS LITTLE KNICKKNACKS."
HOW'S YOUR FIRE, OLD WOMAN?
THE GREEN STUFF.
ELDRITCH OR REAL?
I SEE. YOU WANT ME TO COVER YOU, HUH? I CAN DO IT IF THE GIRLS KEEP 'EM OFF ME.
WE'VE GOT YOUR BACK, MOTHER.

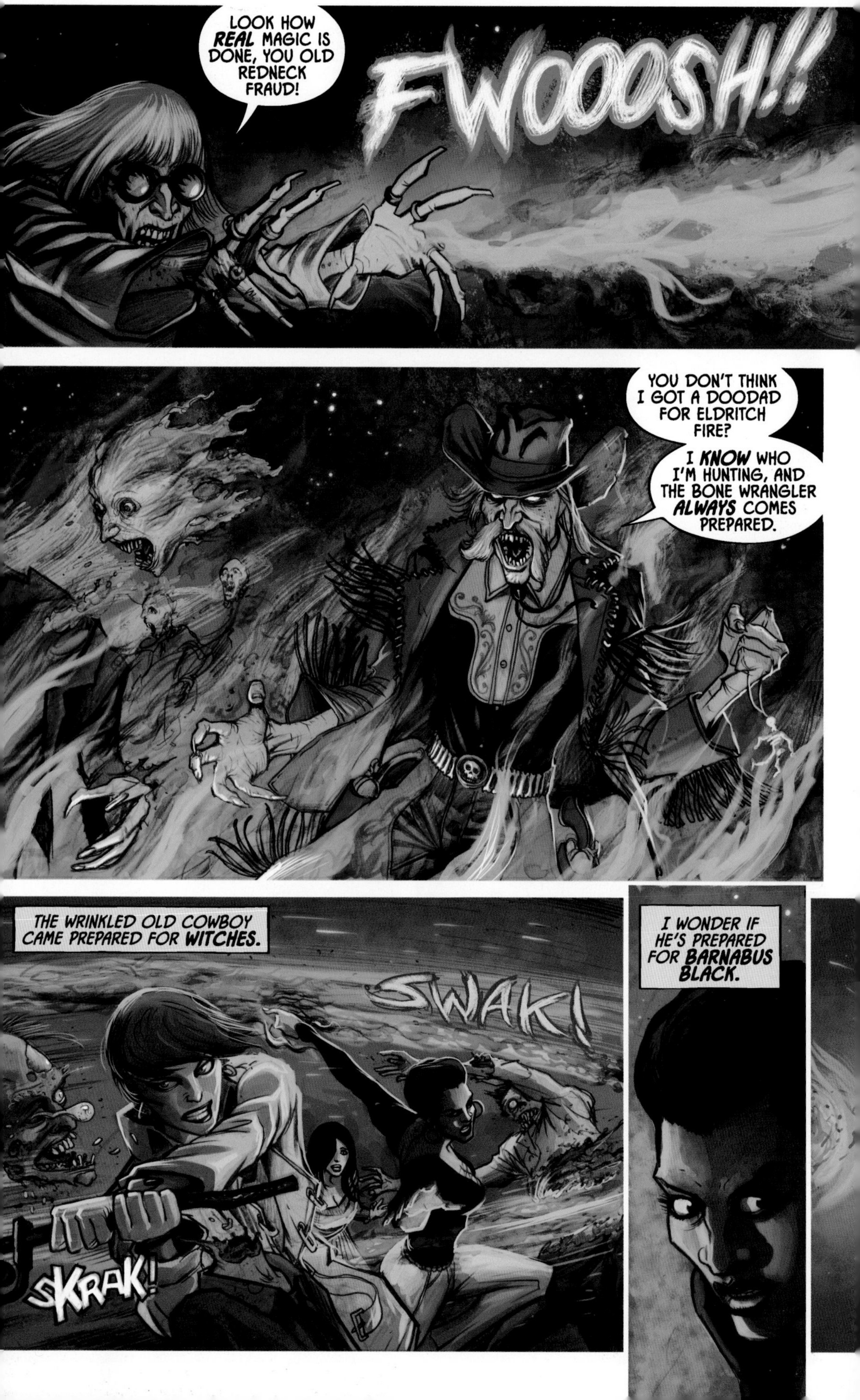

LOOK HOW REAL MAGIC IS DONE, YOU OLD REDNECK FRAUD!
FWOOOSH!!
YOU DON'T THINK I GOT A DOODAD FOR ELDRITCH FIRE?
I KNOW WHO I'M HUNTING, AND THE BONE WRANGLER ALWAYS COMES PREPARED.
THE WRINKLED OLD COWBOY CAME PREPARED FOR WITCHES.
SWAK!
SKRAK!
I WONDER IF HE'S PREPARED FOR BARNABUS BLACK.

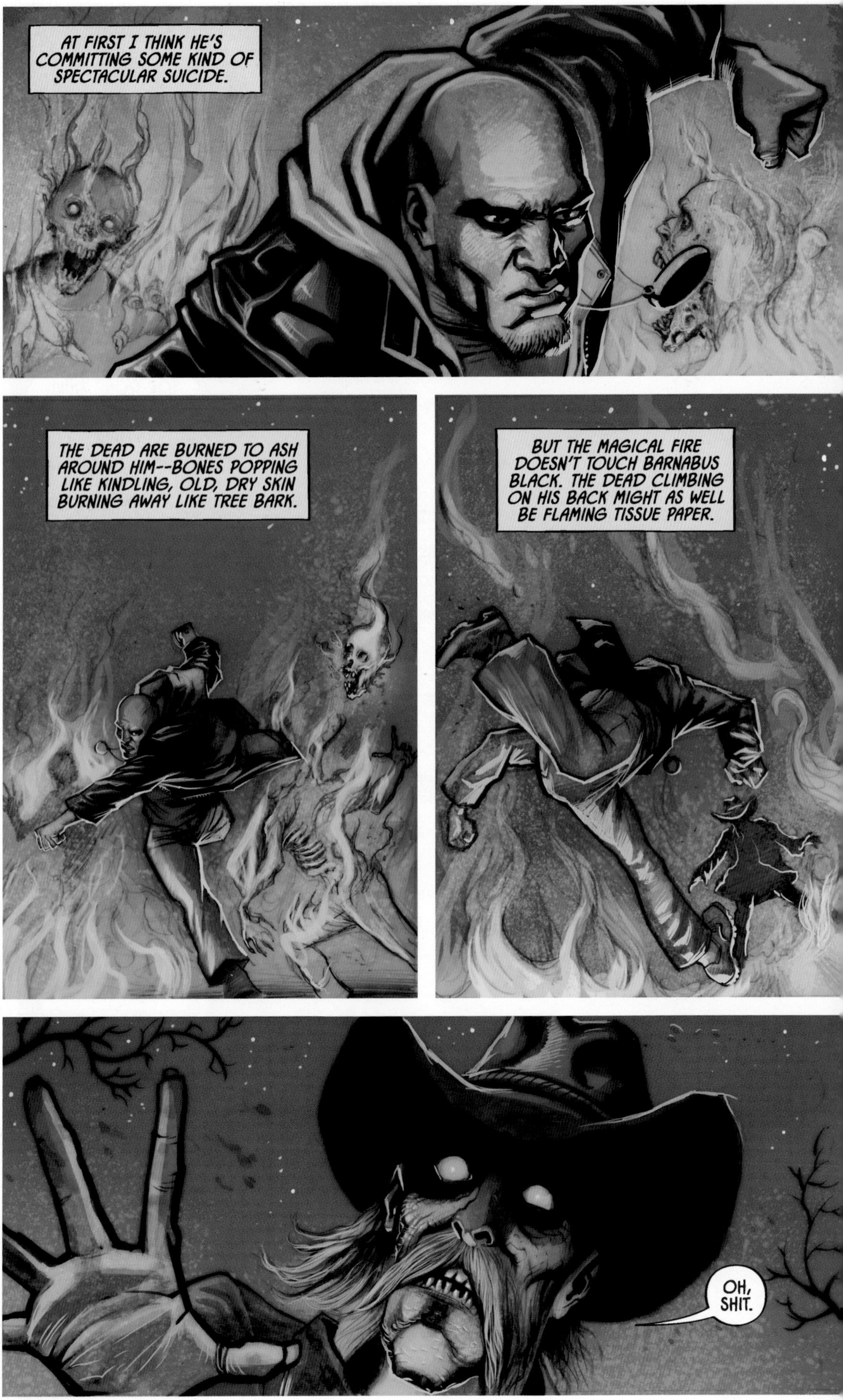
AT FIRST I THINK HE'S COMMITTING SOME KIND OF SPECTACULAR SUICIDE.
THE DEAD ARE BURNED TO ASH AROUND HIM--BONES POPPING LIKE KINDLING, OLD, DRY SKIN BURNING AWAY LIKE TREE BARK.
BUT THE MAGICAL FIRE DOESN'T TOUCH BARNABUS BLACK. THE DEAD CLIMBING ON HIS BACK MIGHT AS WELL BE FLAMING TISSUE PAPER.
OH, SHIT.

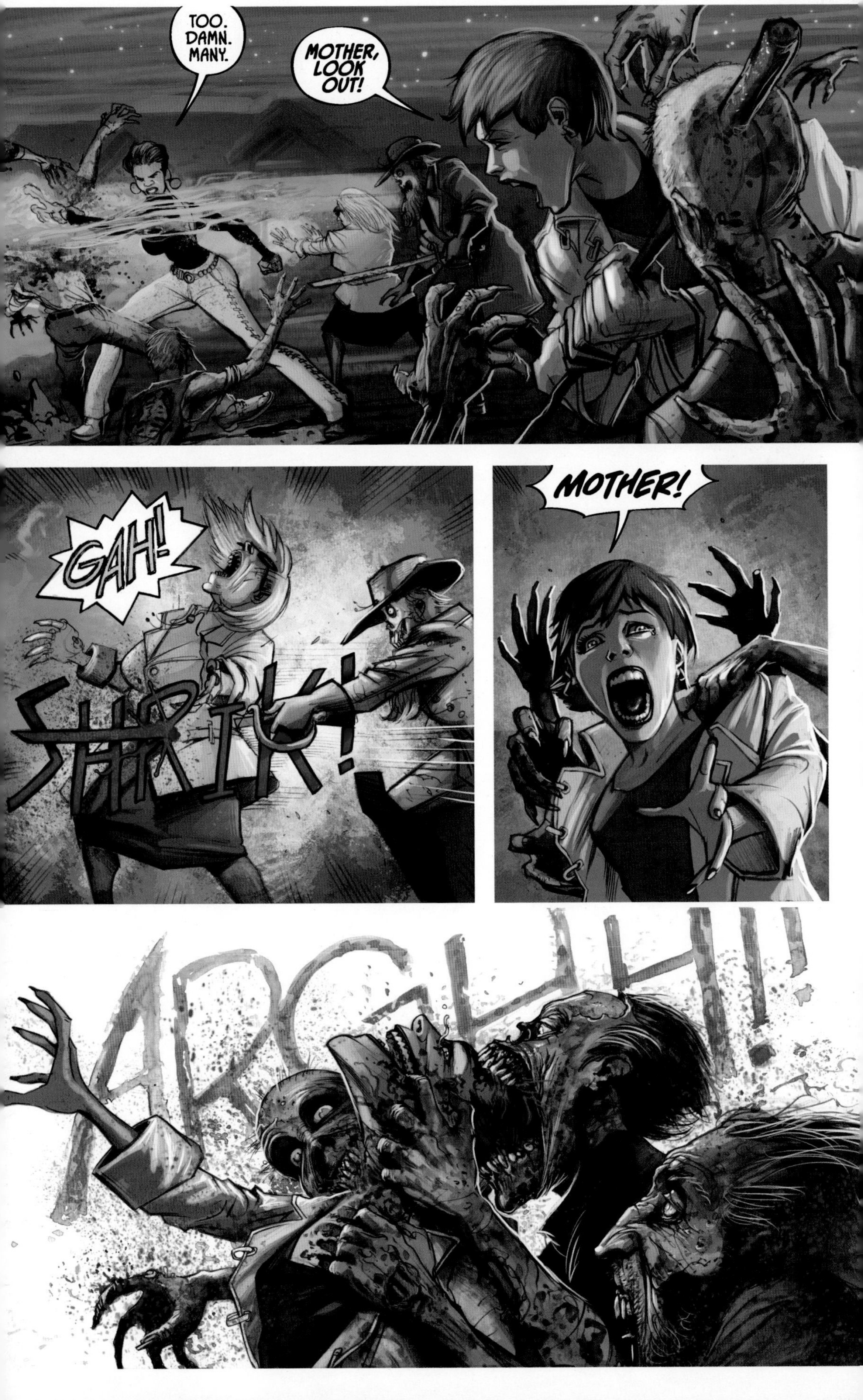
TOO. DAMN. MANY.
MOTHER, LOOK OUT!
GAH!
SHRIK!
MOTHER!
ARGHH!

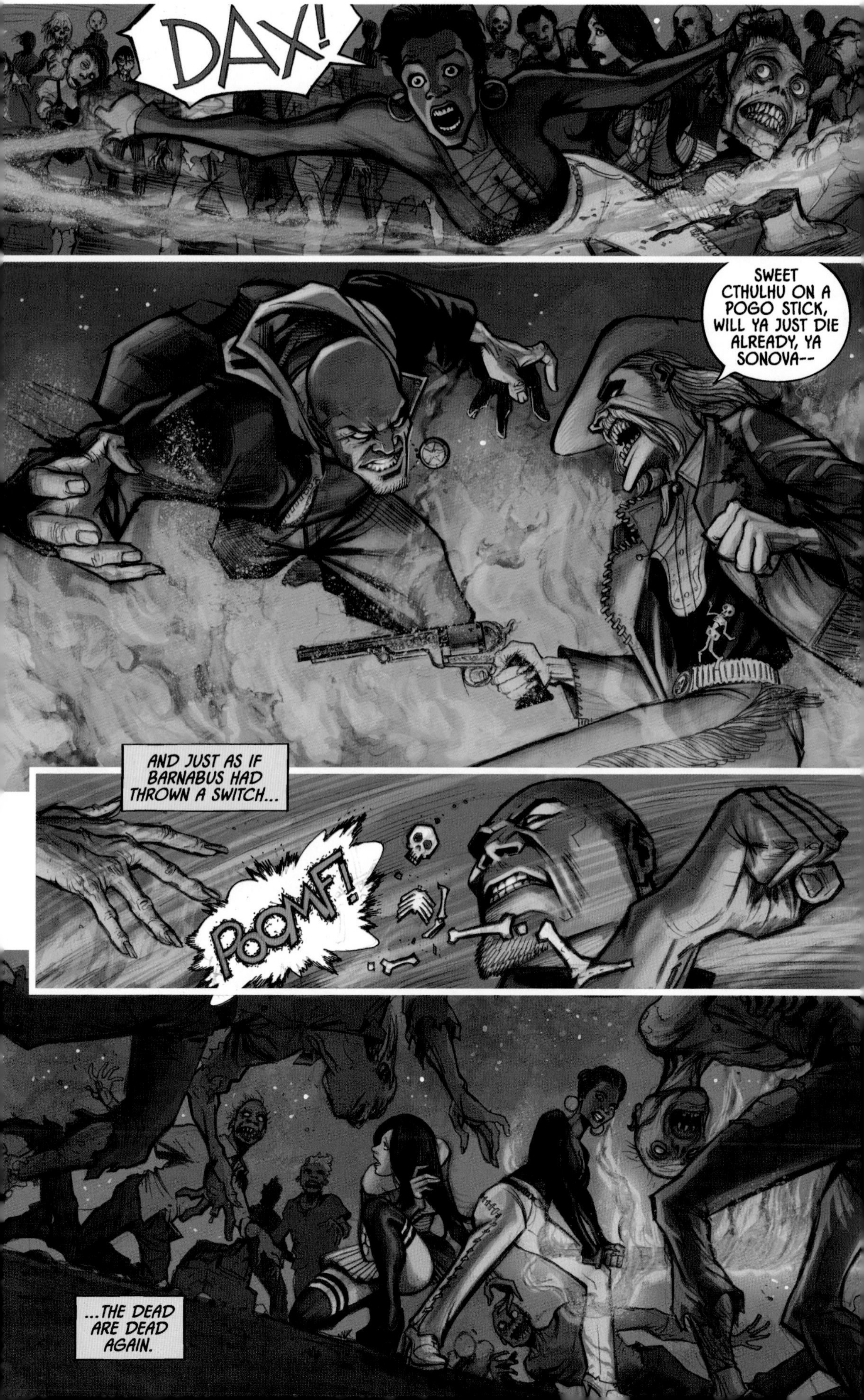
DAX!
SWEET CTHULHU ON A POGO STICK, WILL YA JUST DIE ALREADY, YA SONOVA--
AND JUST AS IF BARNABUS HAD THROWN A SWITCH...
POOMF!
...THE DEAD ARE DEAD AGAIN.

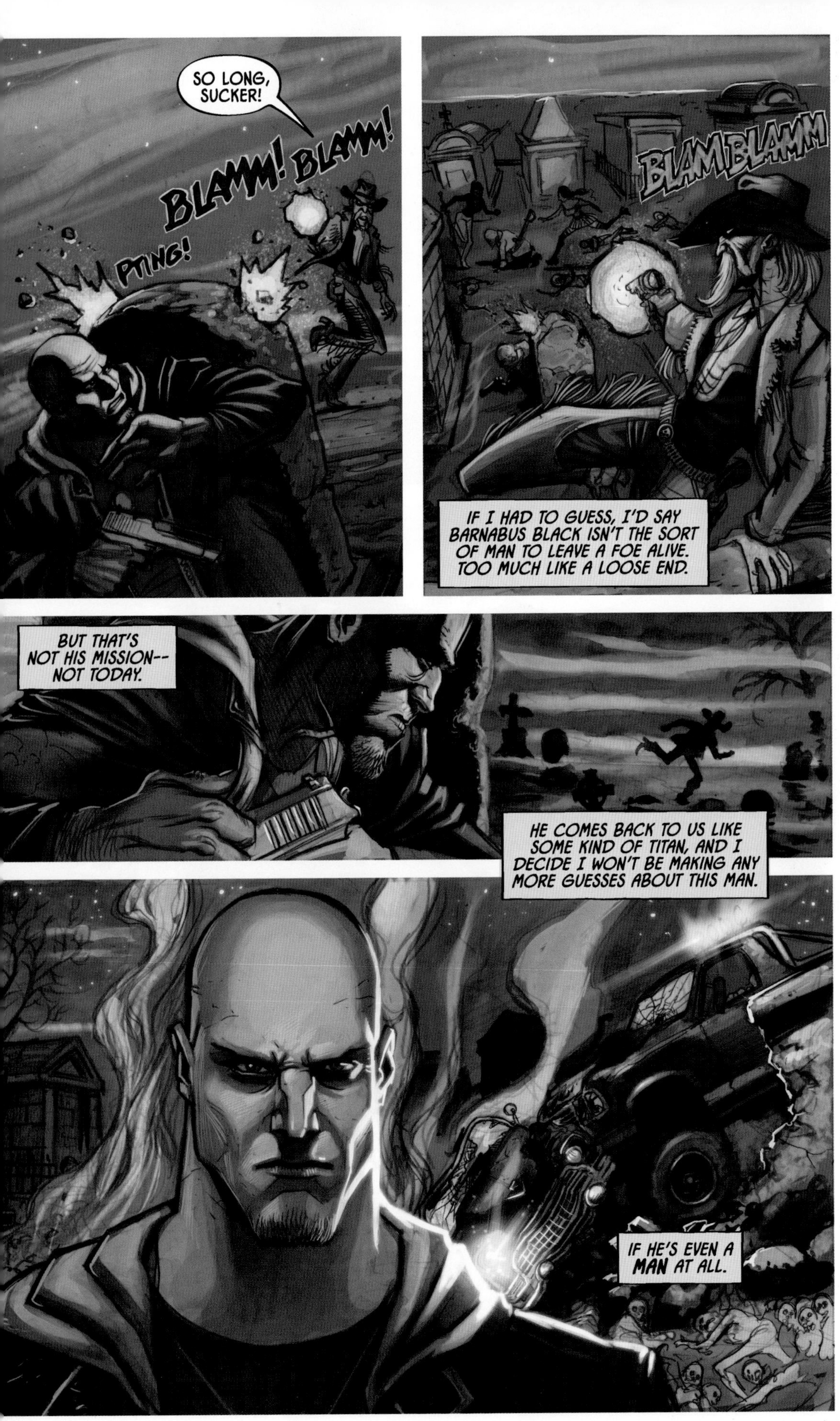
SO LONG, SUCKER!
BLAMM! BLAMM!
PTING!
BLAMBLAMM
IF I HAD TO GUESS, I'D SAY BARNABUS BLACK ISN'T THE SORT OF MAN TO LEAVE A FOE ALIVE. TOO MUCH LIKE A LOOSE END.
BUT THAT'S NOT HIS MISSION-- NOT TODAY.
HE COMES BACK TO US LIKE SOME KIND OF TITAN, AND I DECIDE I WON'T BE MAKING ANY MORE GUESSES ABOUT THIS MAN.
IF HE'S EVEN A MAN AT ALL.

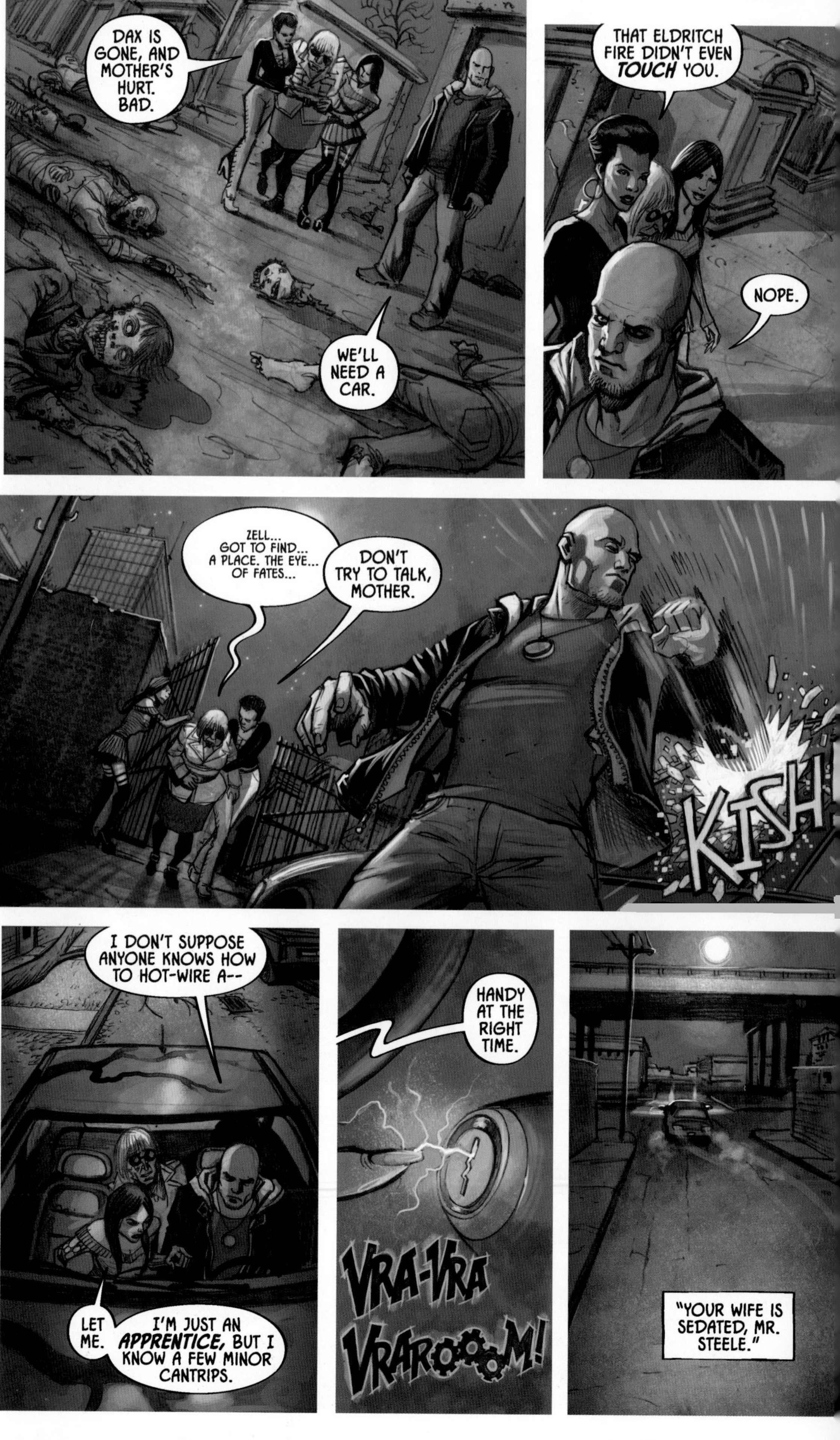

DAX IS GONE, AND MOTHER'S HURT. BAD.
WE'LL NEED A CAR.
THAT ELDRITCH FIRE DIDN'T EVEN TOUCH YOU.
NOPE.
ZELL... GOT TO FIND... A PLACE. THE EYE... OF FATES...
DON'T TRY TO TALK, MOTHER.
KISH
I DON'T SUPPOSE ANYONE KNOWS HOW TO HOT-WIRE A--
LET ME.
I'M JUST AN APPRENTICE, BUT I KNOW A FEW MINOR CANTRIPS.
HANDY AT THE RIGHT TIME.
VRA-VRA VRAROOOOM!
"YOUR WIFE IS SEDATED, MR. STEELE."

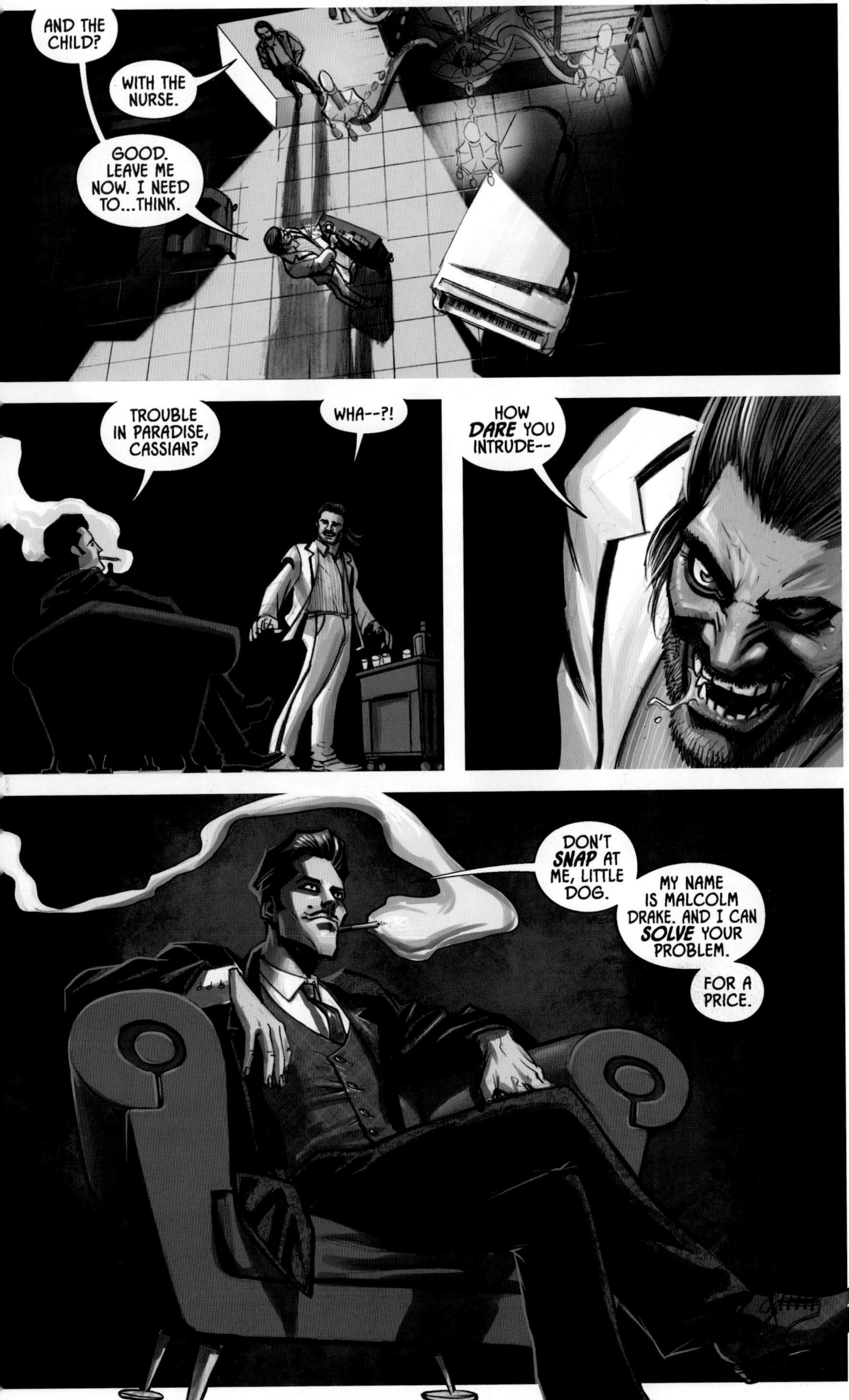
AND THE CHILD?
WITH THE NURSE.
GOOD. LEAVE ME NOW. I NEED TO...THINK.
TROUBLE IN PARADISE, CASSIAN?
WHA--?!
HOW *DARE* YOU INTRUDE--
DON'T *SNAP* AT ME, LITTLE DOG.
MY NAME IS MALCOLM DRAKE. AND I CAN *SOLVE* YOUR PROBLEM.
FOR A PRICE.

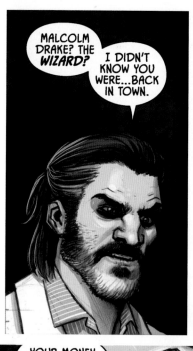

MALCOLM DRAKE? THE *WIZARD?*

I DIDN'T KNOW YOU WERE...BACK IN TOWN.

YOU MEAN YOU DIDN'T KNOW IF I WAS STILL *ALIVE.*

I'M AN AMBITIOUS MAN, AND THAT'S *DANGEROUS.* I'VE HAD SOME CLOSE SCRAPES, BUT I *ALWAYS* COME OUT ON TOP.

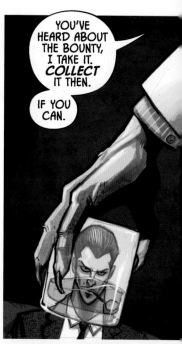

YOU'VE HEARD ABOUT THE BOUNTY, I TAKE IT. *COLLECT* IT THEN.

IF YOU CAN.

YOUR MONEY MEANS NOTHING TO ME.

THE WITCHES HAVE STAMPEDED THE BONE WRANGLER, AND THE VAMPIRE BITCH WAS BUSH LEAGUE. EVERYONE ELSE IS RUNNING IN CIRCLES. YOUR PREY IS SLIPPING *AWAY* FROM YOU.

IF NOT THE BOUNTY, THEN WHAT *DO* YOU WANT?

THE *EYE OF FATES.* THAT'S MY PRICE.

BUT CALL OFF THE REST OF YOUR HIRED KILLERS. I DON'T NEED AMATEURS CLUTTERING THE BATTLEFIELD.

SO THE FAMOUS MALCOLM DRAKE OFFERS HIS SERVICES. HOW CAN I REFUSE? YOU HAVE A *DEAL.*

HAVE A DRINK, WHY DON'T YOU? WE CAN TOAST TO OUR NEW--

HELLO?

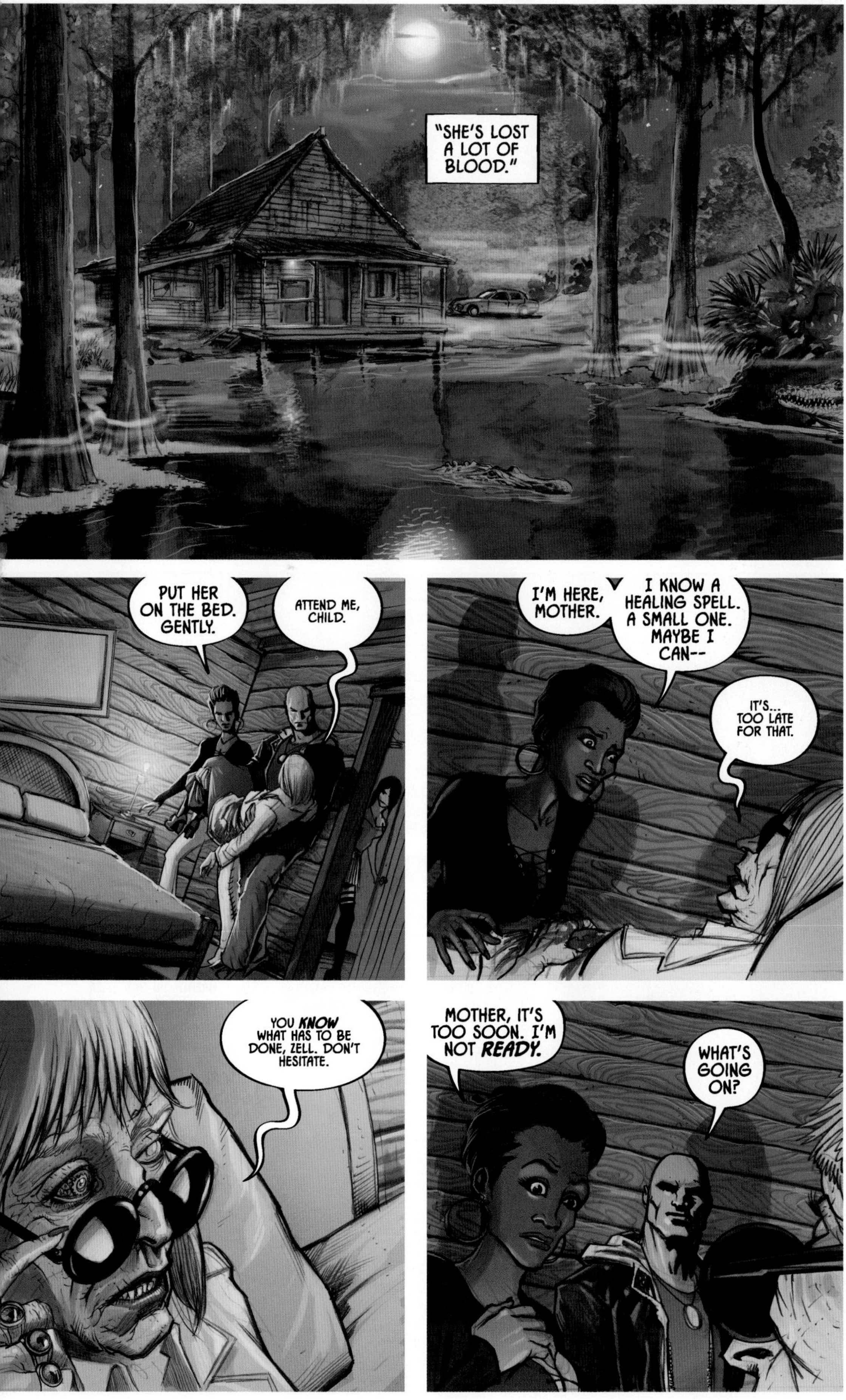
"SHE'S LOST A LOT OF BLOOD."
PUT HER ON THE BED. GENTLY.
ATTEND ME, CHILD.
I'M HERE, MOTHER.
I KNOW A HEALING SPELL. A SMALL ONE. MAYBE I CAN--
IT'S... TOO LATE FOR THAT.
YOU **KNOW** WHAT HAS TO BE DONE, ZELL. DON'T HESITATE.
MOTHER, IT'S TOO SOON. I'M NOT ***READY.***
WHAT'S GOING ON?

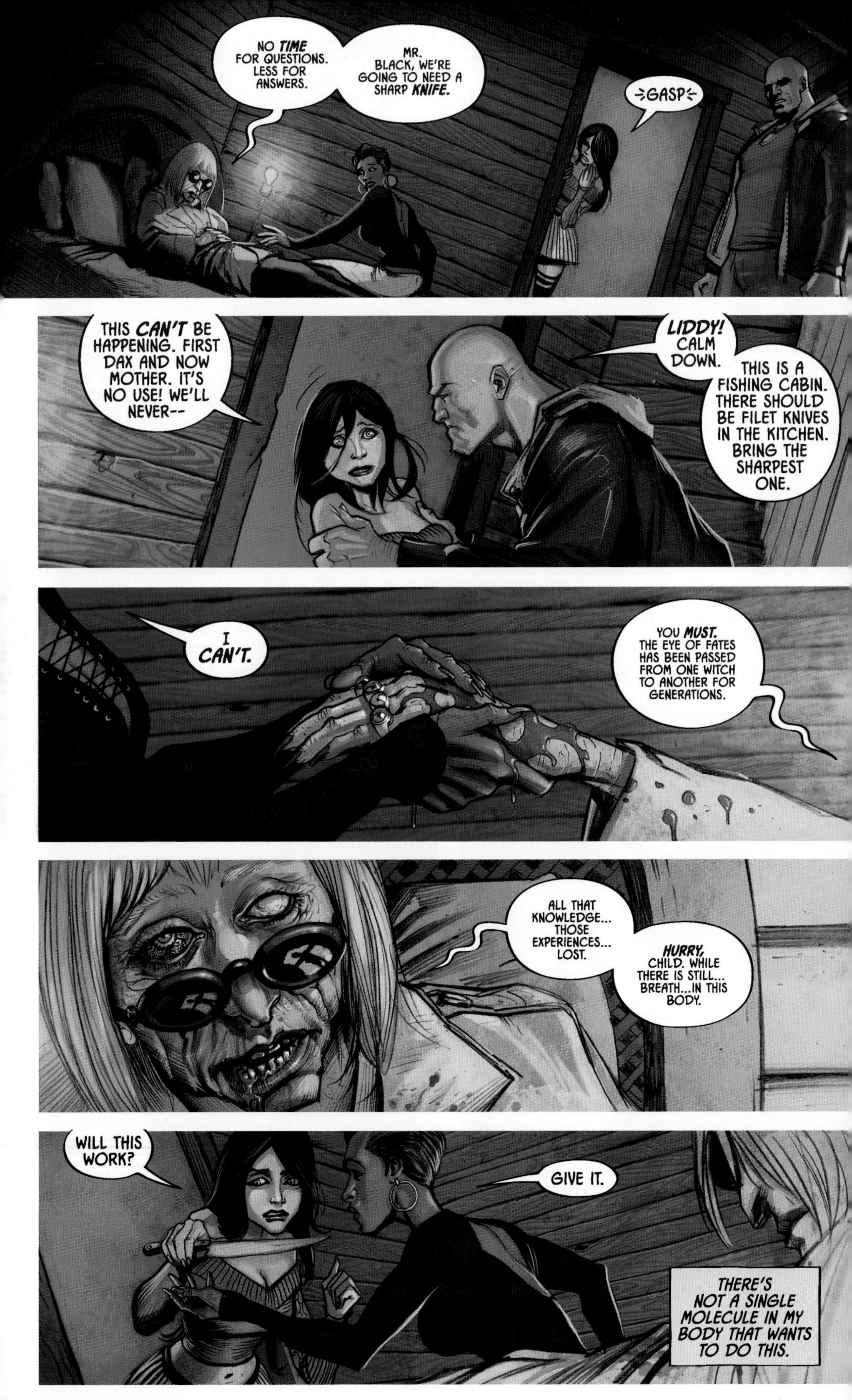
NO TIME FOR QUESTIONS. LESS FOR ANSWERS.
MR. BLACK, WE'RE GOING TO NEED A SHARP KNIFE.
GASP
THIS CAN'T BE HAPPENING. FIRST DAX AND NOW MOTHER. IT'S NO USE! WE'LL NEVER--
LIDDY! CALM DOWN.
THIS IS A FISHING CABIN. THERE SHOULD BE FILET KNIVES IN THE KITCHEN. BRING THE SHARPEST ONE.
I CAN'T.
YOU MUST. THE EYE OF FATES HAS BEEN PASSED FROM ONE WITCH TO ANOTHER FOR GENERATIONS.
ALL THAT KNOWLEDGE... THOSE EXPERIENCES... LOST.
HURRY, CHILD. WHILE THERE IS STILL... BREATH...IN THIS BODY.
WILL THIS WORK?
GIVE IT.
THERE'S NOT A SINGLE MOLECULE IN MY BODY THAT WANTS TO DO THIS.

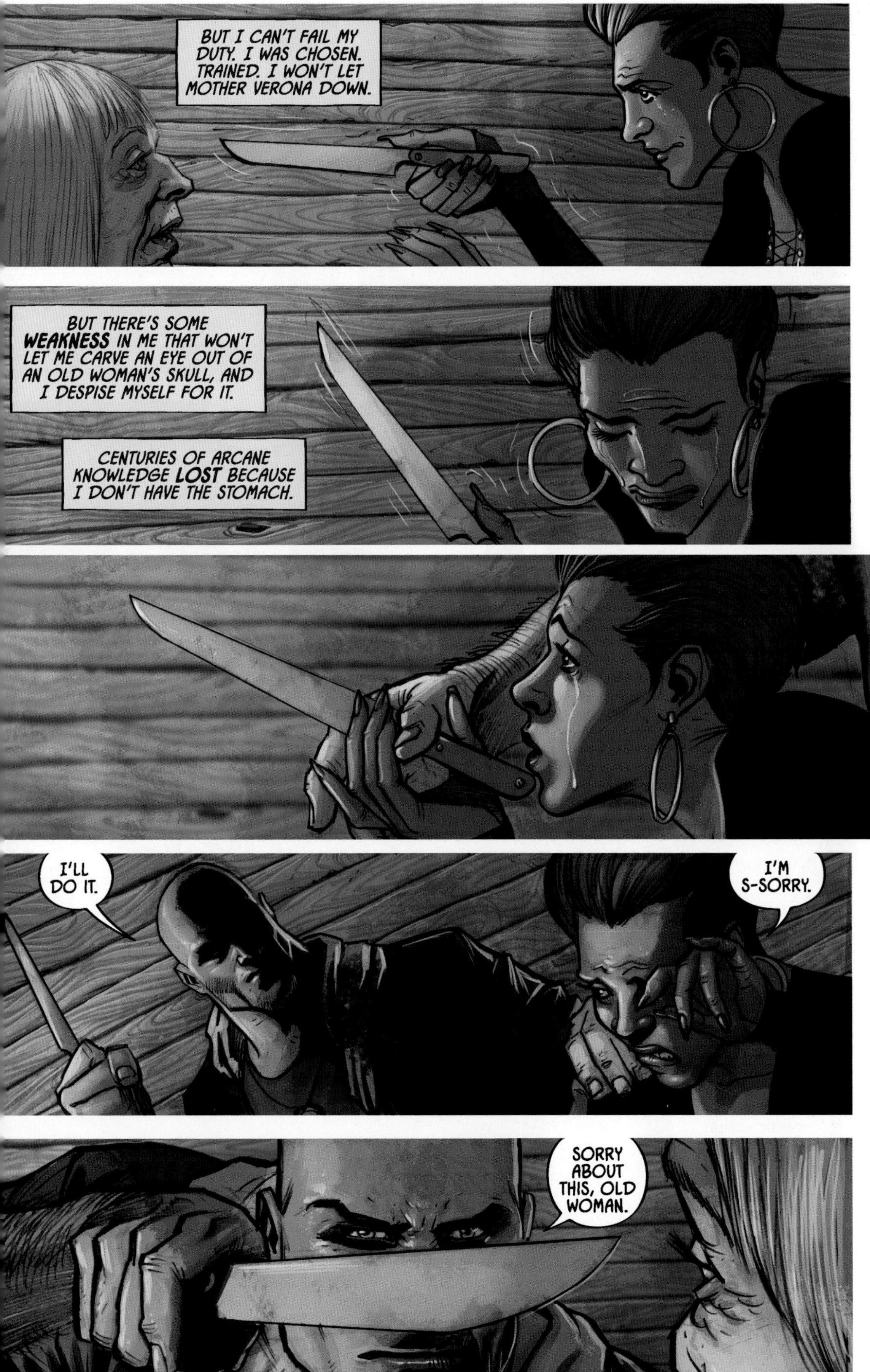
BUT I CAN'T FAIL MY DUTY. I WAS CHOSEN. TRAINED. I WON'T LET MOTHER VERONA DOWN.
BUT THERE'S SOME WEAKNESS IN ME THAT WON'T LET ME CARVE AN EYE OUT OF AN OLD WOMAN'S SKULL, AND I DESPISE MYSELF FOR IT.
CENTURIES OF ARCANE KNOWLEDGE LOST BECAUSE I DON'T HAVE THE STOMACH.
I'LL DO IT.
I'M S-SORRY.
SORRY ABOUT THIS, OLD WOMAN.

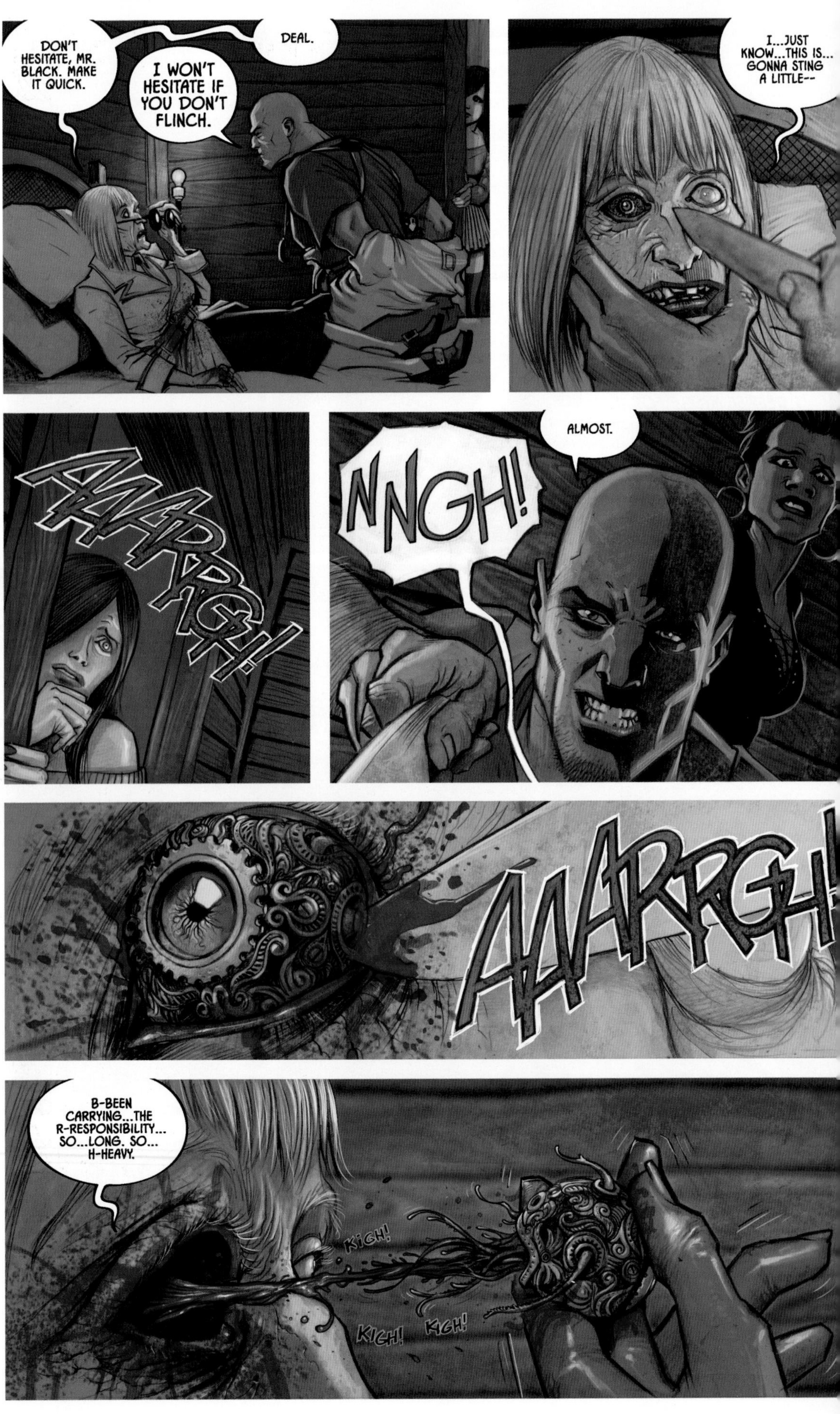

DON'T HESITATE, MR. BLACK. MAKE IT QUICK.
DEAL.
I WON'T HESITATE IF YOU DON'T FLINCH.
I...JUST KNOW...THIS IS... GONNA STING A LITTLE--
AAARRGH!
ALMOST.
NNGH!
AAARRGH!
B-BEEN CARRYING...THE R-RESPONSIBILITY... SO...LONG. SO... H-HEAVY.
KIGH!
KIGH!
KIGH!

THERE'S MORE TO HIS THING THAN MEETS HE...UH... EYE.

MOTHER?

I FEEL... SO... LIGHT.

I'M SO SORRY... THIS BURDEN HAS COME TO YOU, CHILD. SO SOON.

FFfwwwiissssrrSSSS!!

I GLIMPSE MOTHER'S FACE AS SHE PASSES ON, AND I THINK I SEE JOY THERE.

I'D HEARD ABOUT THE RELEASE AT THE END OF A WITCH'S LIFE, BUT IT'S MORE BEAUTIFUL AND FRIGHTENING THAN I'D IMAGINED.

BARNABUS BLACK IS ALMOST IMPRESSED.

IN MY YEARS WALKING THE EARTH, I'VE SEEN SOME UNIQUE SHIT.

THAT'S NEW.

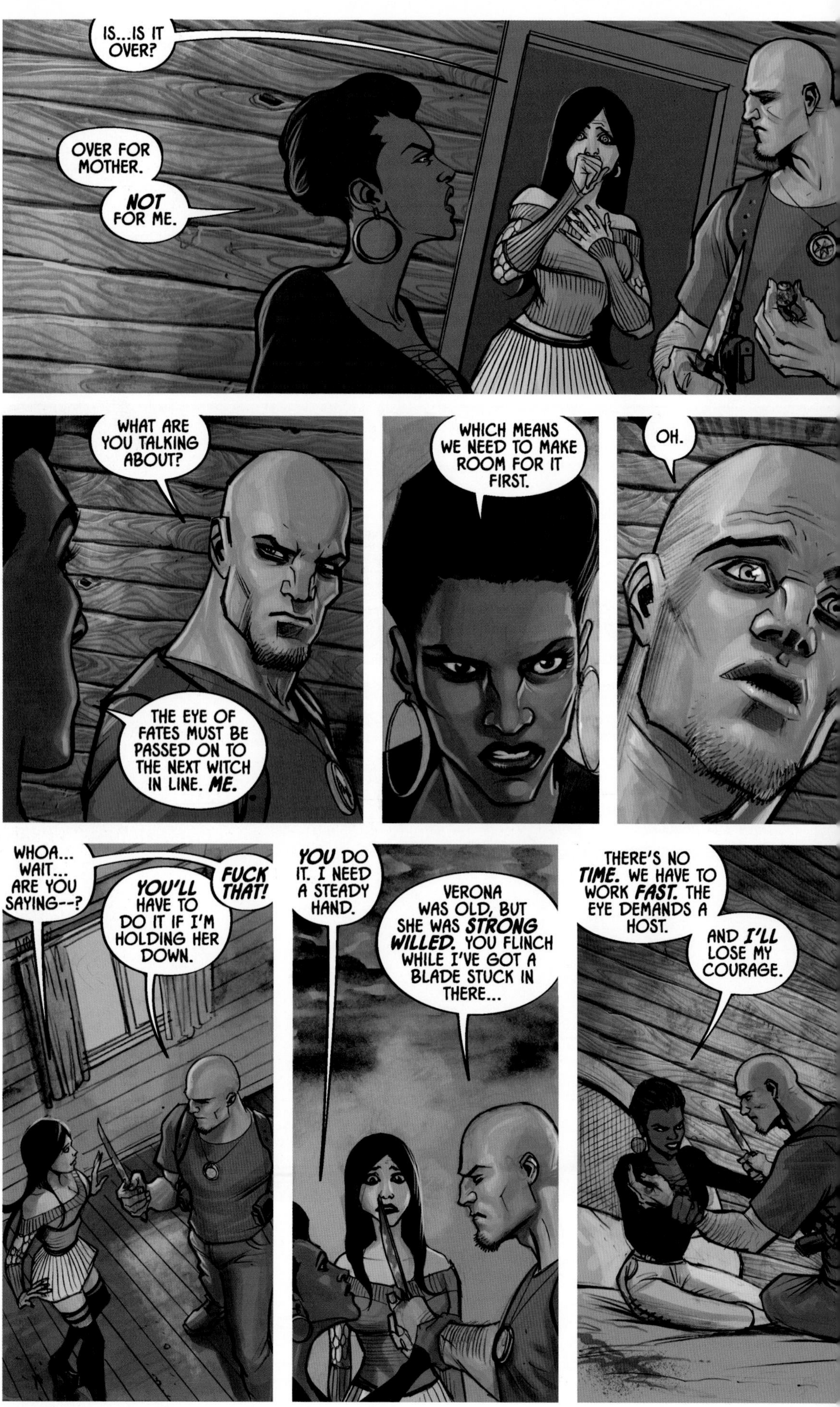

IS...IS IT OVER?
OVER FOR MOTHER.
NOT FOR ME.
WHAT ARE YOU TALKING ABOUT?
THE EYE OF FATES MUST BE PASSED ON TO THE NEXT WITCH IN LINE. ME.
WHICH MEANS WE NEED TO MAKE ROOM FOR IT FIRST.
OH.
WHOA... WAIT... ARE YOU SAYING--?
YOU'LL HAVE TO DO IT IF I'M HOLDING HER DOWN.
FUCK THAT!
YOU DO IT. I NEED A STEADY HAND.
VERONA WAS OLD, BUT SHE WAS STRONG WILLED. YOU FLINCH WHILE I'VE GOT A BLADE STUCK IN THERE...
THERE'S NO TIME. WE HAVE TO WORK FAST. THE EYE DEMANDS A HOST.
AND I'LL LOSE MY COURAGE.

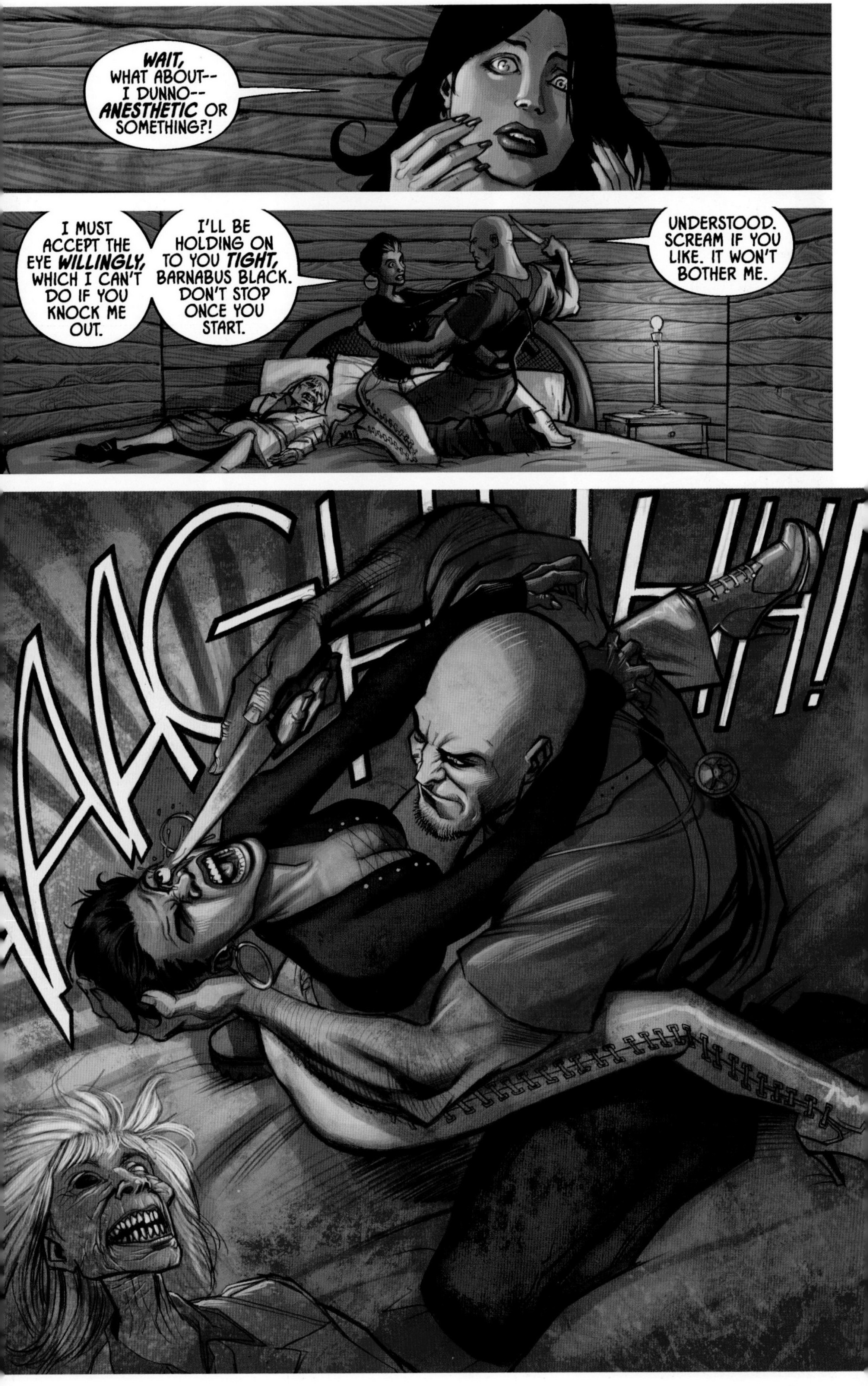
WAIT, WHAT ABOUT-- I DUNNO-- ANESTHETIC OR SOMETHING?!
I MUST ACCEPT THE EYE WILLINGLY, WHICH I CAN'T DO IF YOU KNOCK ME OUT.
I'LL BE HOLDING ON TO YOU TIGHT, BARNABUS BLACK. DON'T STOP ONCE YOU START.
UNDERSTOOD. SCREAM IF YOU LIKE. IT WON'T BOTHER ME.

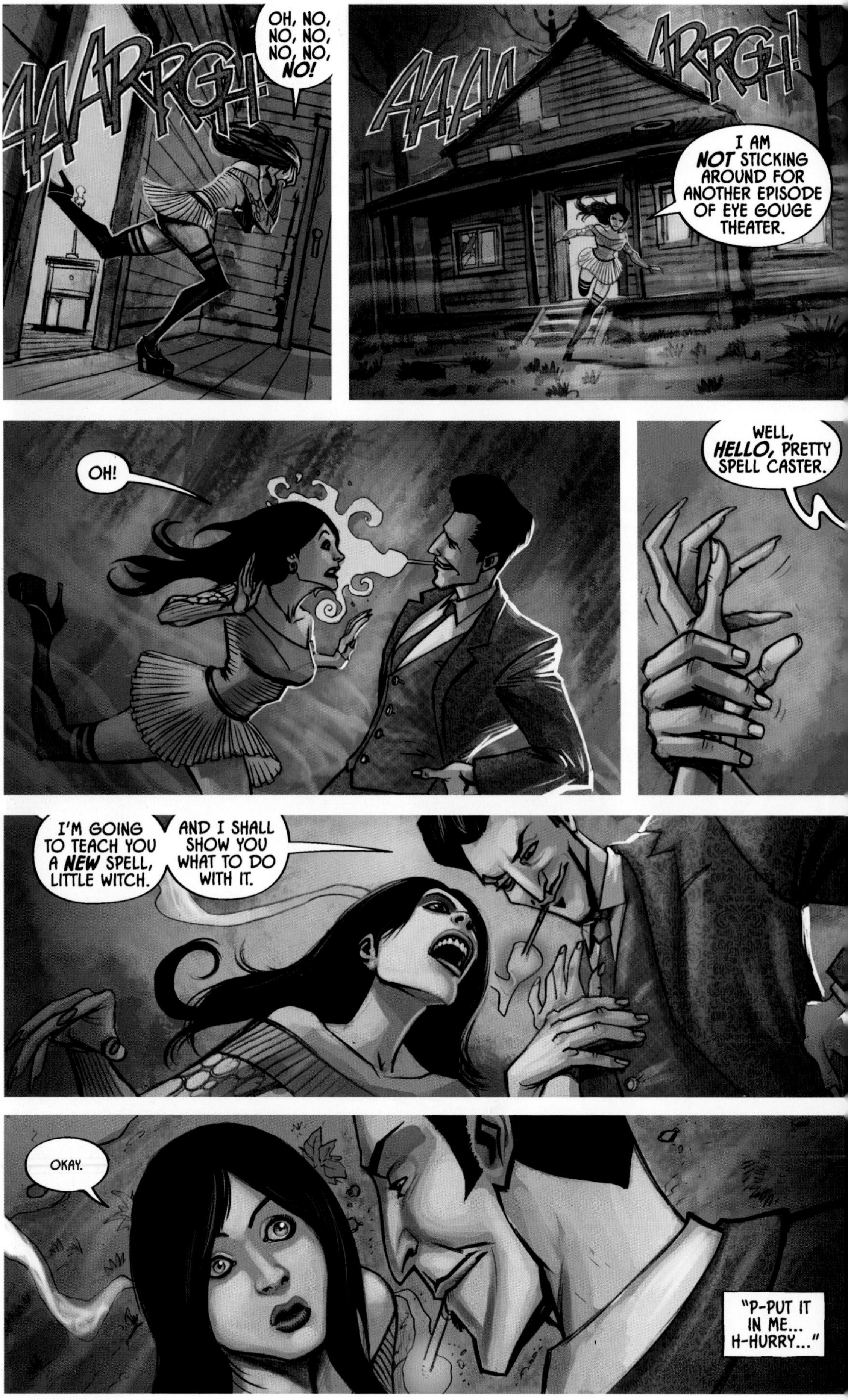
AAARRGH!
OH, NO, NO, NO, NO, NO, NO!
AAAAAARRGH!
I AM NOT STICKING AROUND FOR ANOTHER EPISODE OF EYE GOUGE THEATER.
OH!
WELL, HELLO, PRETTY SPELL CASTER.
I'M GOING TO TEACH YOU A NEW SPELL, LITTLE WITCH.
AND I SHALL SHOW YOU WHAT TO DO WITH IT.
OKAY.
"P-PUT IT IN ME... H-HURRY..."

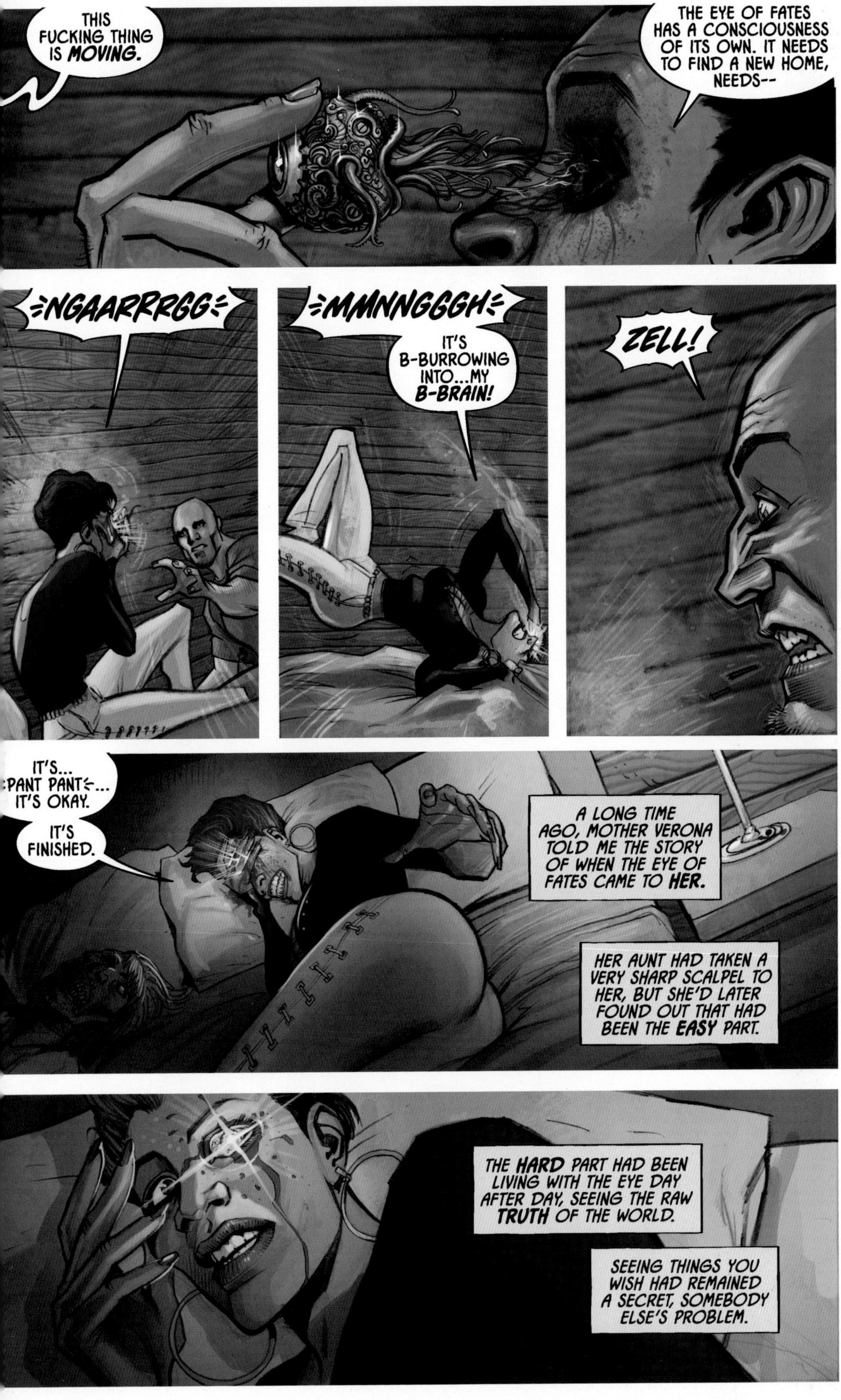
THIS FUCKING THING IS MOVING.
THE EYE OF FATES HAS A CONSCIOUSNESS OF ITS OWN. IT NEEDS TO FIND A NEW HOME, NEEDS--
NGAARRRGG
MMNNGGGH
IT'S B-BURROWING INTO...MY B-BRAIN!
ZELL!
IT'S... PANT PANT... IT'S OKAY.
IT'S FINISHED.
A LONG TIME AGO, MOTHER VERONA TOLD ME THE STORY OF WHEN THE EYE OF FATES CAME TO HER.
HER AUNT HAD TAKEN A VERY SHARP SCALPEL TO HER, BUT SHE'D LATER FOUND OUT THAT HAD BEEN THE EASY PART.
THE HARD PART HAD BEEN LIVING WITH THE EYE DAY AFTER DAY, SEEING THE RAW TRUTH OF THE WORLD.
SEEING THINGS YOU WISH HAD REMAINED A SECRET, SOMEBODY ELSE'S PROBLEM.

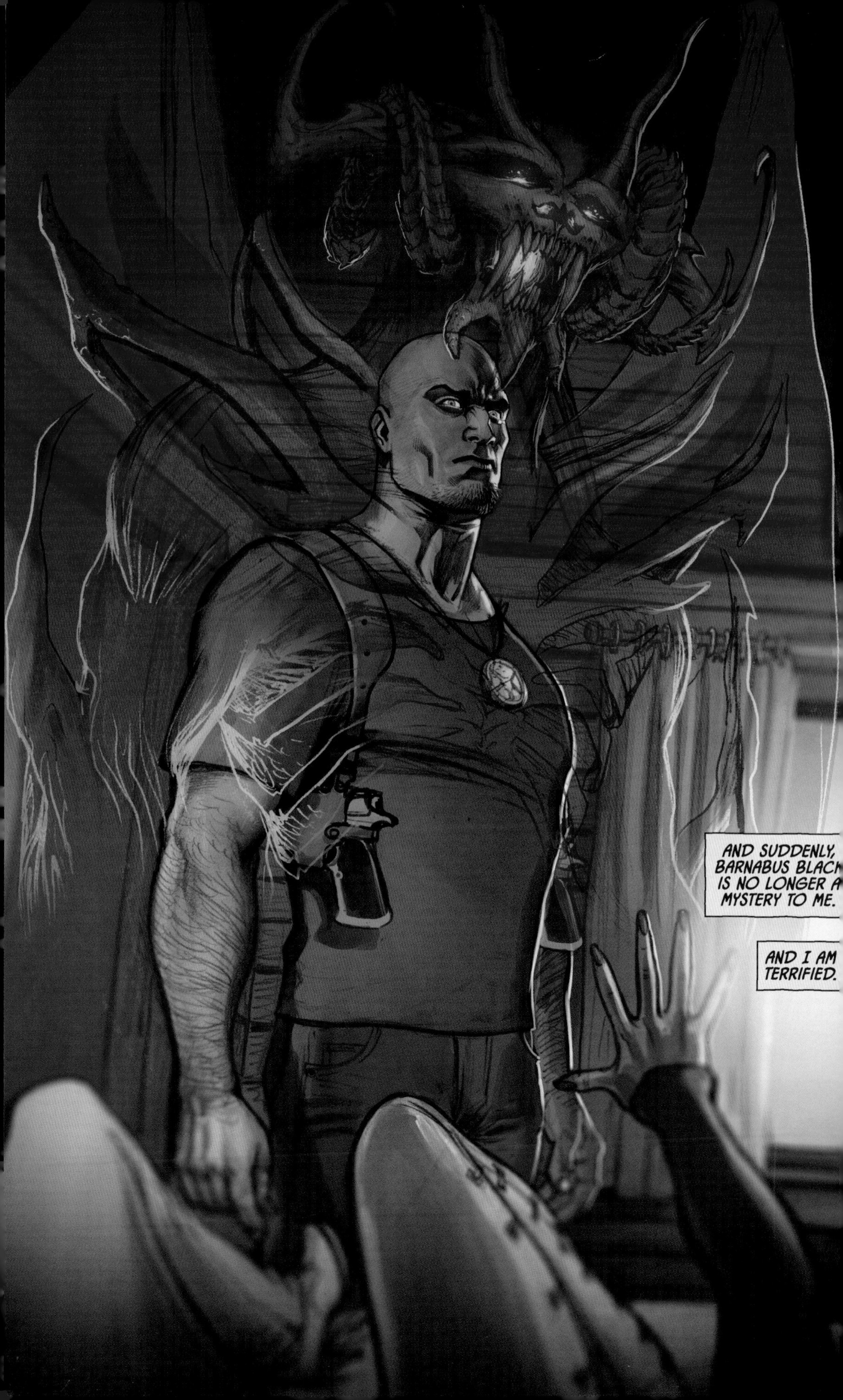
AND SUDDENLY, BARNABUS BLAC IS NO LONGER A MYSTERY TO ME.
AND I AM TERRIFIED.

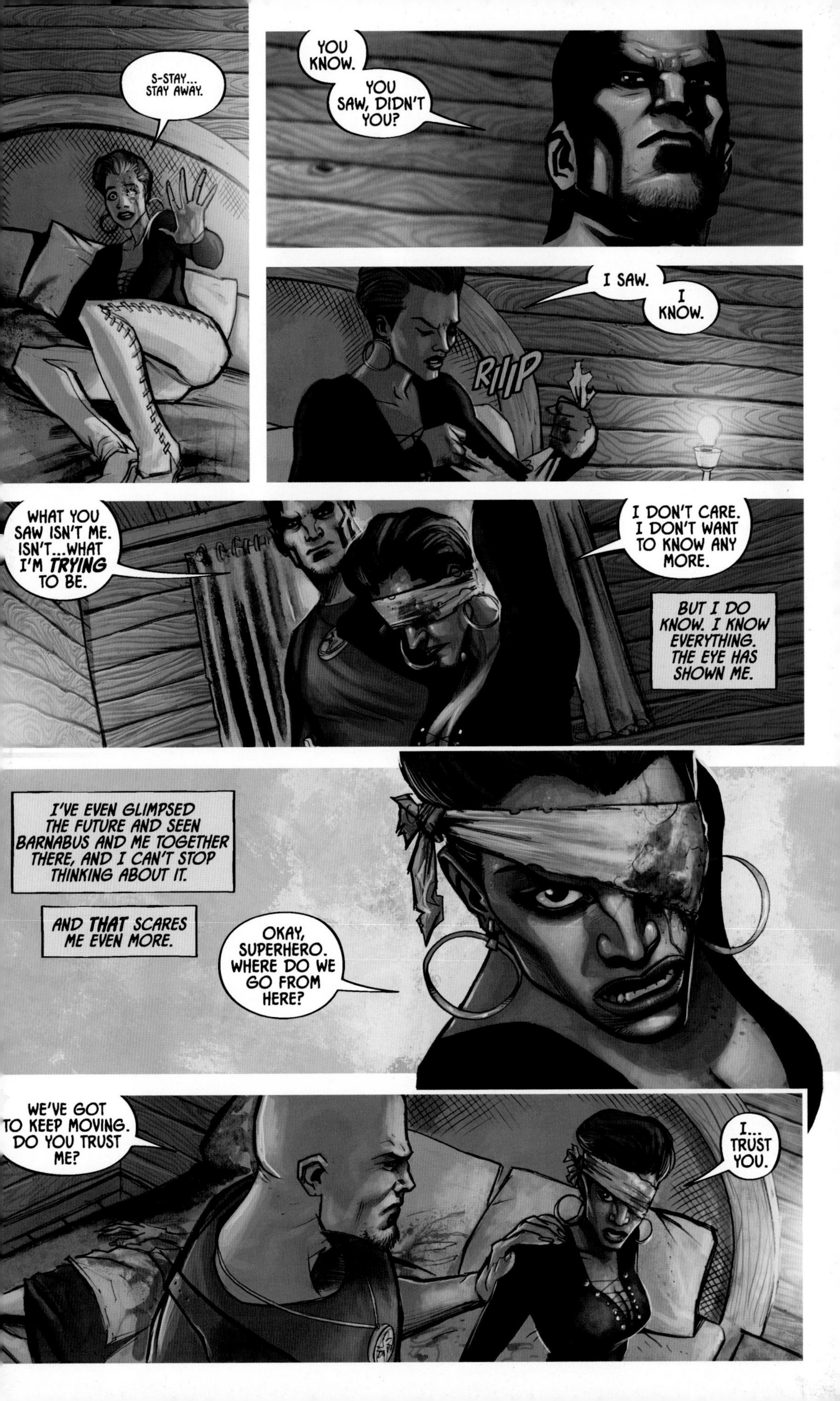
S-STAY... STAY AWAY.
YOU KNOW.
YOU SAW, DIDN'T YOU?
I SAW.
I KNOW.
RIIP
WHAT YOU SAW ISN'T ME. ISN'T...WHAT I'M TRYING TO BE.
I DON'T CARE. I DON'T WANT TO KNOW ANY MORE.
BUT I DO KNOW. I KNOW EVERYTHING. THE EYE HAS SHOWN ME.
I'VE EVEN GLIMPSED THE FUTURE AND SEEN BARNABUS AND ME TOGETHER THERE, AND I CAN'T STOP THINKING ABOUT IT.
AND THAT SCARES ME EVEN MORE.
OKAY, SUPERHERO. WHERE DO WE GO FROM HERE?
WE'VE GOT TO KEEP MOVING. DO YOU TRUST ME?
I... TRUST YOU.

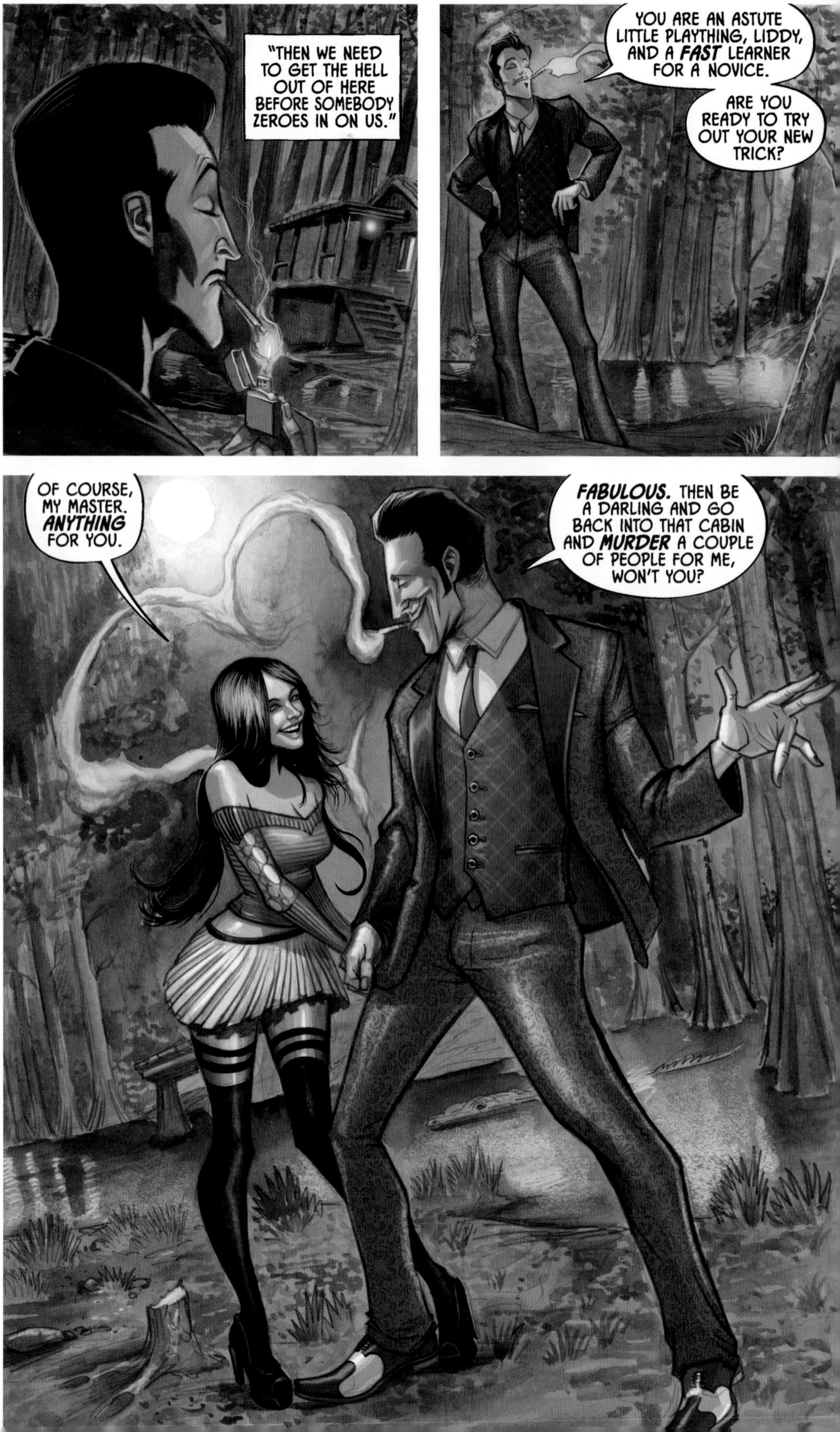
"THEN WE NEED TO GET THE HELL OUT OF HERE BEFORE SOMEBODY ZEROES IN ON US."
YOU ARE AN ASTUTE LITTLE PLAYTHING, LIDDY, AND A FAST LEARNER FOR A NOVICE.
ARE YOU READY TO TRY OUT YOUR NEW TRICK?
OF COURSE, MY MASTER. ANYTHING FOR YOU.
FABULOUS. THEN BE A DARLING AND GO BACK INTO THAT CABIN AND MURDER A COUPLE OF PEOPLE FOR ME, WON'T YOU?

CHAPTER IV

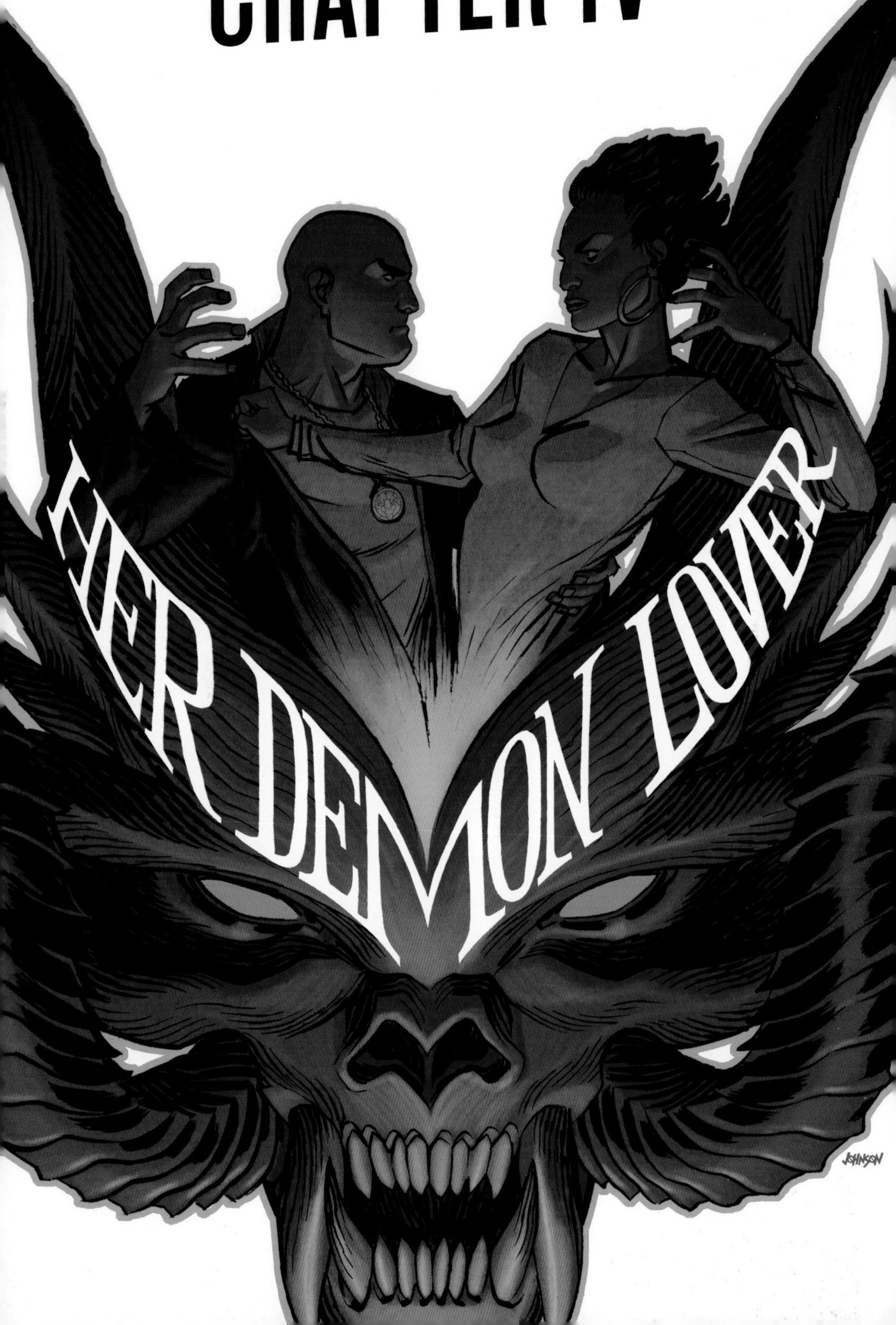
HER DEMON LOVER
JOHNSON

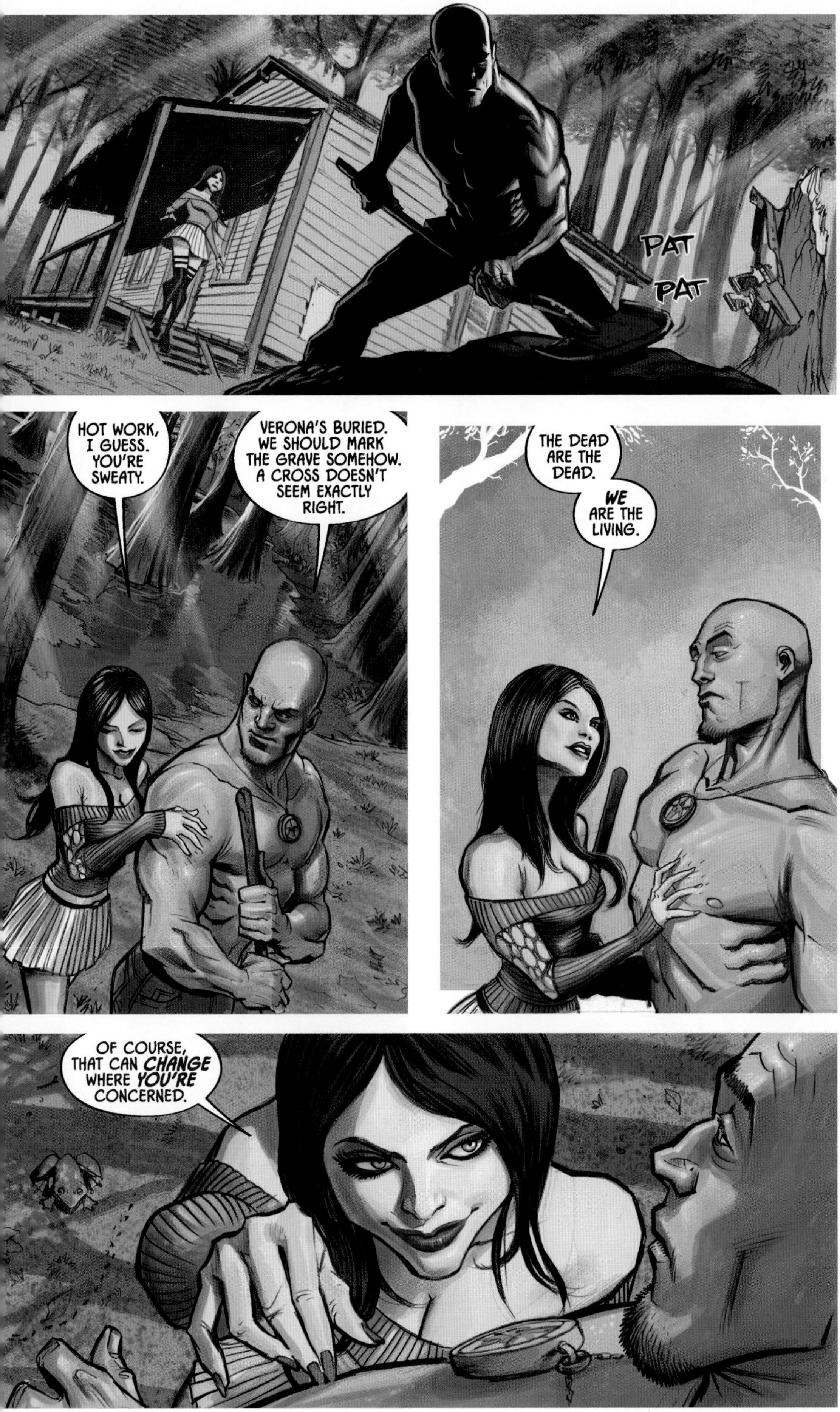
PAT
PAT
HOT WORK, I GUESS. YOU'RE SWEATY.
VERONA'S BURIED. WE SHOULD MARK THE GRAVE SOMEHOW. A CROSS DOESN'T SEEM EXACTLY RIGHT.
THE DEAD ARE THE DEAD.
WE ARE THE LIVING.
OF COURSE, THAT CAN CHANGE WHERE YOU'RE CONCERNED.

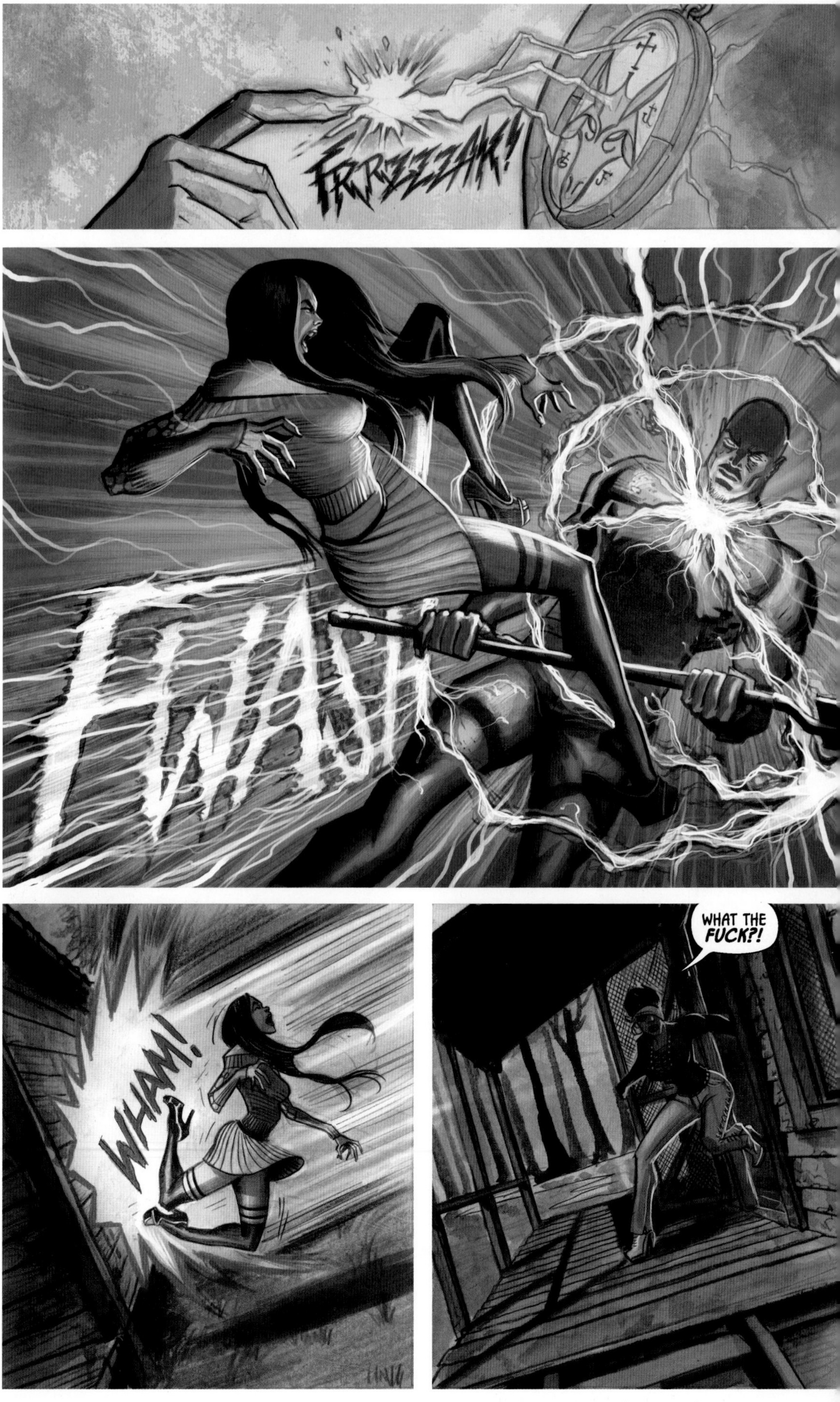
FRRZZZAK!
FWASH
WHAM!
WHAT THE FUCK?!

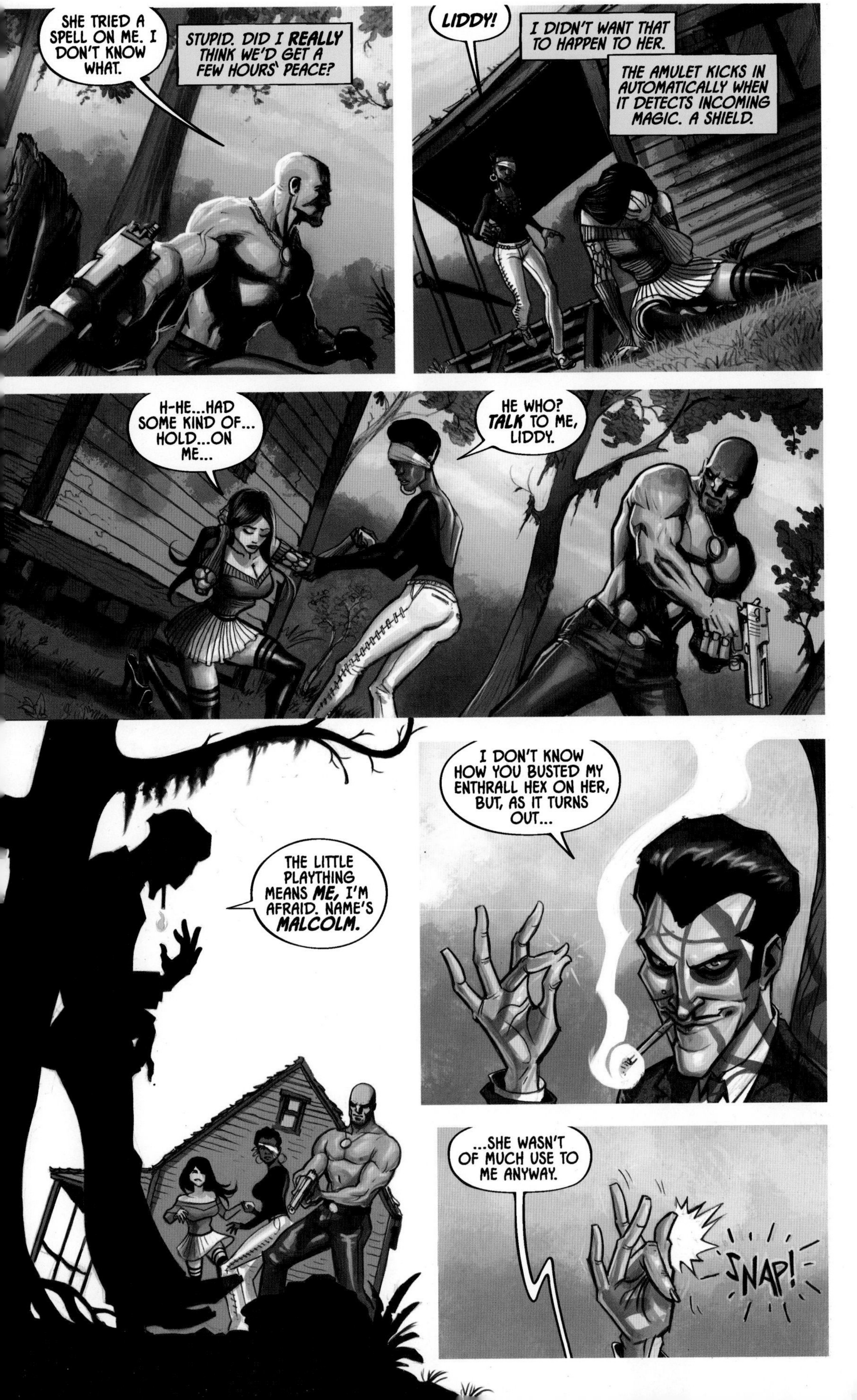
SHE TRIED A SPELL ON ME. I DON'T KNOW WHAT.
STUPID. DID I **REALLY** THINK WE'D GET A FEW HOURS' PEACE?
LIDDY!
I DIDN'T WANT THAT TO HAPPEN TO HER.
THE AMULET KICKS IN AUTOMATICALLY WHEN IT DETECTS INCOMING MAGIC. A SHIELD.
H-HE...HAD SOME KIND OF... HOLD...ON ME...
HE WHO? **TALK** TO ME, LIDDY.
THE LITTLE PLAYTHING MEANS **ME,** I'M AFRAID. NAME'S **MALCOLM.**
I DON'T KNOW HOW YOU BUSTED MY ENTHRALL HEX ON HER, BUT, AS IT TURNS OUT...
...SHE WASN'T OF MUCH USE TO ME ANYWAY.
SNAP!

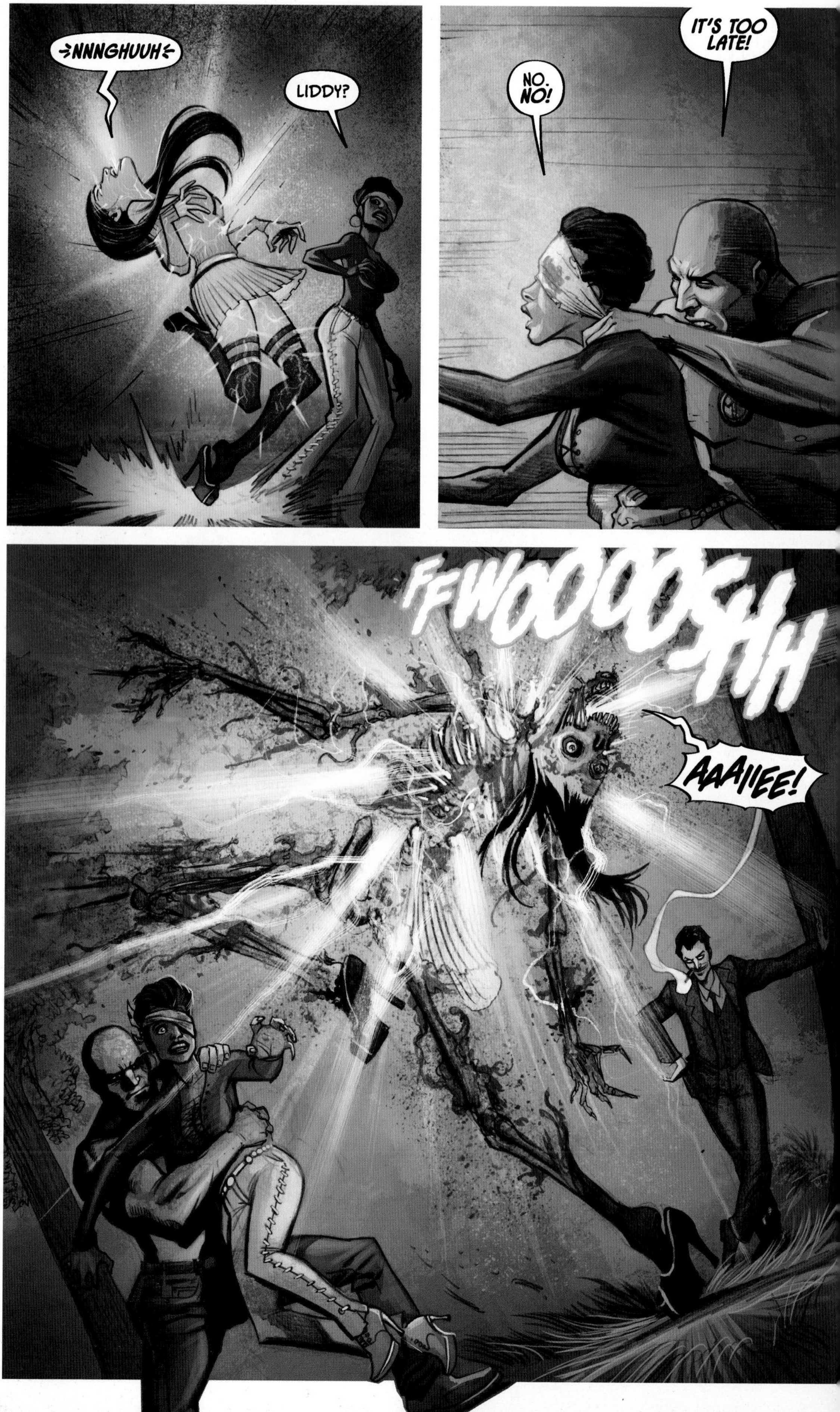

NNNGHUUH
LIDDY?
IT'S TOO LATE!
NO. NO!
FFWOOOOSHH
AAAIIEE!

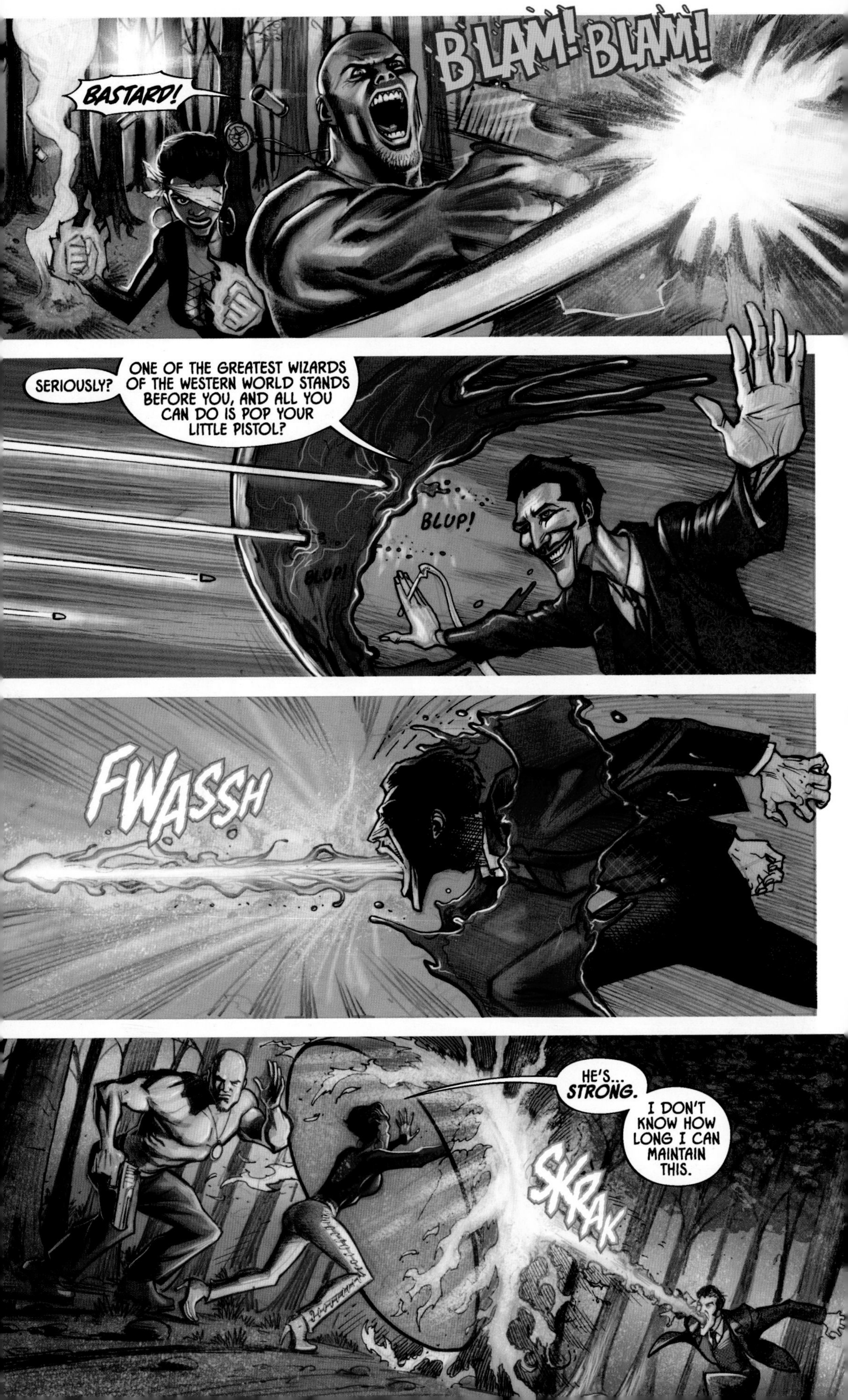
BASTARD!
BLAM! BLAM!
SERIOUSLY?
ONE OF THE GREATEST WIZARDS OF THE WESTERN WORLD STANDS BEFORE YOU, AND ALL YOU CAN DO IS POP YOUR LITTLE PISTOL?
BLUP!
BLUP!
FWASSH
HE'S... STRONG.
I DON'T KNOW HOW LONG I CAN MAINTAIN THIS.
SKRAK

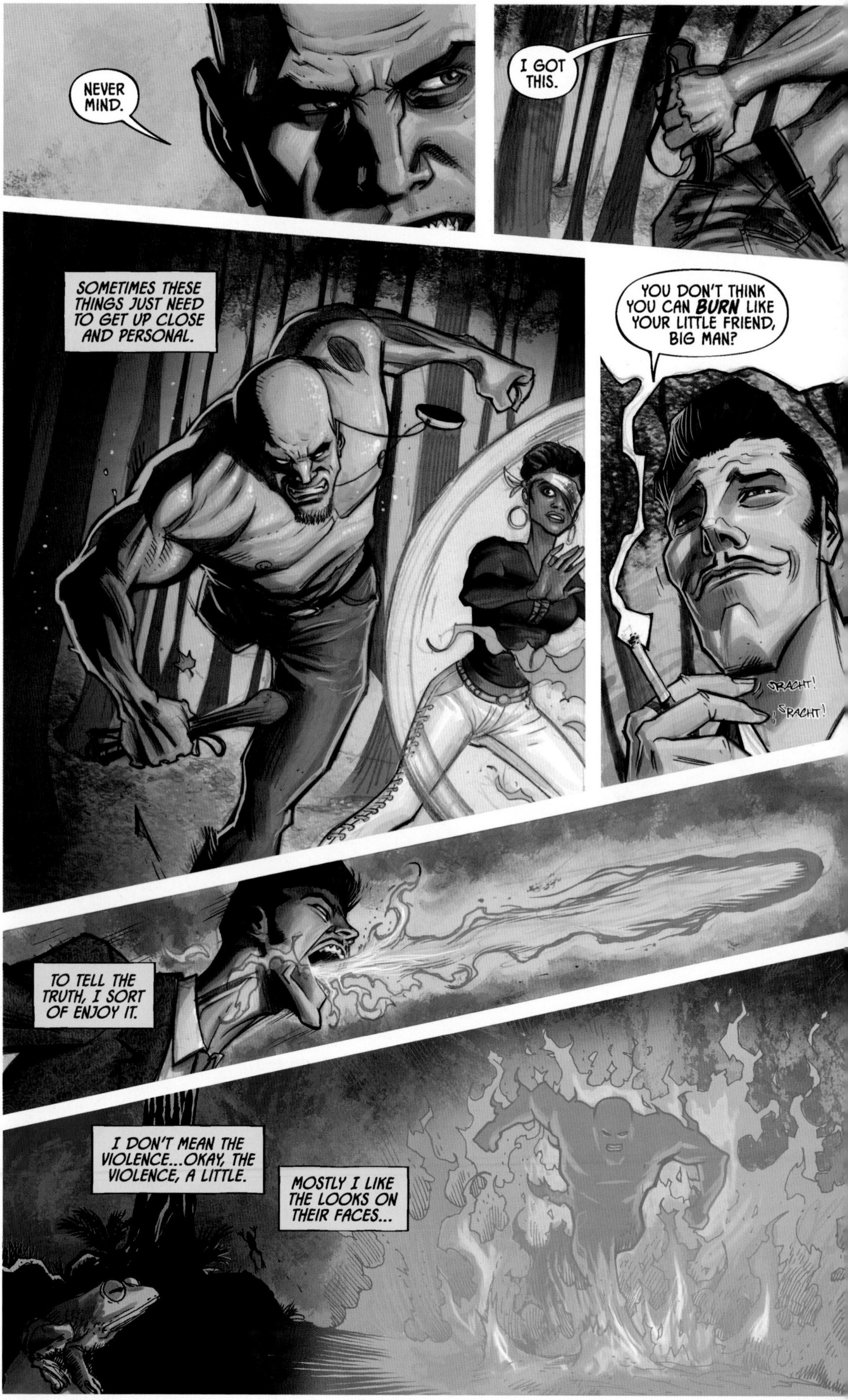
NEVER MIND.
I GOT THIS.
SOMETIMES THESE THINGS JUST NEED TO GET UP CLOSE AND PERSONAL.
YOU DON'T THINK YOU CAN BURN LIKE YOUR LITTLE FRIEND, BIG MAN?
SRACHT!
SRACHT!
TO TELL THE TRUTH, I SORT OF ENJOY IT.
I DON'T MEAN THE VIOLENCE...OKAY, THE VIOLENCE, A LITTLE.
MOSTLY I LIKE THE LOOKS ON THEIR FACES...

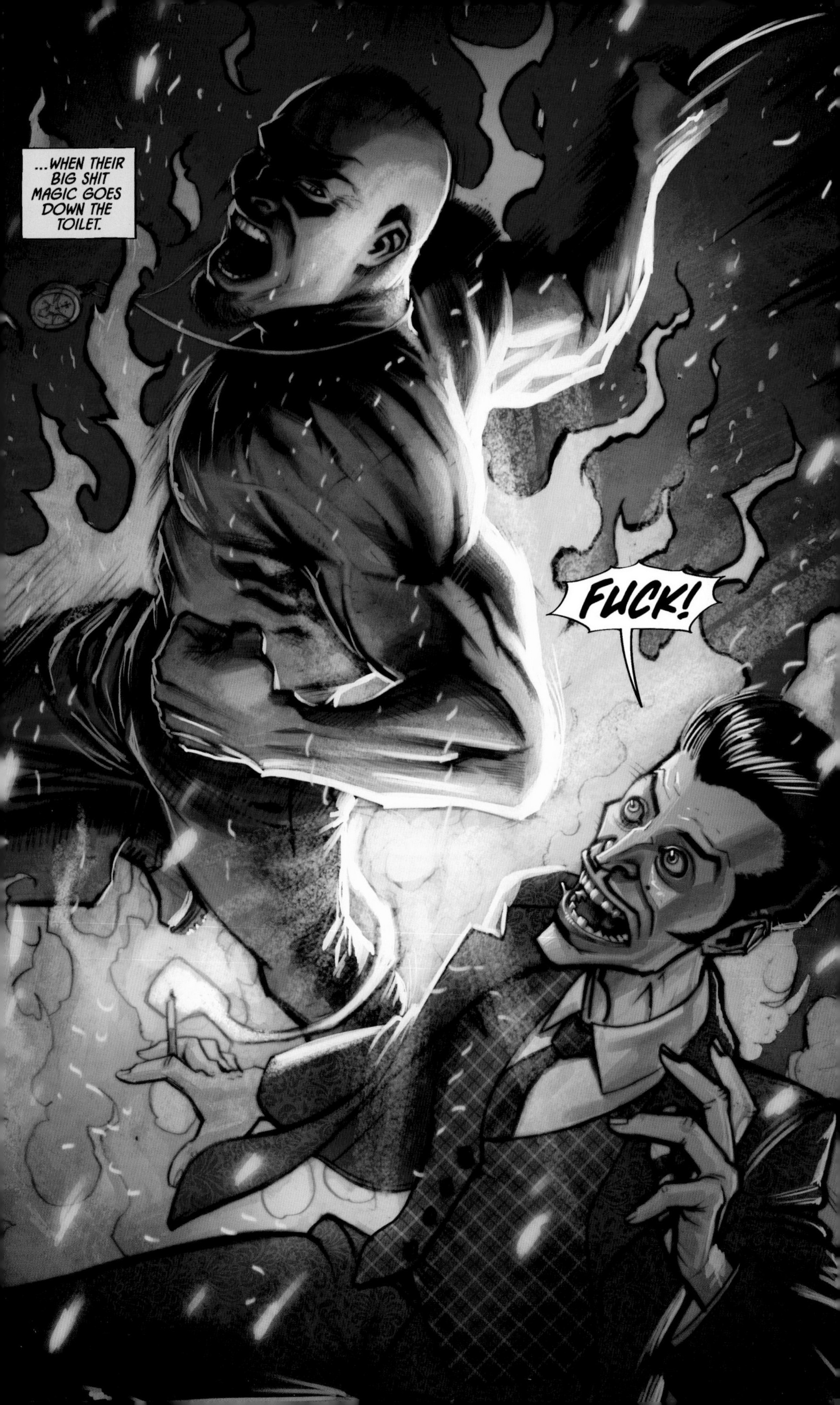
...WHEN THEIR BIG SHIT MAGIC GOES DOWN THE TOILET.
FUCK!

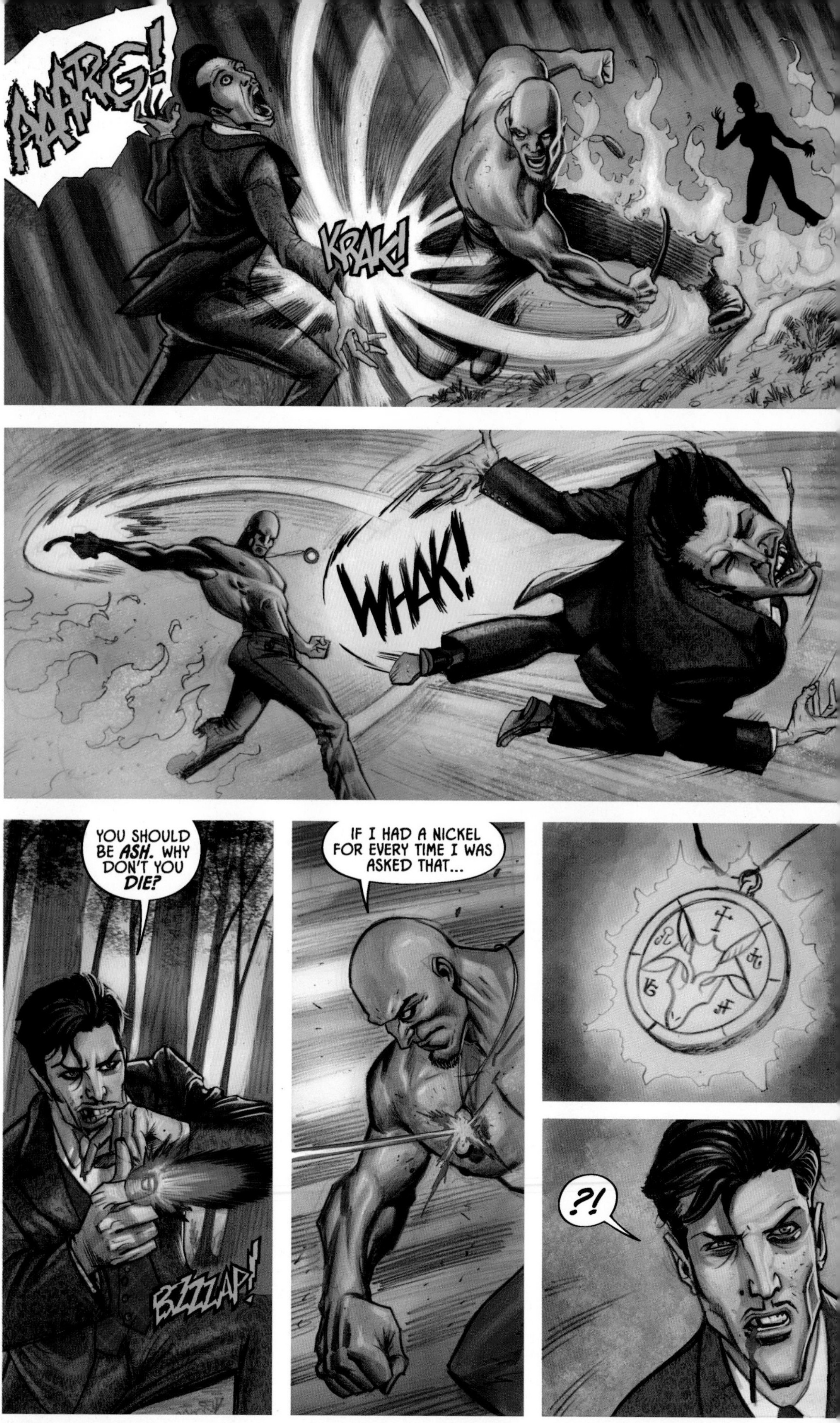
AAARG!
KRAK!
WHAK!
YOU SHOULD BE ASH. WHY DON'T YOU DIE?
BZZZAP!
IF I HAD A NICKEL FOR EVERY TIME I WAS ASKED THAT...
?!

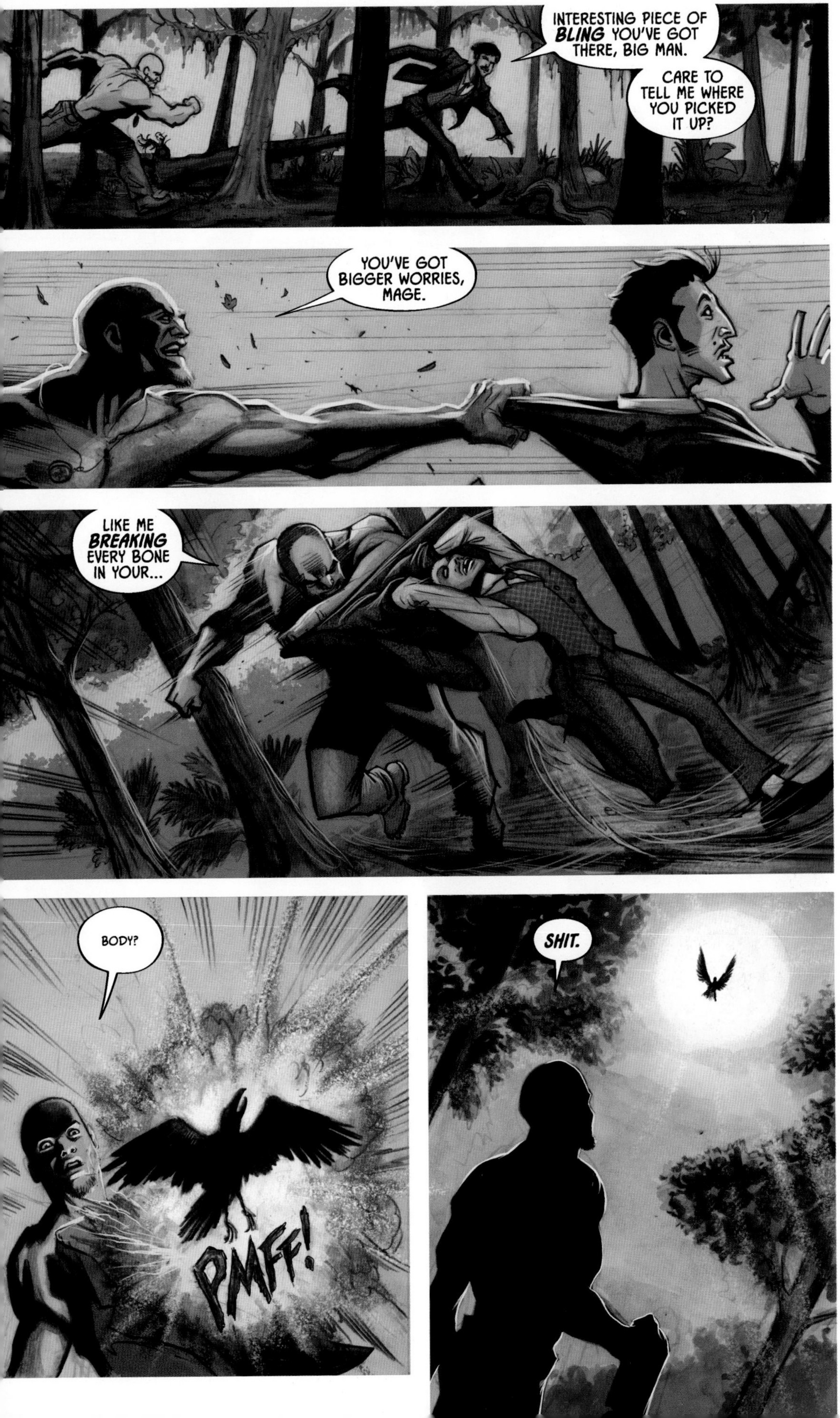
INTERESTING PIECE OF BLING YOU'VE GOT THERE, BIG MAN.
CARE TO TELL ME WHERE YOU PICKED IT UP?
YOU'VE GOT BIGGER WORRIES, MAGE.
LIKE ME BREAKING EVERY BONE IN YOUR...
BODY?
PMFF!
SHIT.

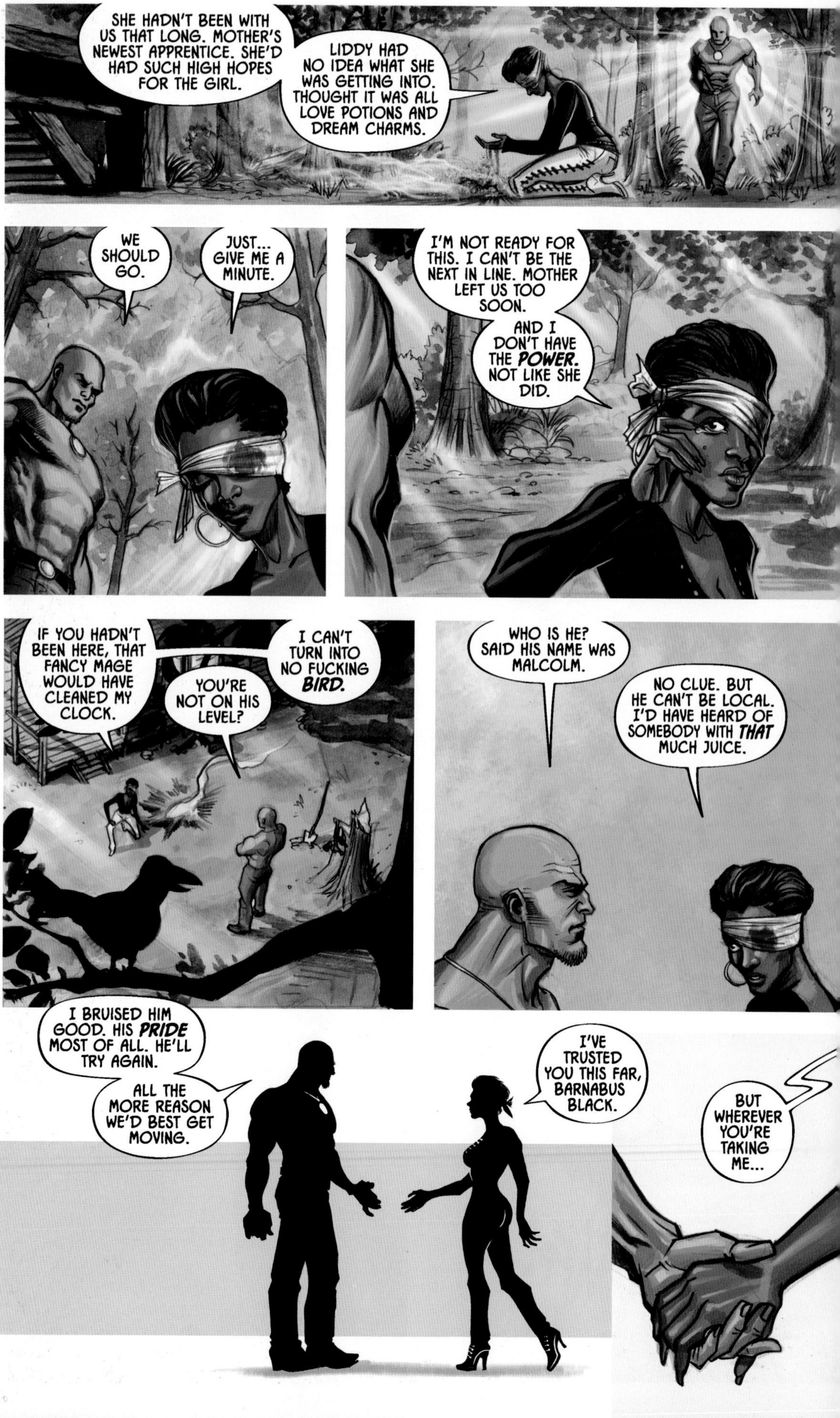
SHE HADN'T BEEN WITH US THAT LONG. MOTHER'S NEWEST APPRENTICE. SHE'D HAD SUCH HIGH HOPES FOR THE GIRL.
LIDDY HAD NO IDEA WHAT SHE WAS GETTING INTO. THOUGHT IT WAS ALL LOVE POTIONS AND DREAM CHARMS.
WE SHOULD GO.
JUST... GIVE ME A MINUTE.
I'M NOT READY FOR THIS. I CAN'T BE THE NEXT IN LINE. MOTHER LEFT US TOO SOON.
AND I DON'T HAVE THE POWER. NOT LIKE SHE DID.
IF YOU HADN'T BEEN HERE, THAT FANCY MAGE WOULD HAVE CLEANED MY CLOCK.
YOU'RE NOT ON HIS LEVEL?
I CAN'T TURN INTO NO FUCKING BIRD.
WHO IS HE? SAID HIS NAME WAS MALCOLM.
NO CLUE. BUT HE CAN'T BE LOCAL. I'D HAVE HEARD OF SOMEBODY WITH THAT MUCH JUICE.
I BRUISED HIM GOOD. HIS PRIDE MOST OF ALL. HE'LL TRY AGAIN.
ALL THE MORE REASON WE'D BEST GET MOVING.
I'VE TRUSTED YOU THIS FAR, BARNABUS BLACK.
BUT WHEREVER YOU'RE TAKING ME...

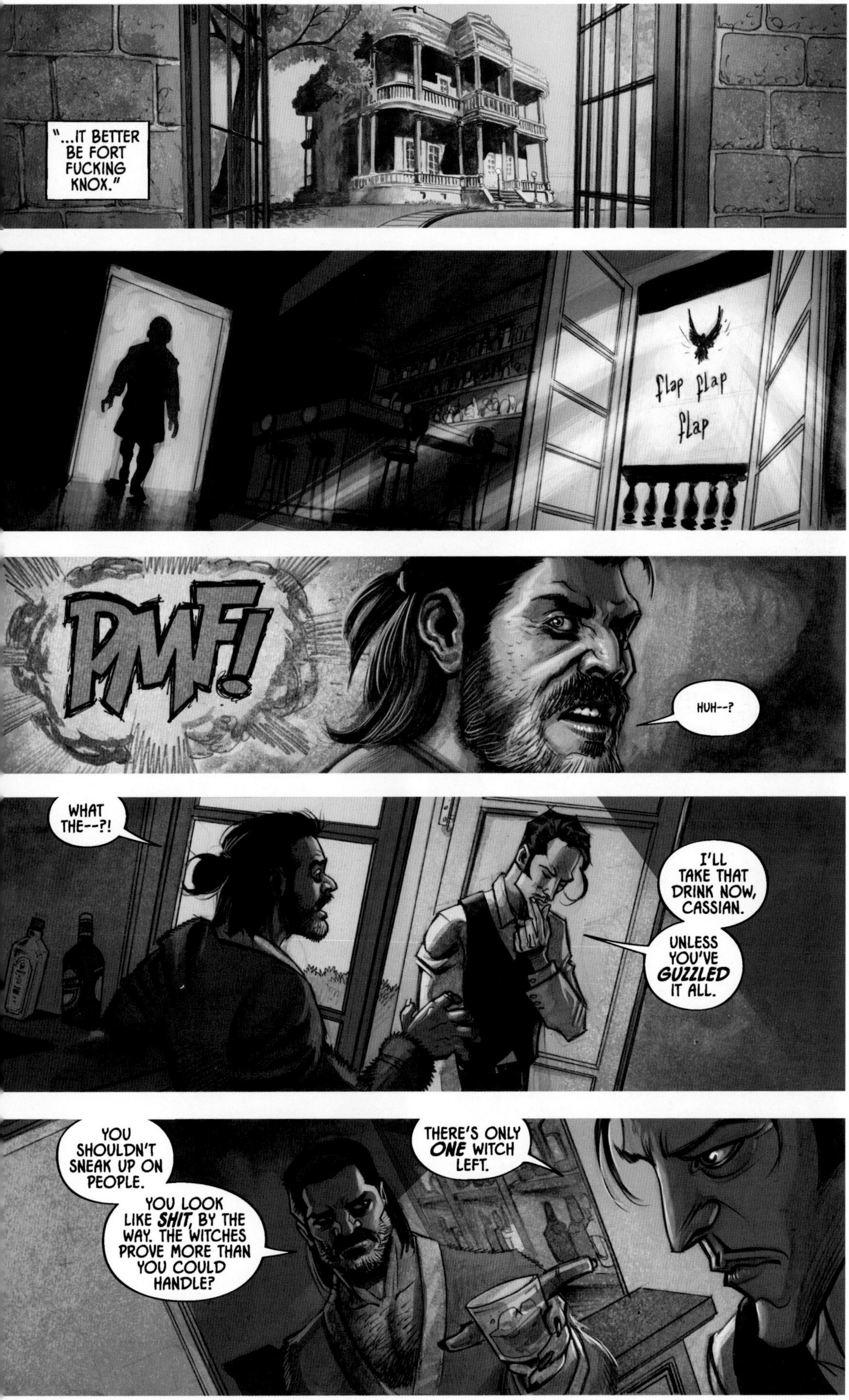

"...IT BETTER BE FORT FUCKING KNOX."
flap flap flap
PMF!
HUH--?
WHAT THE--?!
I'LL TAKE THAT DRINK NOW, CASSIAN.
UNLESS YOU'VE GUZZLED IT ALL.
YOU SHOULDN'T SNEAK UP ON PEOPLE.
YOU LOOK LIKE SHIT, BY THE WAY. THE WITCHES PROVE MORE THAN YOU COULD HANDLE?
THERE'S ONLY ONE WITCH LEFT.

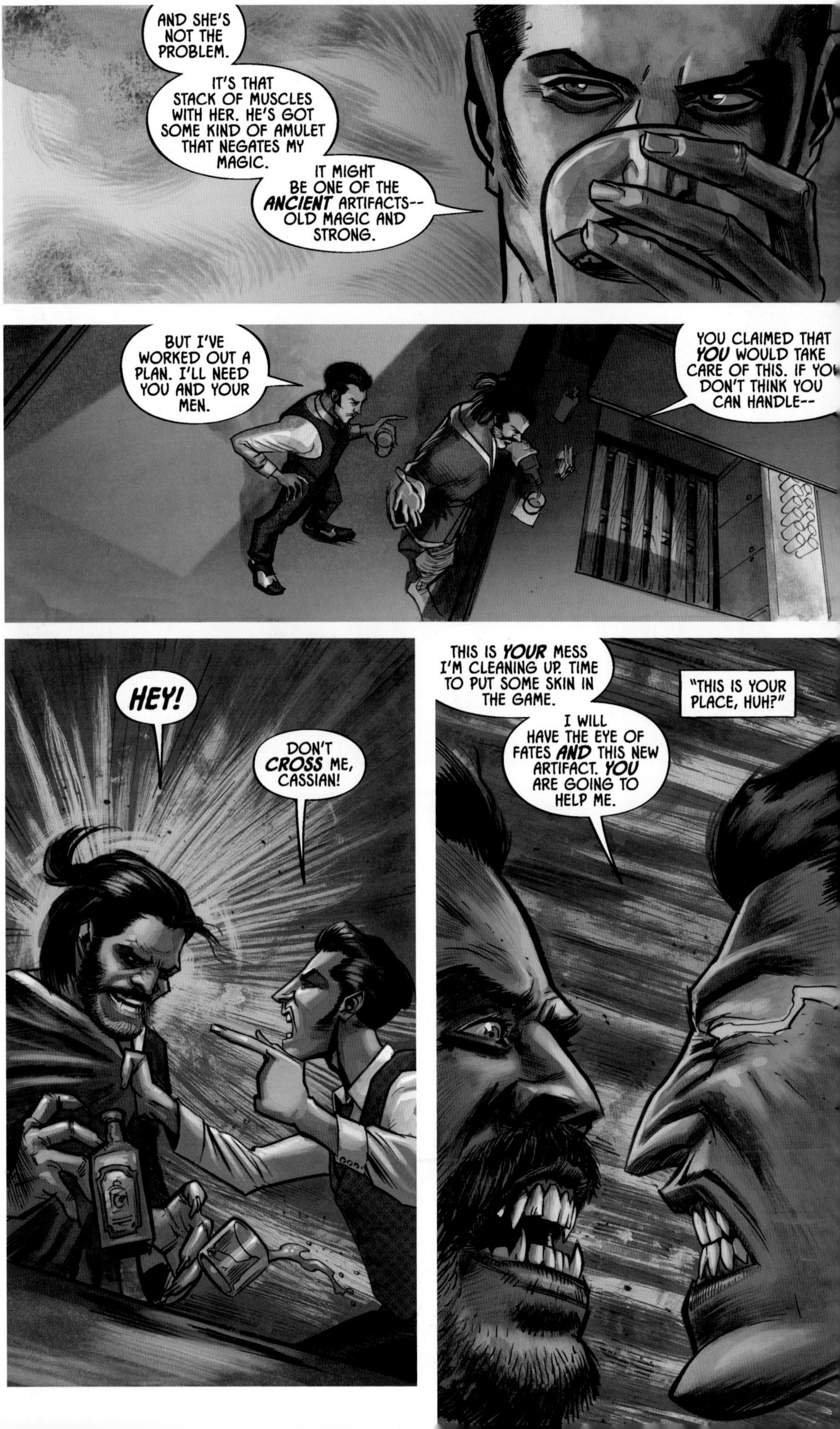

AND SHE'S NOT THE PROBLEM.
IT'S THAT STACK OF MUSCLES WITH HER. HE'S GOT SOME KIND OF AMULET THAT NEGATES MY MAGIC.
IT MIGHT BE ONE OF THE *ANCIENT* ARTIFACTS-- OLD MAGIC AND STRONG.
BUT I'VE WORKED OUT A PLAN. I'LL NEED YOU AND YOUR MEN.
YOU CLAIMED THAT *YOU* WOULD TAKE CARE OF THIS. IF YO DON'T THINK YOU CAN HANDLE--
HEY!
DON'T *CROSS* ME, CASSIAN!
THIS IS *YOUR* MESS I'M CLEANING UP. TIME TO PUT SOME SKIN IN THE GAME.
I WILL HAVE THE EYE OF FATES *AND* THIS NEW ARTIFACT. *YOU* ARE GOING TO HELP ME.
"THIS IS YOUR PLACE, HUH?"

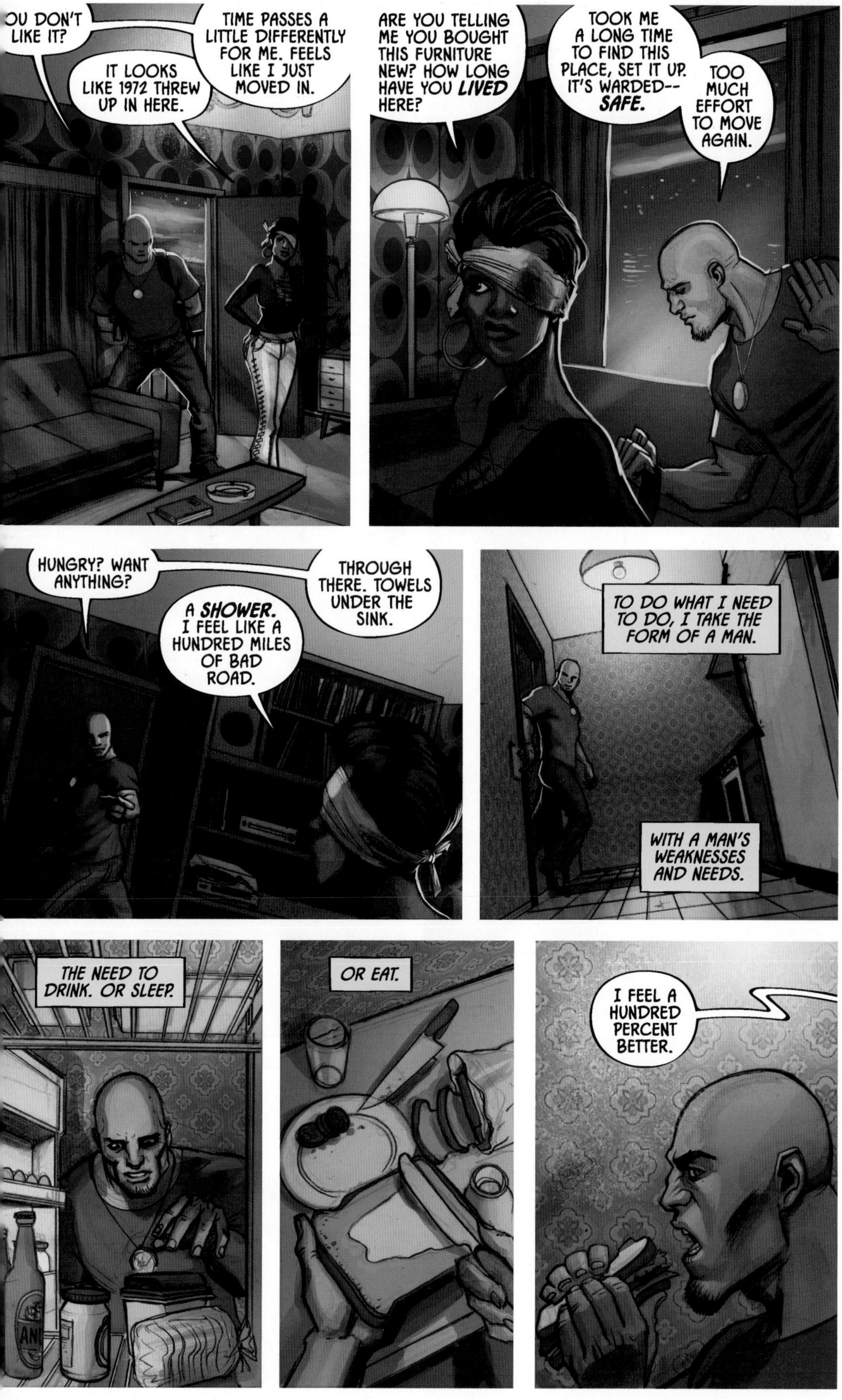
OU DON'T LIKE IT?
IT LOOKS LIKE 1972 THREW UP IN HERE.
TIME PASSES A LITTLE DIFFERENTLY FOR ME. FEELS LIKE I JUST MOVED IN.
ARE YOU TELLING ME YOU BOUGHT THIS FURNITURE NEW? HOW LONG HAVE YOU LIVED HERE?
TOOK ME A LONG TIME TO FIND THIS PLACE, SET IT UP. IT'S WARDED-- SAFE.
TOO MUCH EFFORT TO MOVE AGAIN.
HUNGRY? WANT ANYTHING?
A SHOWER. I FEEL LIKE A HUNDRED MILES OF BAD ROAD.
THROUGH THERE. TOWELS UNDER THE SINK.
TO DO WHAT I NEED TO DO, I TAKE THE FORM OF A MAN.
WITH A MAN'S WEAKNESSES AND NEEDS.
THE NEED TO DRINK. OR SLEEP.
OR EAT.
I FEEL A HUNDRED PERCENT BETTER.

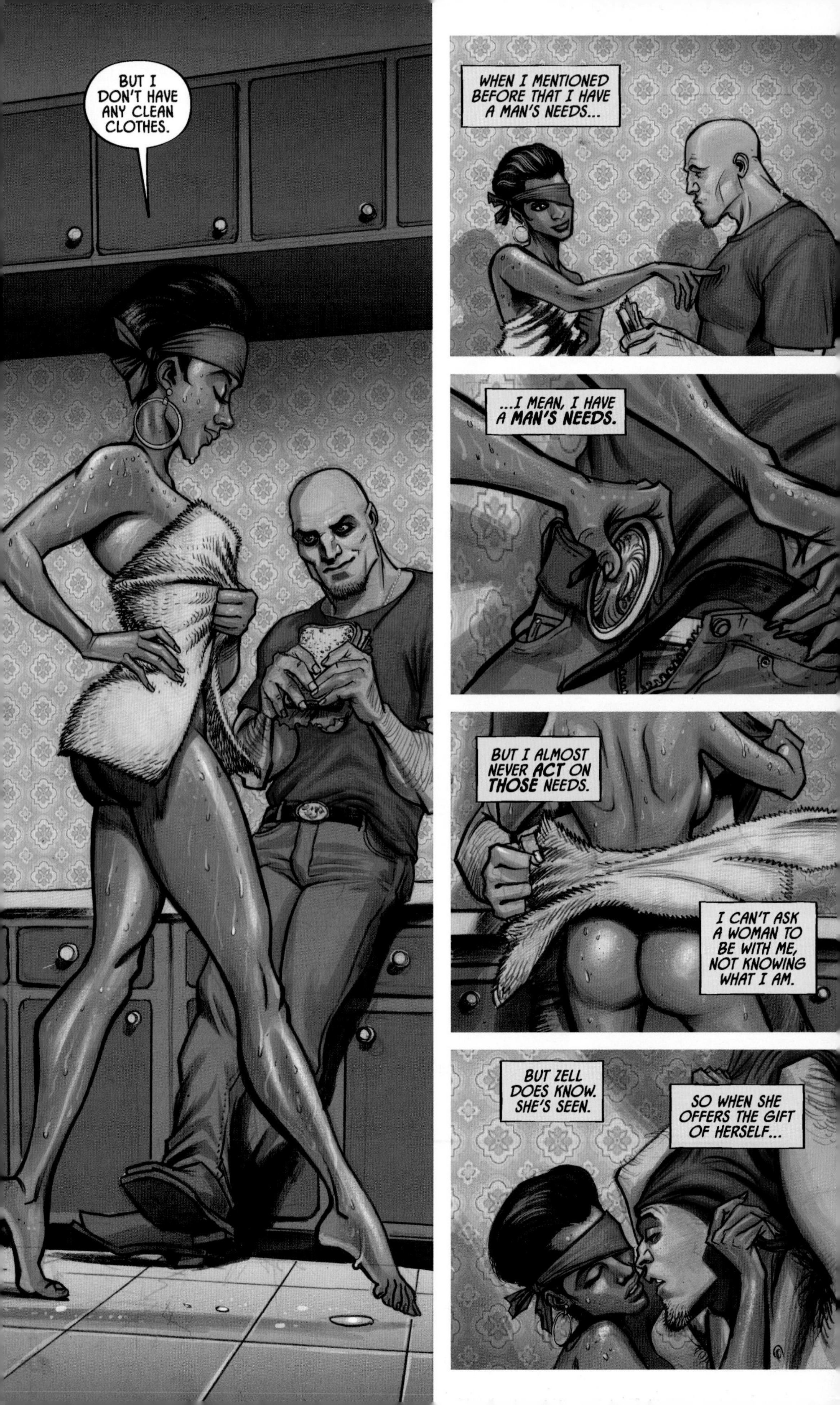
BUT I DON'T HAVE ANY CLEAN CLOTHES.
WHEN I MENTIONED BEFORE THAT I HAVE A MAN'S NEEDS...
...I MEAN, I HAVE A **MAN'S NEEDS.**
BUT I ALMOST NEVER **ACT** ON **THOSE** NEEDS.
I CAN'T ASK A WOMAN TO BE WITH ME, NOT KNOWING WHAT I AM.
BUT ZELL DOES KNOW. SHE'S SEEN.
SO WHEN SHE OFFERS THE GIFT OF HERSELF...

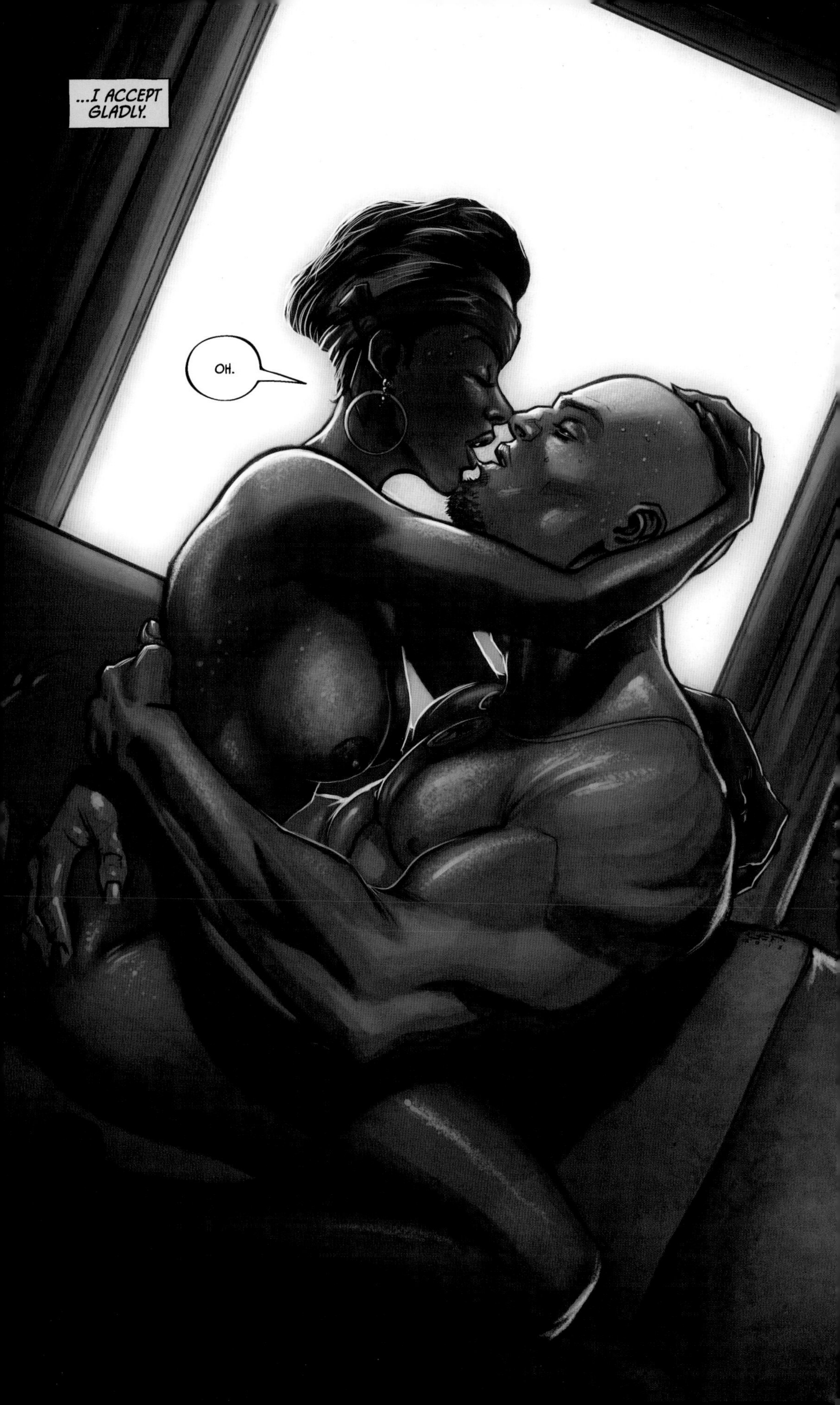
...I ACCEPT GLADLY.
OH.

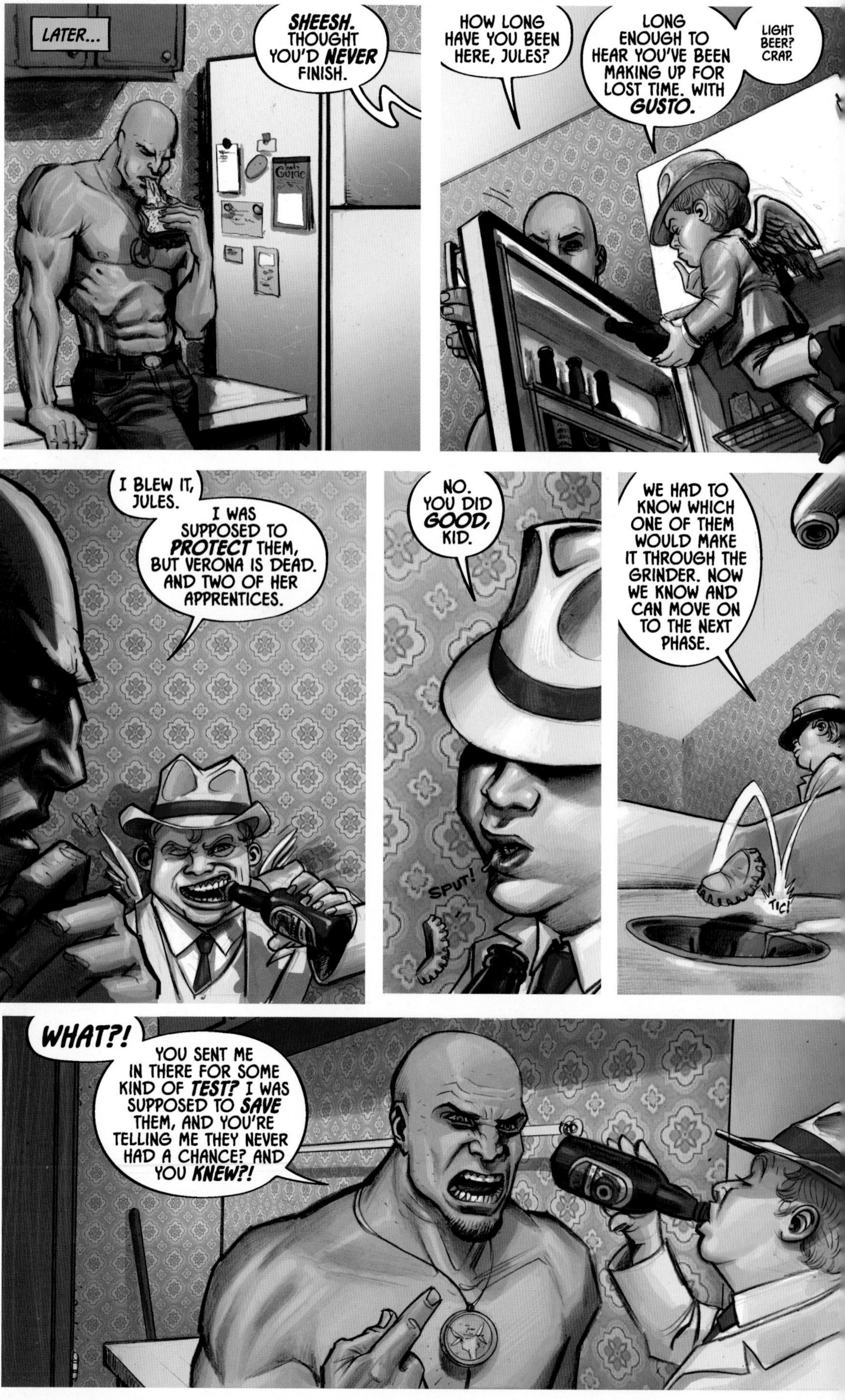
LATER...
SHEESH. THOUGHT YOU'D NEVER FINISH.
HOW LONG HAVE YOU BEEN HERE, JULES?
LONG ENOUGH TO HEAR YOU'VE BEEN MAKING UP FOR LOST TIME. WITH GUSTO.
LIGHT BEER? CRAP.
I BLEW IT, JULES.
I WAS SUPPOSED TO PROTECT THEM, BUT VERONA IS DEAD. AND TWO OF HER APPRENTICES.
NO. YOU DID GOOD, KID.
SPUT!
WE HAD TO KNOW WHICH ONE OF THEM WOULD MAKE IT THROUGH THE GRINDER. NOW WE KNOW AND CAN MOVE ON TO THE NEXT PHASE.
TIC!
WHAT?!
YOU SENT ME IN THERE FOR SOME KIND OF TEST? I WAS SUPPOSED TO SAVE THEM, AND YOU'RE TELLING ME THEY NEVER HAD A CHANCE? AND YOU KNEW?!

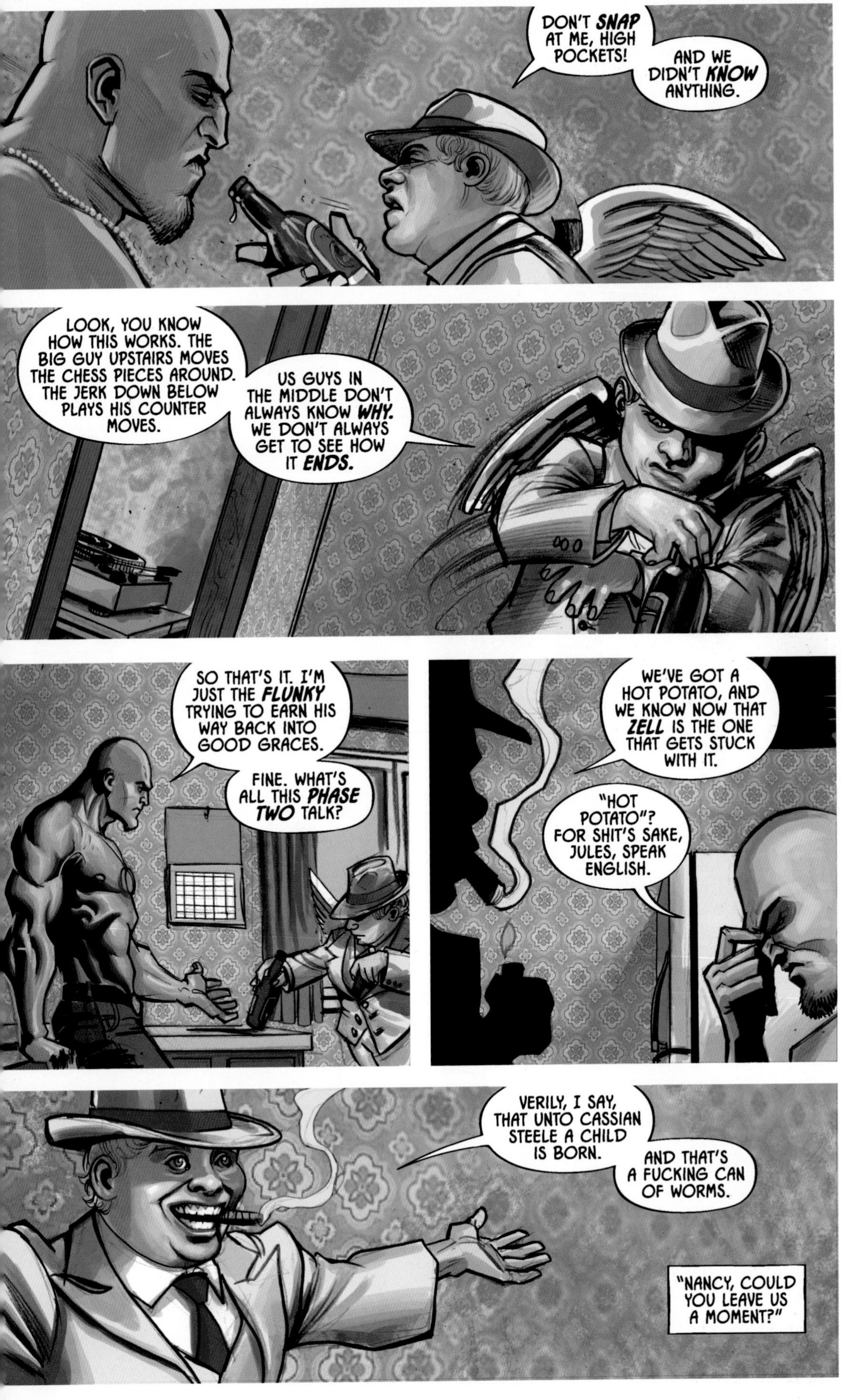
DON'T SNAP AT ME, HIGH POCKETS!
AND WE DIDN'T KNOW ANYTHING.
LOOK, YOU KNOW HOW THIS WORKS. THE BIG GUY UPSTAIRS MOVES THE CHESS PIECES AROUND. THE JERK DOWN BELOW PLAYS HIS COUNTER MOVES.
US GUYS IN THE MIDDLE DON'T ALWAYS KNOW WHY. WE DON'T ALWAYS GET TO SEE HOW IT ENDS.
SO THAT'S IT. I'M JUST THE FLUNKY TRYING TO EARN HIS WAY BACK INTO GOOD GRACES.
FINE. WHAT'S ALL THIS PHASE TWO TALK?
WE'VE GOT A HOT POTATO, AND WE KNOW NOW THAT ZELL IS THE ONE THAT GETS STUCK WITH IT.
"HOT POTATO"? FOR SHIT'S SAKE, JULES, SPEAK ENGLISH.
VERILY, I SAY, THAT UNTO CASSIAN STEELE A CHILD IS BORN.
AND THAT'S A FUCKING CAN OF WORMS.
"NANCY, COULD YOU LEAVE US A MOMENT?"

OF COURSE, MR. STEELE. IF YOU LIKE, I CAN--

YES, SIR.

JUST GO.

HELLO... SON.

I FELT WE SHOULD TALK.

I KNOW YOU WON'T UNDERSTAND, BUT I NEED TO SAY THIS OUT LOUD. MAYBE IT WILL MAKE A DIFFERENCE.

I'VE... WORKED HARD.

YOU DON'T KNOW WHAT IT'S LIKE TO BE A MAN LIKE ME. TO BE IN MY POSITION.

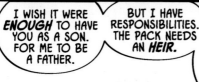

I WISH IT WERE *ENOUGH* TO HAVE YOU AS A SON. FOR ME TO BE A FATHER.

BUT I HAVE RESPONSIBILITIES. THE PACK NEEDS AN *HEIR.*

IT'S NOT MY FATE TO HAVE A SIMPLE LIFE, A SIMPLE FAMILY. I HAVE A...DUTY.

AND YOU DON'T HAVE THE MARK OF THE LYCAN UPON YOU, MY BOY.

AND THAT'S... WELL, THAT'S *EVERYTHING,* ISN'T IT?

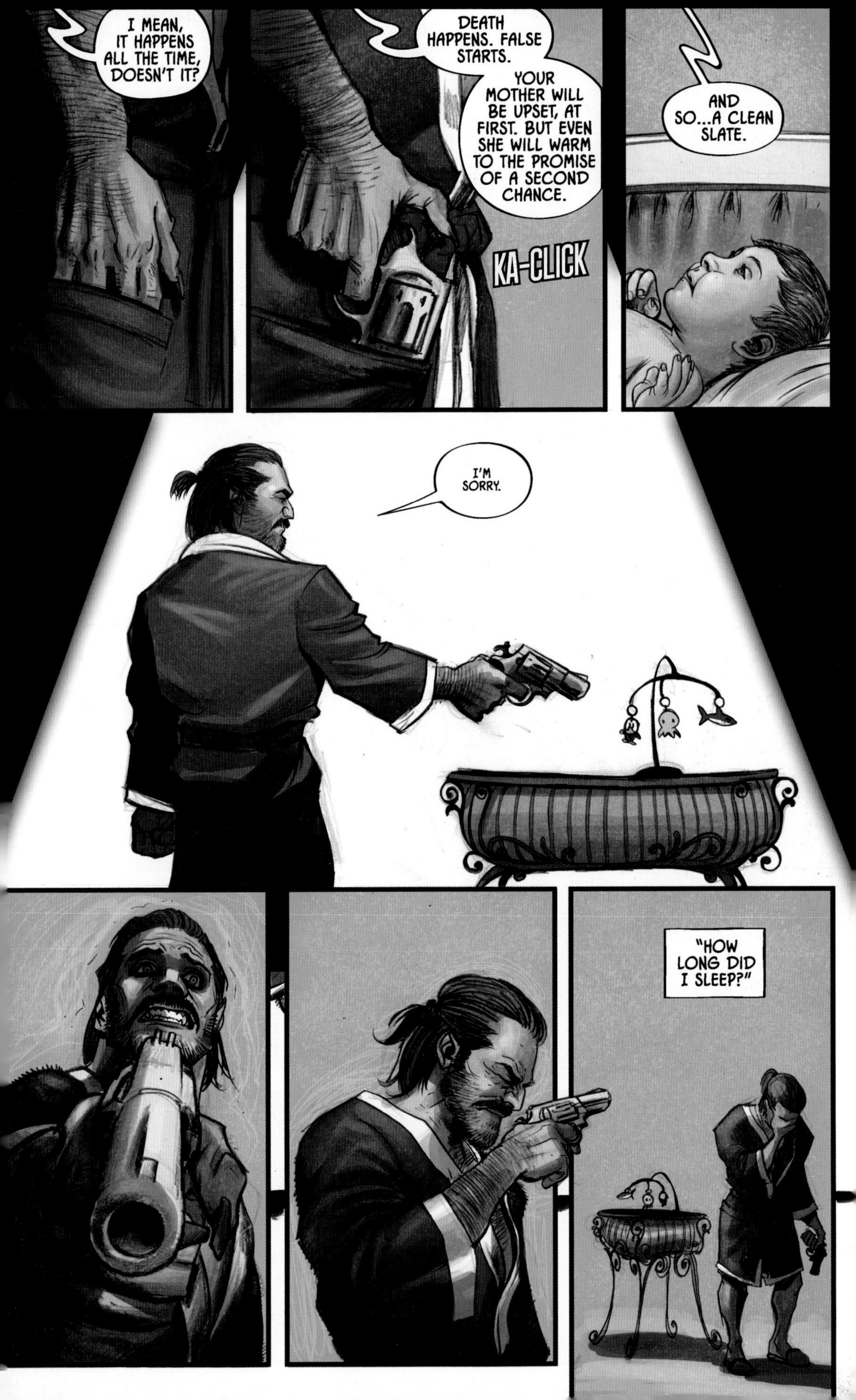

I MEAN, IT HAPPENS ALL THE TIME, DOESN'T IT?
DEATH HAPPENS. FALSE STARTS.
YOUR MOTHER WILL BE UPSET, AT FIRST. BUT EVEN SHE WILL WARM TO THE PROMISE OF A SECOND CHANCE.
KA-CLICK
AND SO...A CLEAN SLATE.
I'M SORRY.
"HOW LONG DID I SLEEP?"

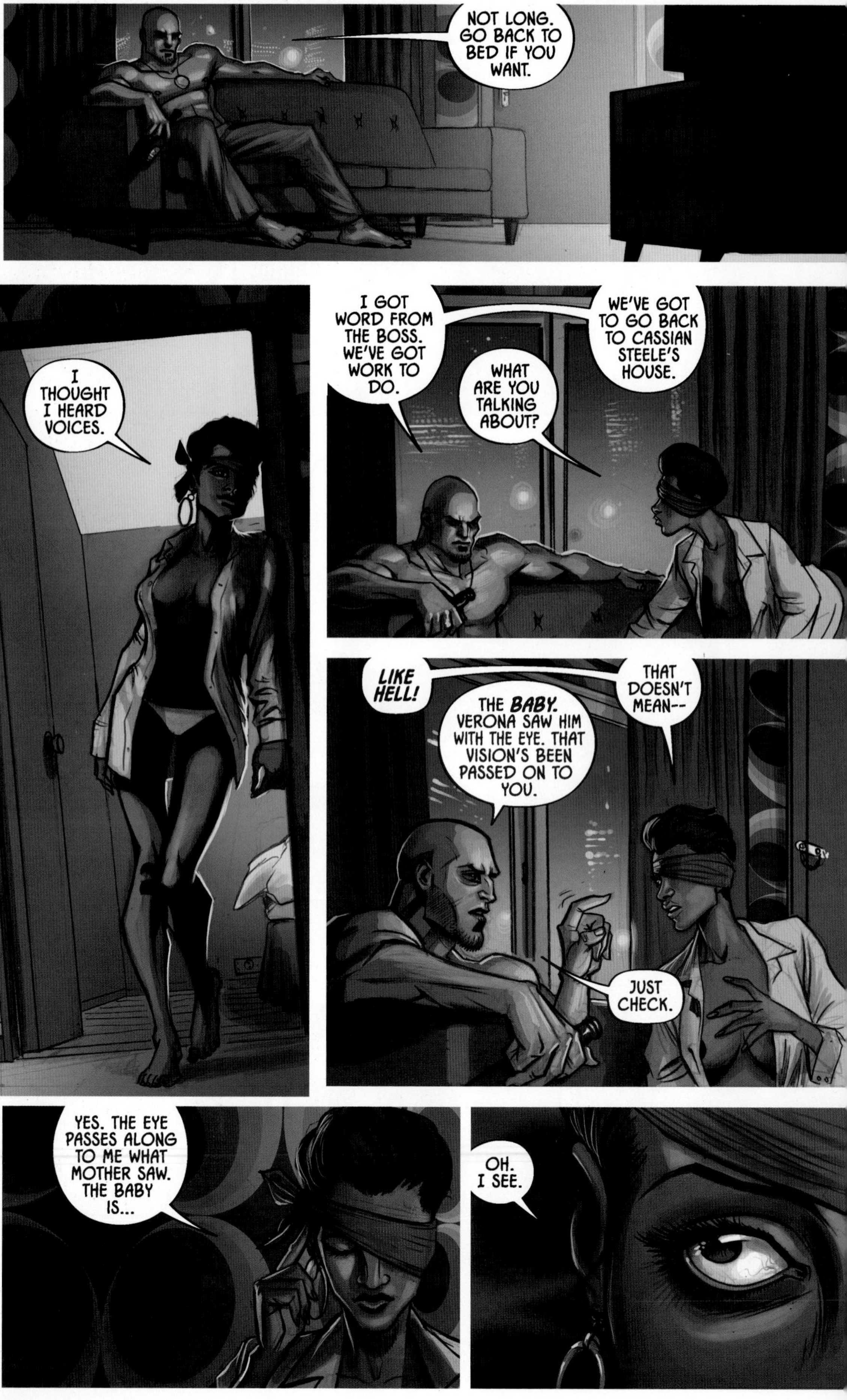
NOT LONG. GO BACK TO BED IF YOU WANT.
I THOUGHT I HEARD VOICES.
I GOT WORD FROM THE BOSS. WE'VE GOT WORK TO DO.
WHAT ARE YOU TALKING ABOUT?
WE'VE GOT TO GO BACK TO CASSIAN STEELE'S HOUSE.
THAT DOESN'T MEAN--
LIKE HELL!
THE BABY. VERONA SAW HIM WITH THE EYE. THAT VISION'S BEEN PASSED ON TO YOU.
JUST CHECK.
YES. THE EYE PASSES ALONG TO ME WHAT MOTHER SAW. THE BABY IS...
OH. I SEE.

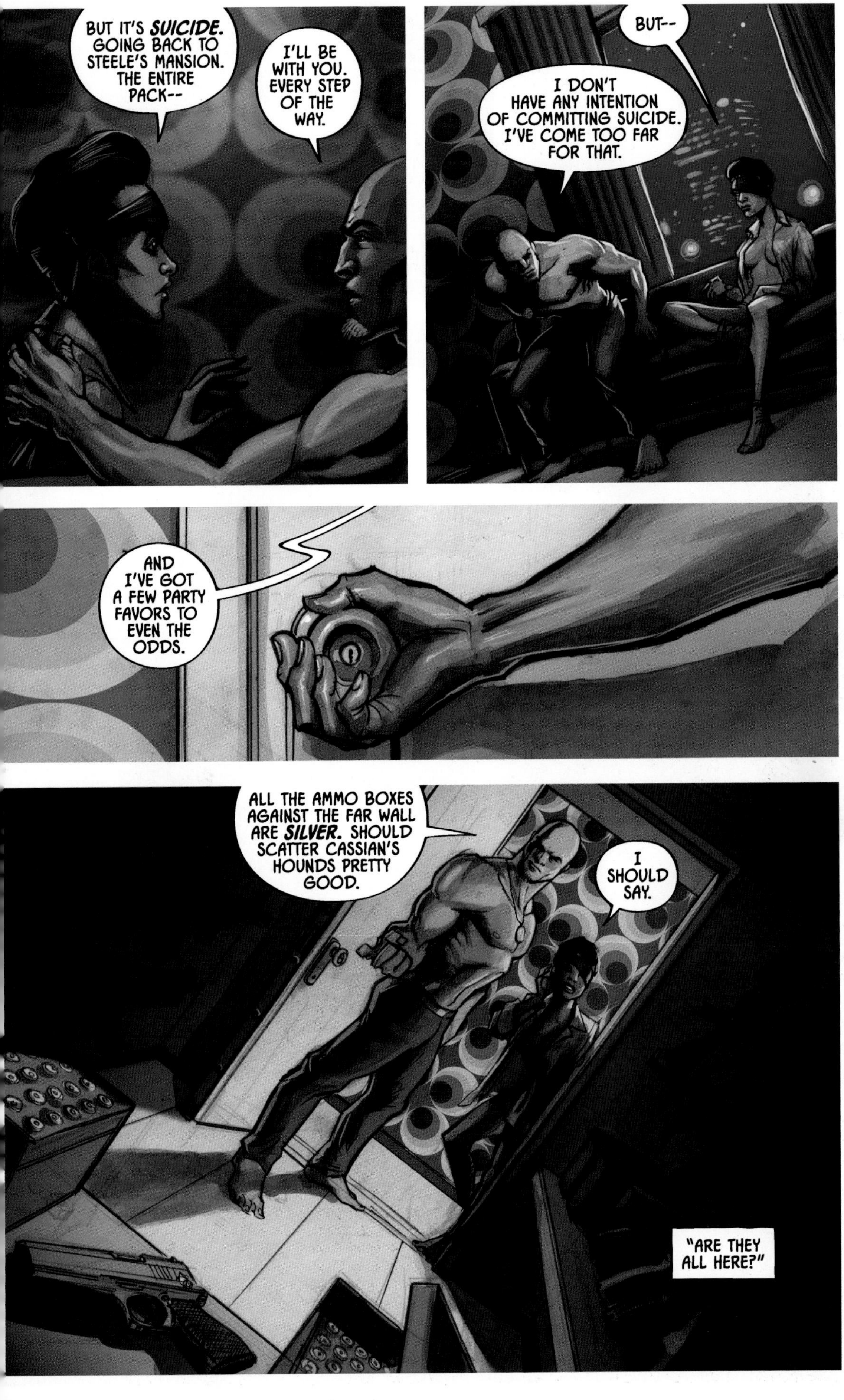
BUT IT'S SUICIDE. GOING BACK TO STEELE'S MANSION. THE ENTIRE PACK--
I'LL BE WITH YOU. EVERY STEP OF THE WAY.
BUT--
I DON'T HAVE ANY INTENTION OF COMMITTING SUICIDE. I'VE COME TOO FAR FOR THAT.
AND I'VE GOT A FEW PARTY FAVORS TO EVEN THE ODDS.
ALL THE AMMO BOXES AGAINST THE FAR WALL ARE SILVER. SHOULD SCATTER CASSIAN'S HOUNDS PRETTY GOOD.
I SHOULD SAY.
"ARE THEY ALL HERE?"

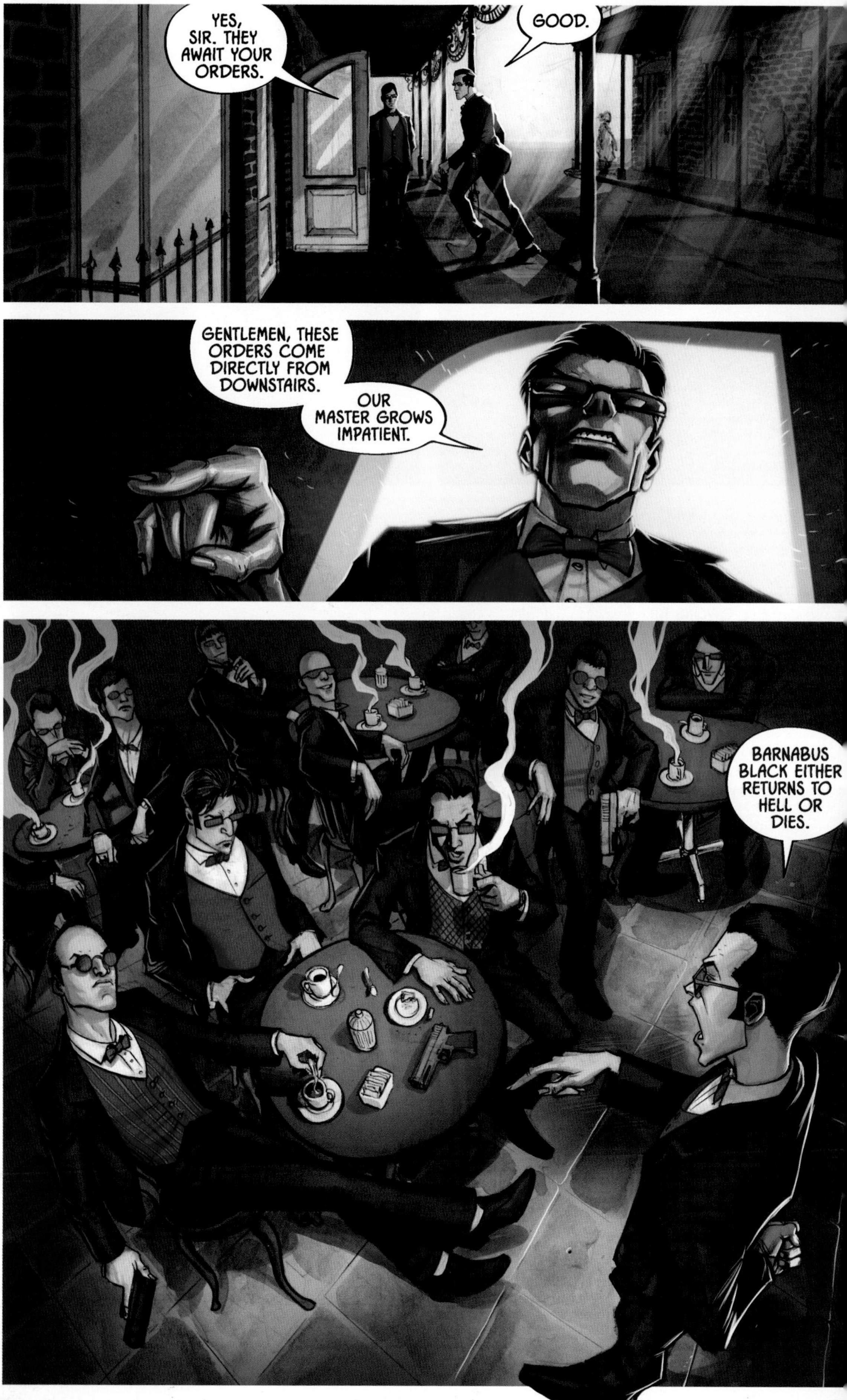
YES, SIR. THEY AWAIT YOUR ORDERS.
GOOD.
GENTLEMEN, THESE ORDERS COME DIRECTLY FROM DOWNSTAIRS.
OUR MASTER GROWS IMPATIENT.
BARNABUS BLACK EITHER RETURNS TO HELL OR DIES.

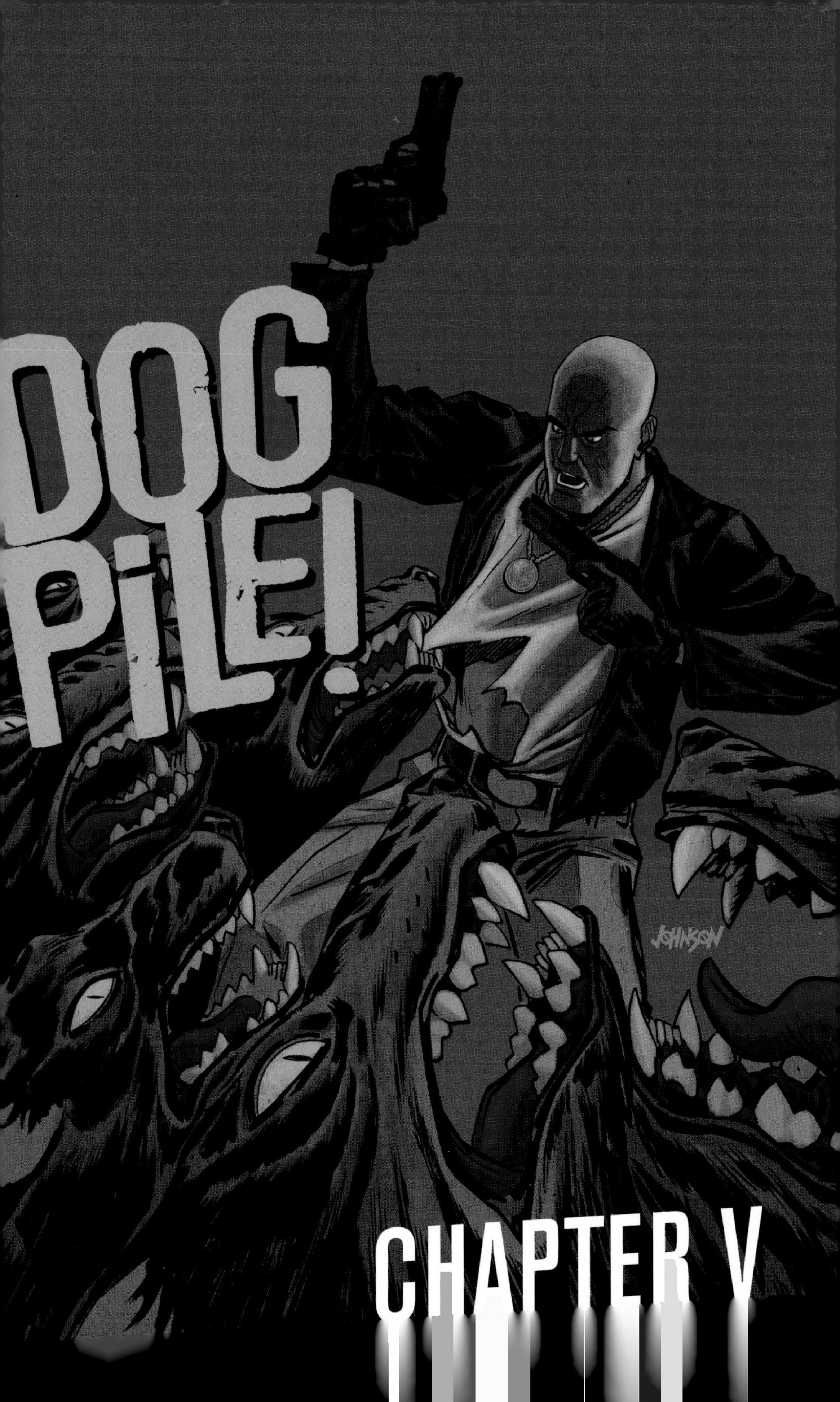
DOG PILE!
JOHNSON

CHAPTER V

"SHE'S *LAGGED*, FATHER.

VZZZZZZZ!

"THE FACIAL RECOGNITION SOFTWARE PICKED HER UP WHEN SHE CAME IN."

REC 0:2

HMMMM. LOOKS LIKE OUR LOCAL KINGPIN, CASSIAN STEELE, AS PUT A BOUNTY ON OUR YOUNG LADY.

WE DON'T SERVE CASSIAN STEELE IN THIS HOUSE, SISTER. WE SERVE A *HIGHER* POWER.

BUT LOOK. CASSIAN *RESCINDED* THE KILL ORDER.

SHE *SEEMS* HARMLESS ENOUGH, FATHER.

"THOU SHALT NOT SUFFER A WITCH TO LIVE."

EXODUS 22:18.

GET A BITE TO EAT AFTER THIS?

SURE.

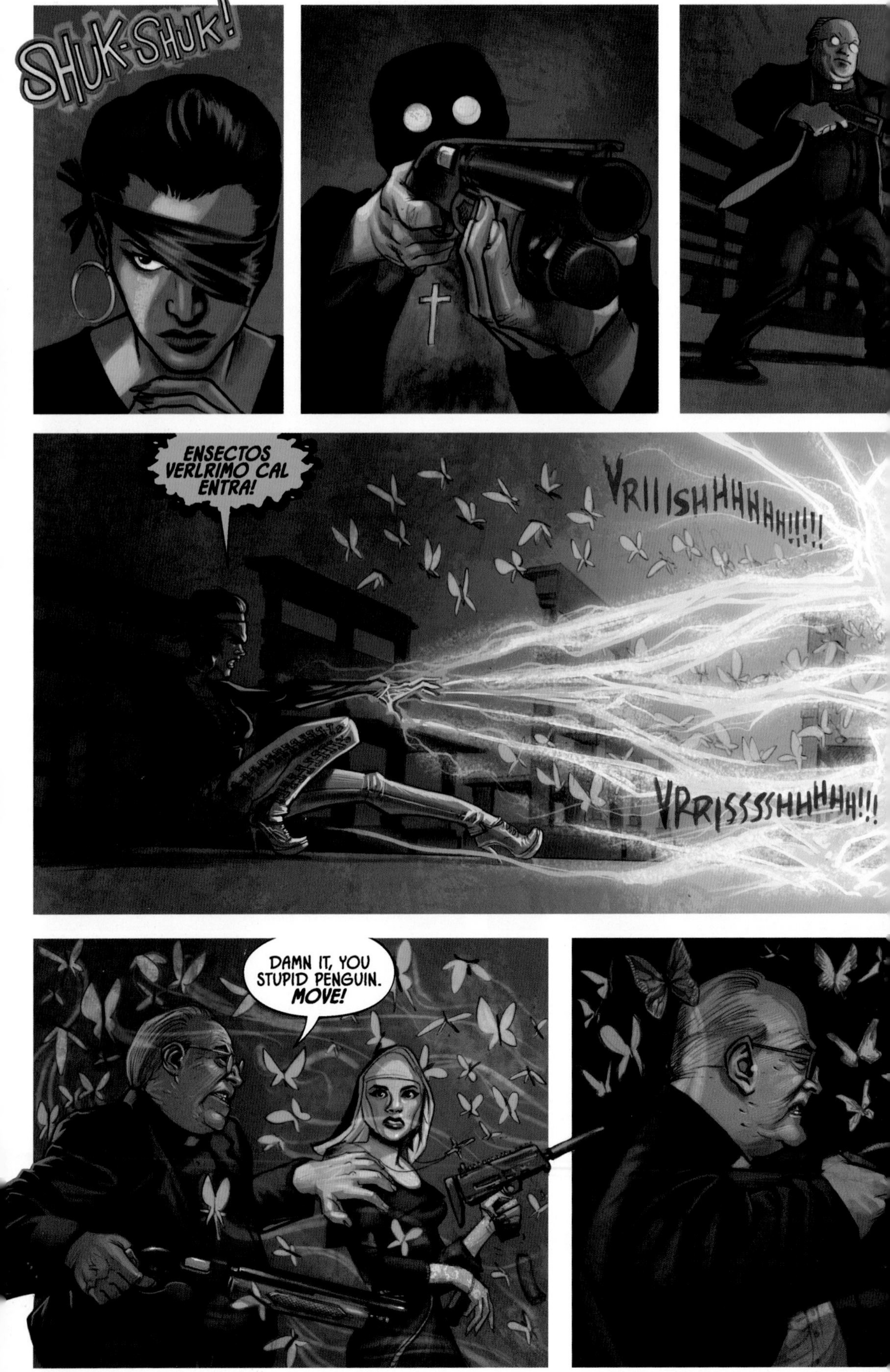
SHUK-SHUK!
ENSECTOS VERLRIMO CAL ENTRA!
VRIIISHHHHHH!!!!!
VRRISSSSHHHHH!!!
DAMN IT, YOU STUPID PENGUIN. MOVE!

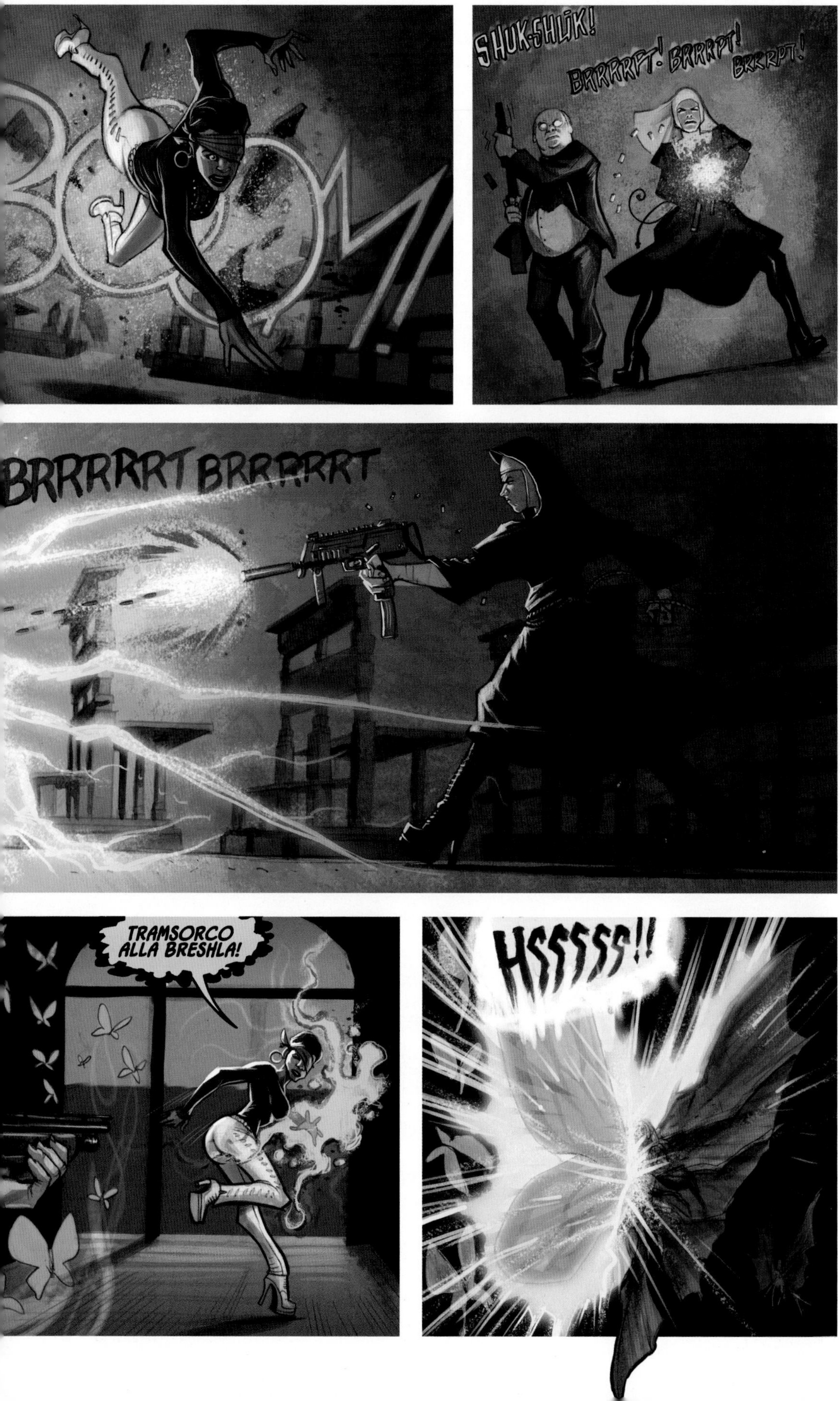

SHUK-SHLIK!
BRRRRPT! BRRRPT!
BRRRPT!
BRRRRRT BRRRRRT
TRAMSORCO ALLA BRESHLA!
HSSSSS!!

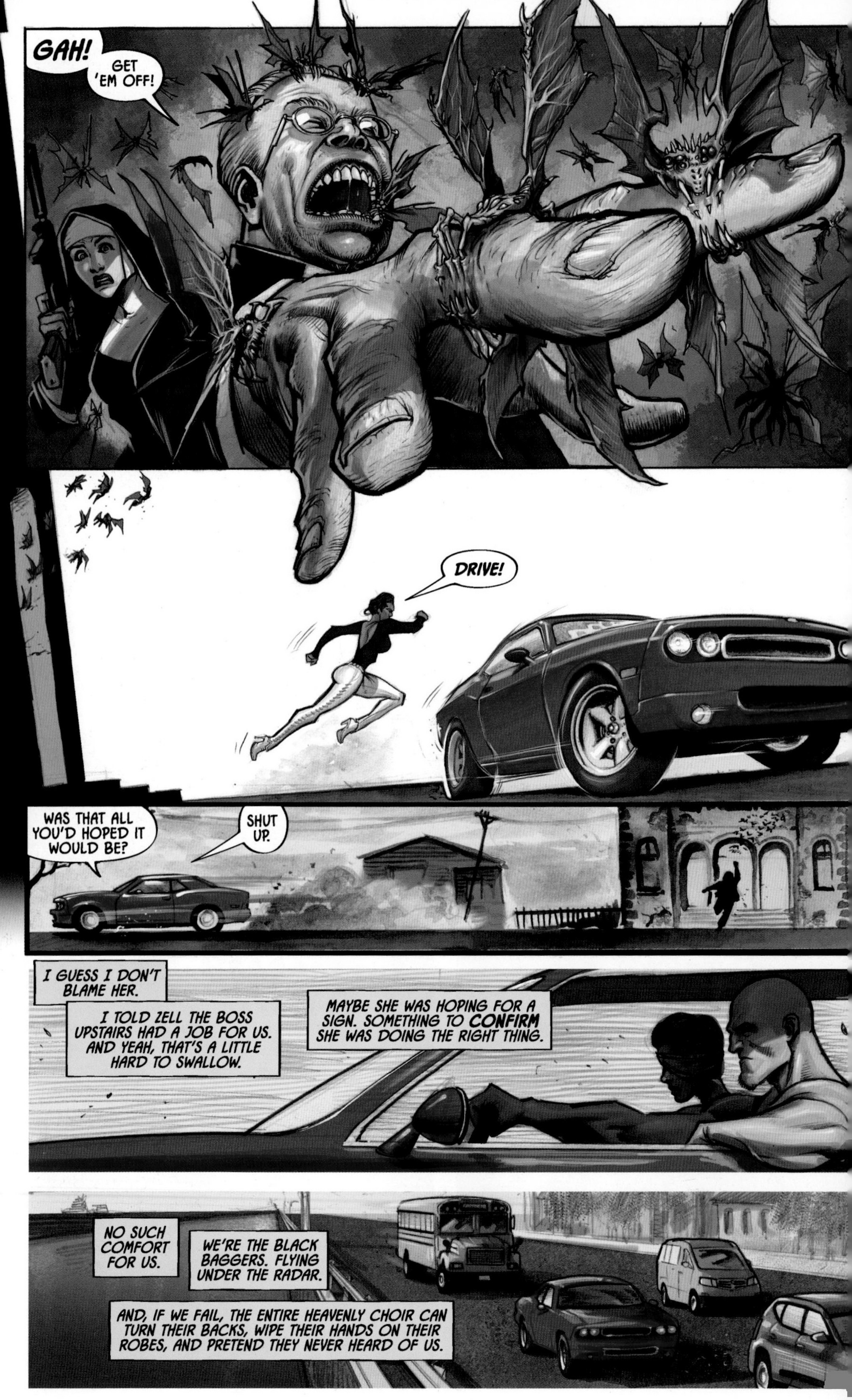
GAH!
GET 'EM OFF!
DRIVE!
WAS THAT ALL YOU'D HOPED IT WOULD BE?
SHUT UP.
I GUESS I DON'T BLAME HER.
I TOLD ZELL THE BOSS UPSTAIRS HAD A JOB FOR US. AND YEAH, THAT'S A LITTLE HARD TO SWALLOW.
MAYBE SHE WAS HOPING FOR A SIGN. SOMETHING TO CONFIRM SHE WAS DOING THE RIGHT THING.
NO SUCH COMFORT FOR US.
WE'RE THE BLACK BAGGERS. FLYING UNDER THE RADAR.
AND, IF WE FAIL, THE ENTIRE HEAVENLY CHOIR CAN TURN THEIR BACKS, WIPE THEIR HANDS ON THEIR ROBES, AND PRETEND THEY NEVER HEARD OF US.

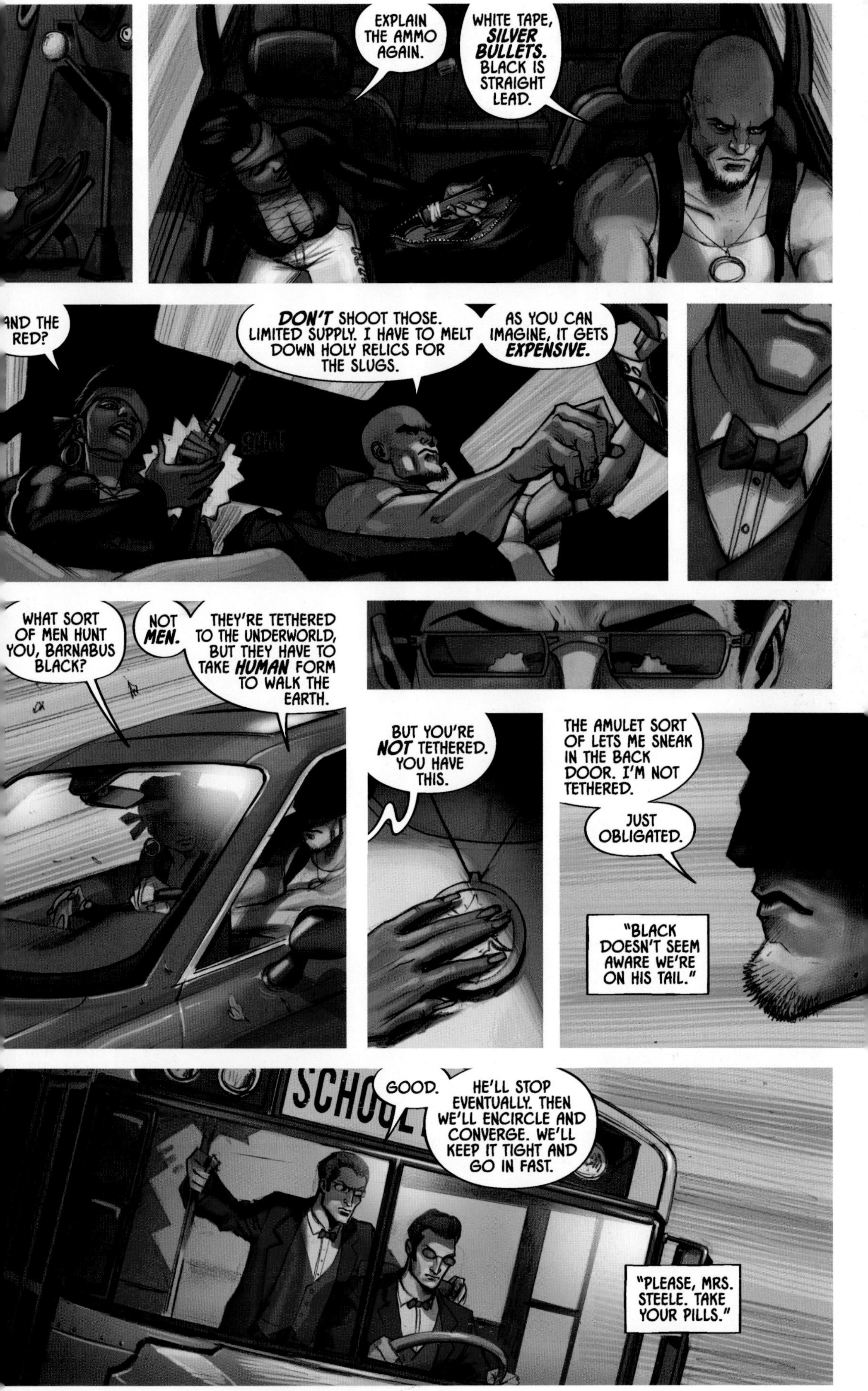
EXPLAIN THE AMMO AGAIN.
WHITE TAPE, SILVER BULLETS. BLACK IS STRAIGHT LEAD.
AND THE RED?
DON'T SHOOT THOSE. LIMITED SUPPLY. I HAVE TO MELT DOWN HOLY RELICS FOR THE SLUGS.
AS YOU CAN IMAGINE, IT GETS EXPENSIVE.
WHAT SORT OF MEN HUNT YOU, BARNABUS BLACK?
NOT MEN.
THEY'RE TETHERED TO THE UNDERWORLD, BUT THEY HAVE TO TAKE HUMAN FORM TO WALK THE EARTH.
BUT YOU'RE NOT TETHERED. YOU HAVE THIS.
THE AMULET SORT OF LETS ME SNEAK IN THE BACK DOOR. I'M NOT TETHERED.
JUST OBLIGATED.
"BLACK DOESN'T SEEM AWARE WE'RE ON HIS TAIL."
SCHOOL
GOOD.
HE'LL STOP EVENTUALLY. THEN WE'LL ENCIRCLE AND CONVERGE. WE'LL KEEP IT TIGHT AND GO IN FAST.
"PLEASE, MRS. STEELE. TAKE YOUR PILLS."

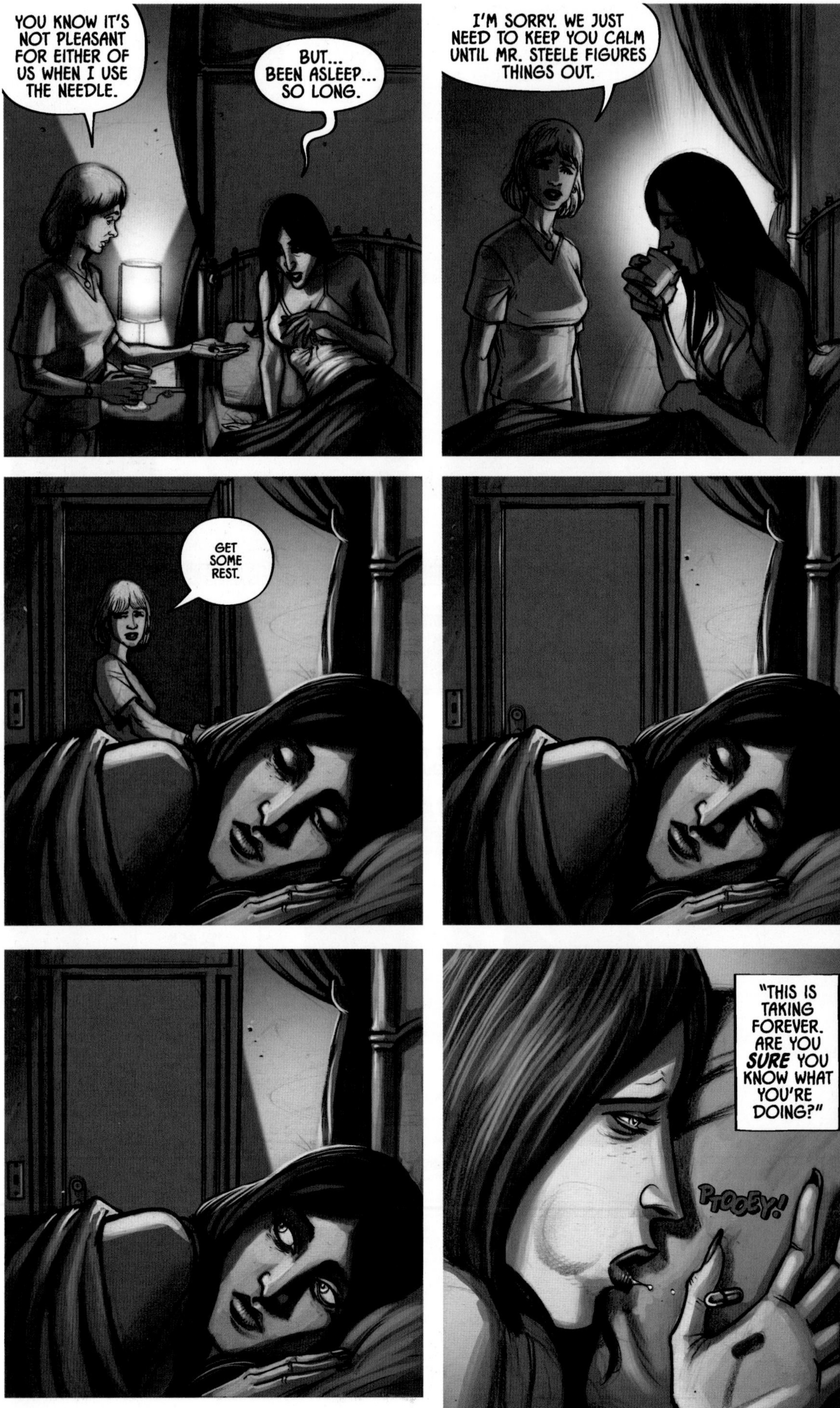
YOU KNOW IT'S NOT PLEASANT FOR EITHER OF US WHEN I USE THE NEEDLE.
BUT... BEEN ASLEEP... SO LONG.
I'M SORRY. WE JUST NEED TO KEEP YOU CALM UNTIL MR. STEELE FIGURES THINGS OUT.
GET SOME REST.
"THIS IS TAKING FOREVER. ARE YOU SURE YOU KNOW WHAT YOU'RE DOING?"
PTOOEY!

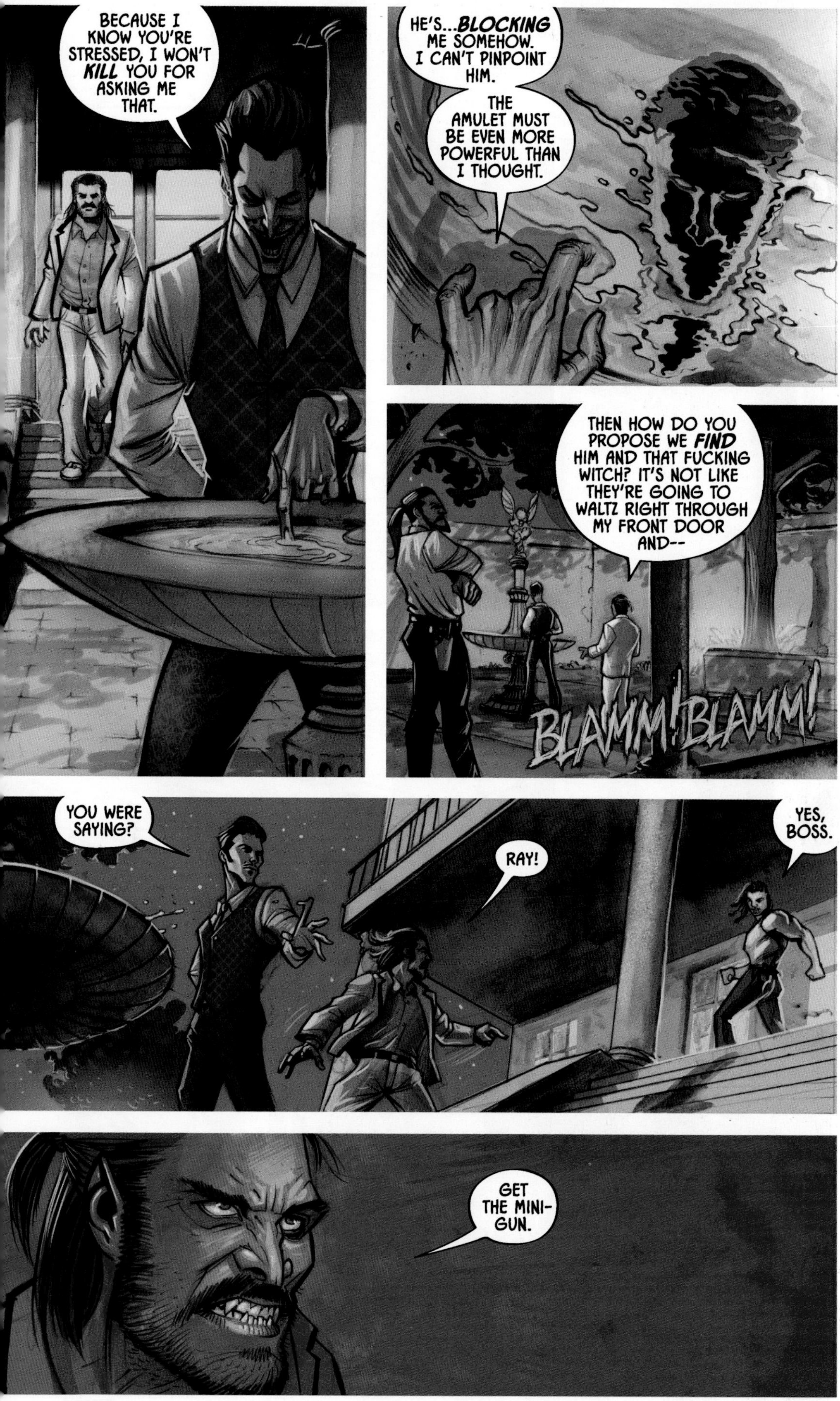

BECAUSE I KNOW YOU'RE STRESSED, I WON'T KILL YOU FOR ASKING ME THAT.
HE'S...BLOCKING ME SOMEHOW. I CAN'T PINPOINT HIM.
THE AMULET MUST BE EVEN MORE POWERFUL THAN I THOUGHT.
THEN HOW DO YOU PROPOSE WE FIND HIM AND THAT FUCKING WITCH? IT'S NOT LIKE THEY'RE GOING TO WALTZ RIGHT THROUGH MY FRONT DOOR AND--
BLAMM! BLAMM!
YOU WERE SAYING?
RAY!
YES, BOSS.
GET THE MINI-GUN.

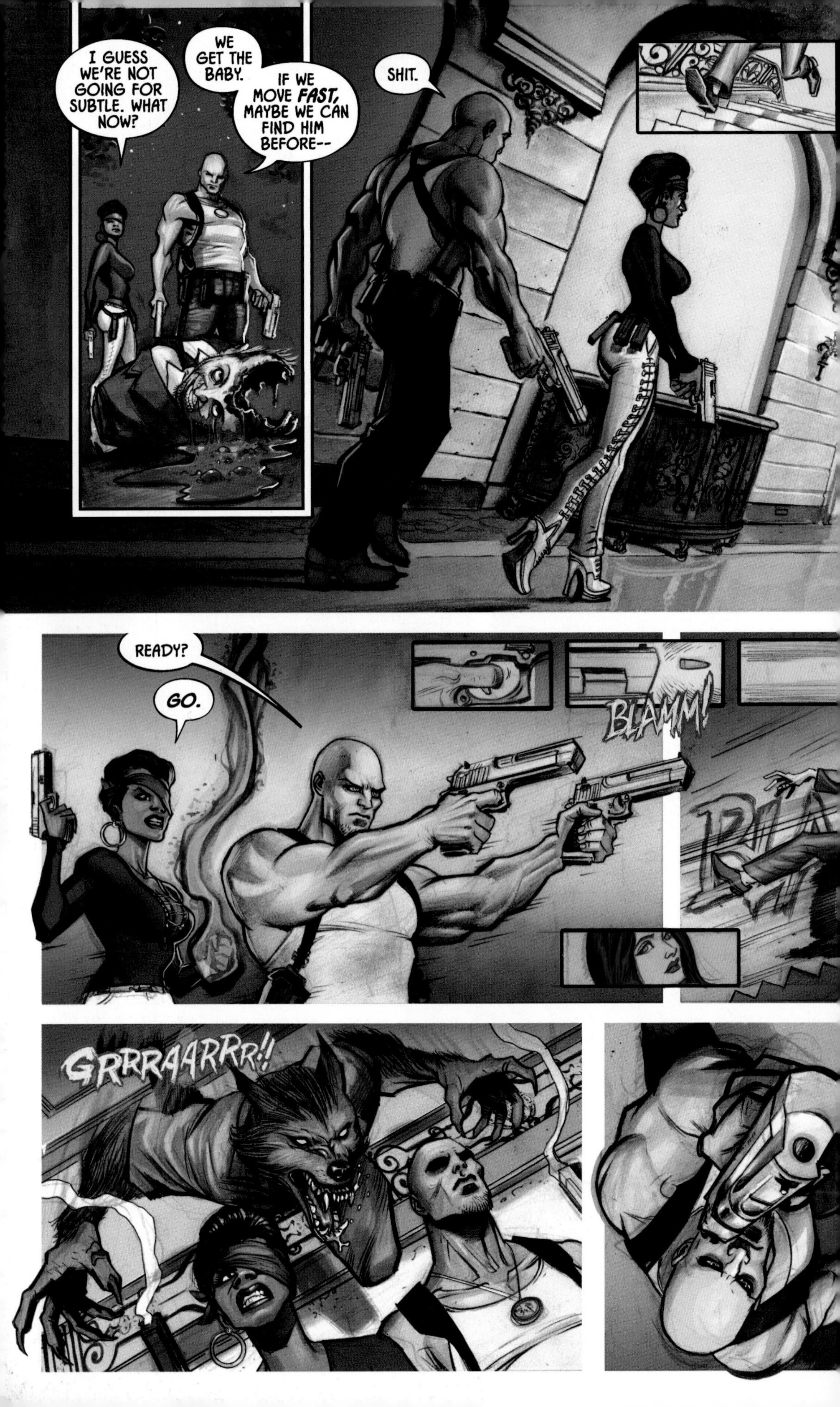
I GUESS WE'RE NOT GOING FOR SUBTLE. WHAT NOW?
WE GET THE BABY.
IF WE MOVE FAST, MAYBE WE CAN FIND HIM BEFORE--
SHIT.
READY?
GO.
BLAMM!
GRRRAARRR!!

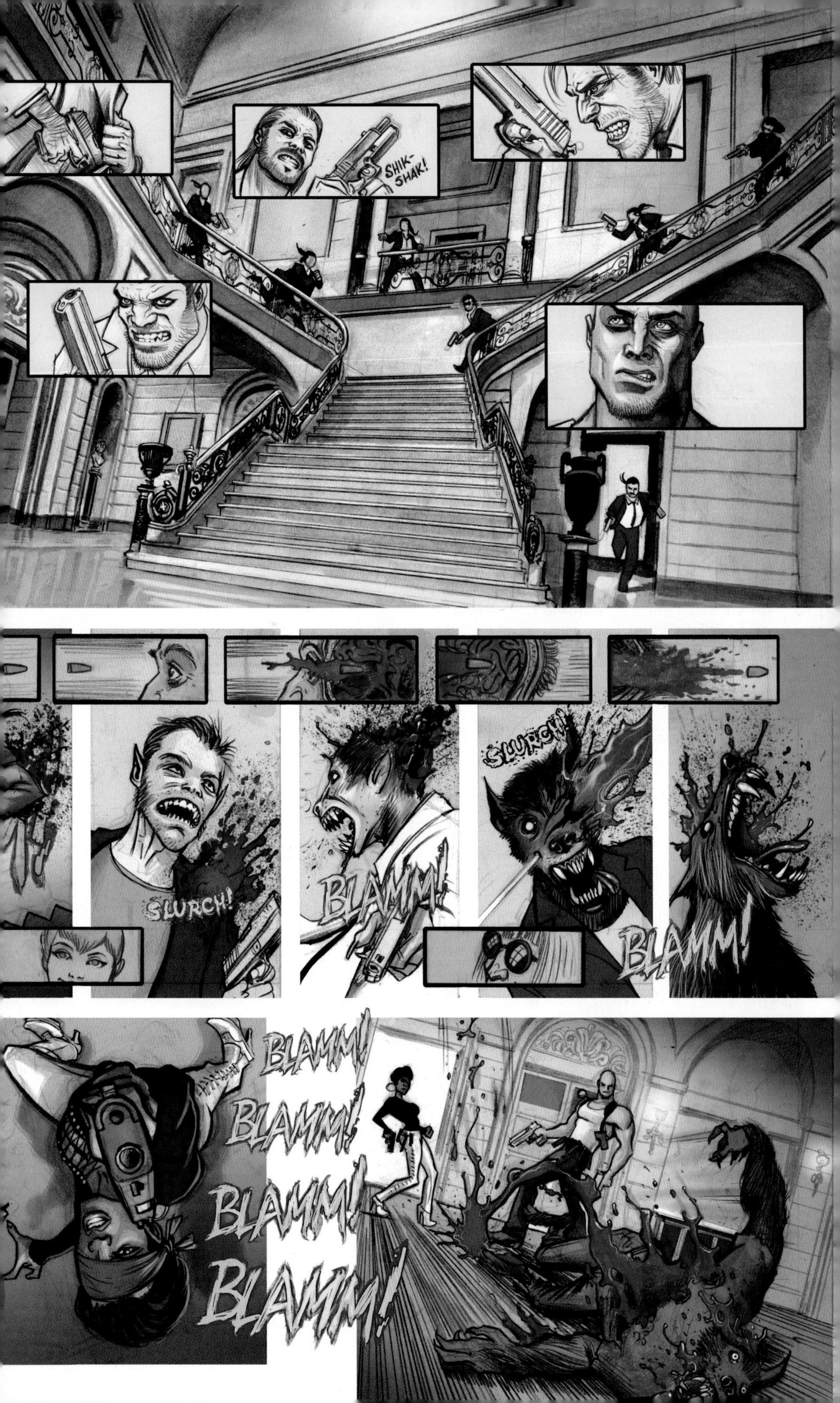

SHIK-SHAK!
SLURCH!
BLAMM!
SLURCH!
BLAMM!
BLAMM!
BLAMM!
BLAMM!
BLAMM!

FWHAM!

DOWN!

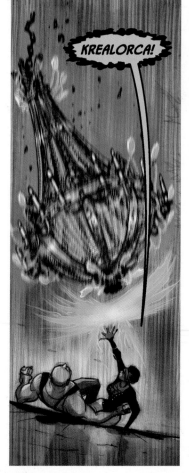

KREALORCA!

HUH.

I'M GOING TO HAVE TO HANDLE THIS. ALONE.

BUT I--

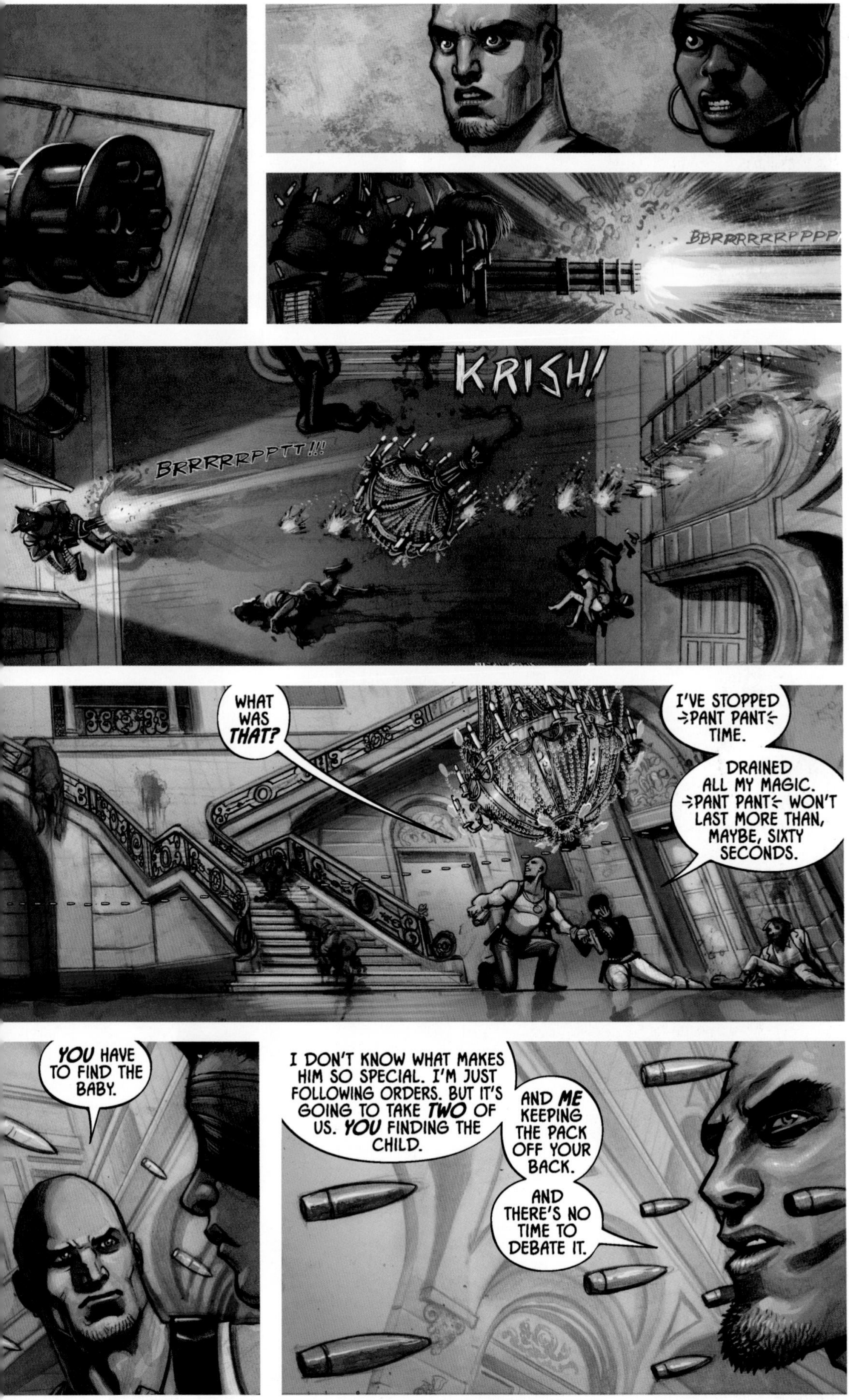
BBRRRRRRPPPP
KRISH!
BRRRRRPPTT!!!
WHAT WAS THAT?
I'VE STOPPED ⇒PANT PANT⇐ TIME.
DRAINED ALL MY MAGIC. ⇒PANT PANT⇐ WON'T LAST MORE THAN, MAYBE, SIXTY SECONDS.
YOU HAVE TO FIND THE BABY.
I DON'T KNOW WHAT MAKES HIM SO SPECIAL. I'M JUST FOLLOWING ORDERS. BUT IT'S GOING TO TAKE TWO OF US. YOU FINDING THE CHILD.
AND ME KEEPING THE PACK OFF YOUR BACK.
AND THERE'S NO TIME TO DEBATE IT.

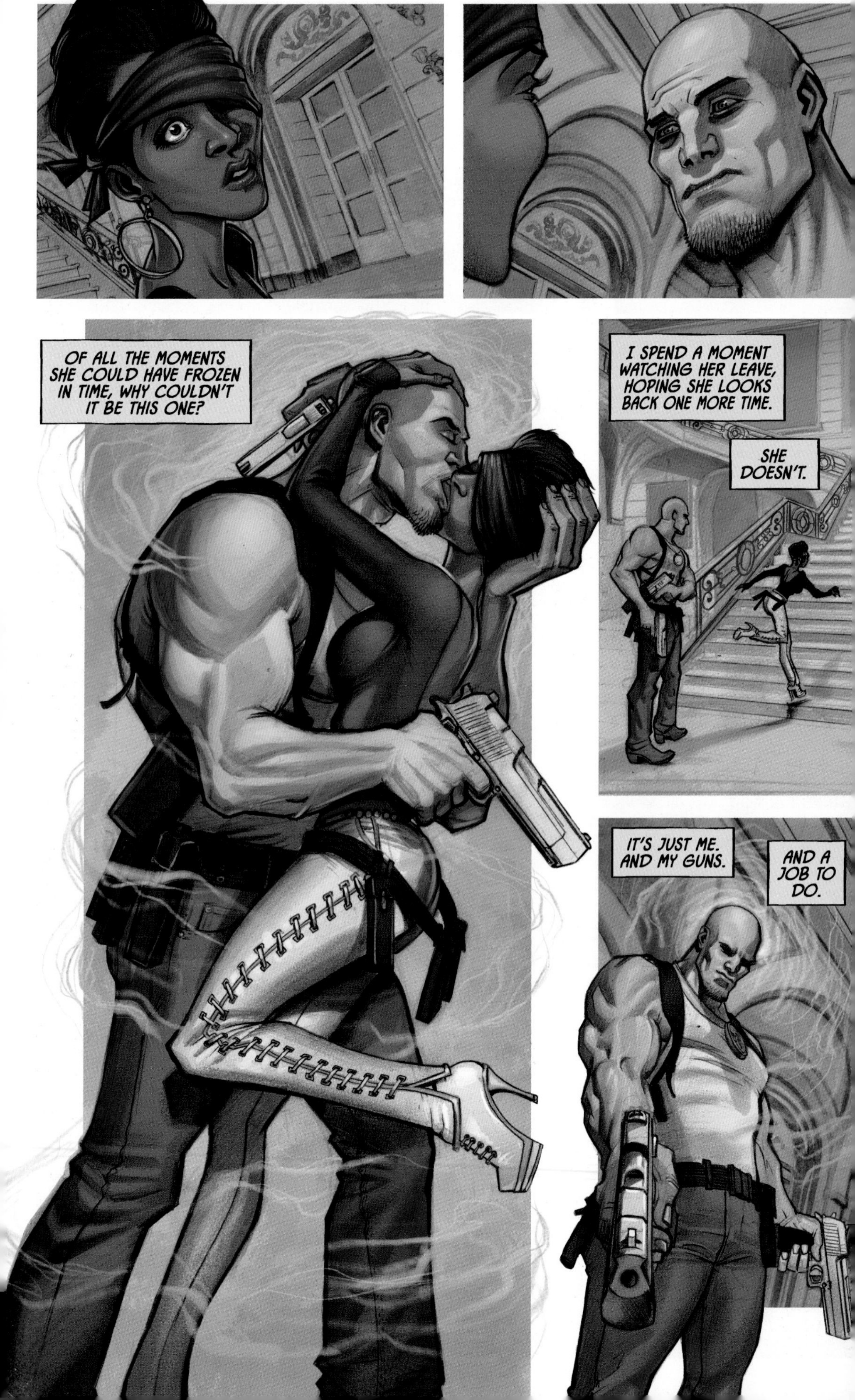
OF ALL THE MOMENTS SHE COULD HAVE FROZEN IN TIME, WHY COULDN'T IT BE THIS ONE?
I SPEND A MOMENT WATCHING HER LEAVE, HOPING SHE LOOKS BACK ONE MORE TIME.
SHE DOESN'T.
IT'S JUST ME. AND MY GUNS.
AND A JOB TO DO.

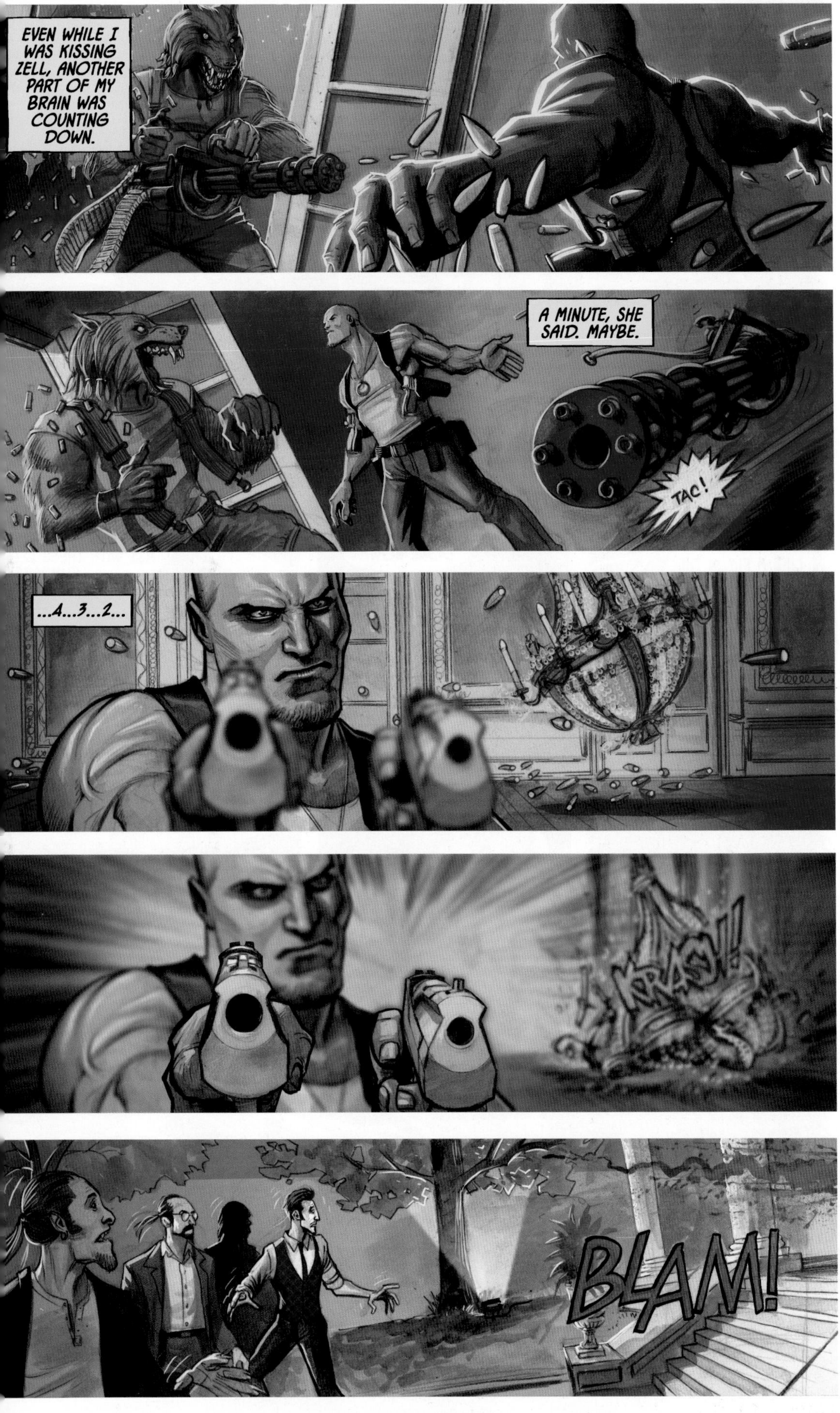
EVEN WHILE I WAS KISSING ZELL, ANOTHER PART OF MY BRAIN WAS COUNTING DOWN.
A MINUTE, SHE SAID. MAYBE.
TAC!
...4...3...2...
KRASH!!
BLAM!

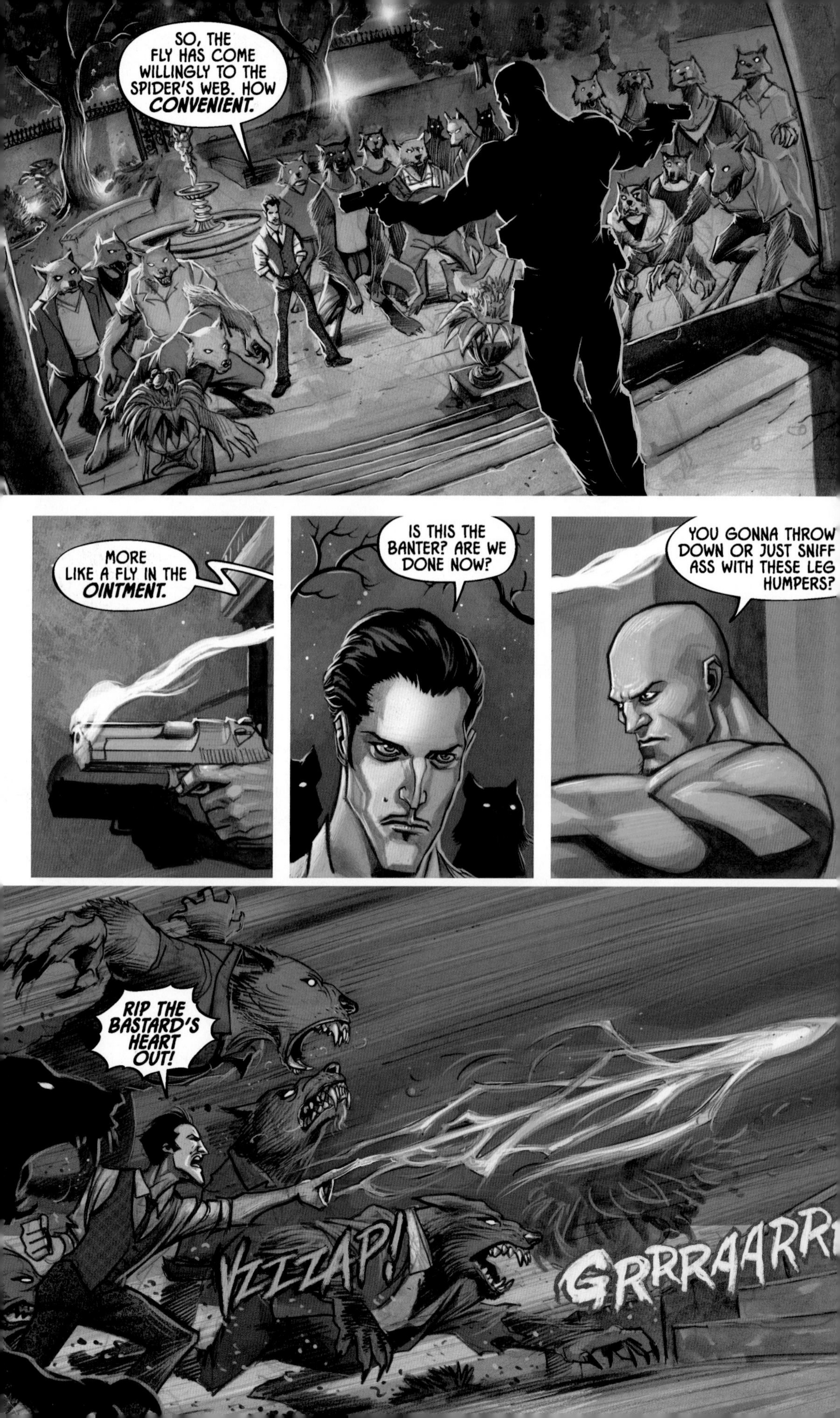
SO, THE FLY HAS COME WILLINGLY TO THE SPIDER'S WEB. HOW CONVENIENT.
MORE LIKE A FLY IN THE OINTMENT.
IS THIS THE BANTER? ARE WE DONE NOW?
YOU GONNA THROW DOWN OR JUST SNIFF ASS WITH THESE LEG HUMPERS?
RIP THE BASTARD'S HEART OUT!
VZZZAP!
GRRRAARR

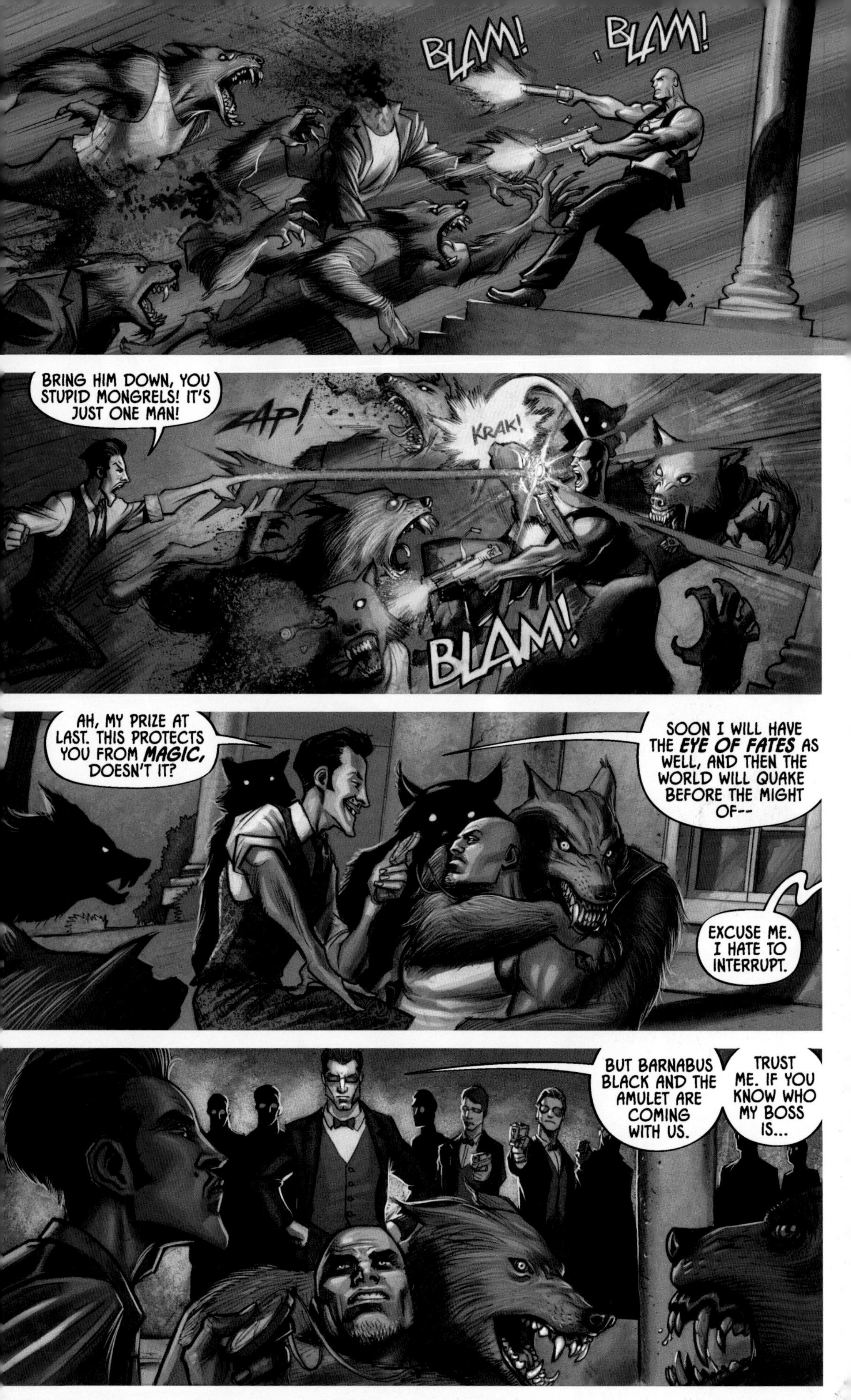

BLAM!
BLAM!
BRING HIM DOWN, YOU STUPID MONGRELS! IT'S JUST ONE MAN!
ZAP!
KRAK!
BLAM!
AH, MY PRIZE AT LAST. THIS PROTECTS YOU FROM MAGIC, DOESN'T IT?
SOON I WILL HAVE THE EYE OF FATES AS WELL, AND THEN THE WORLD WILL QUAKE BEFORE THE MIGHT OF--
EXCUSE ME. I HATE TO INTERRUPT.
BUT BARNABUS BLACK AND THE AMULET ARE COMING WITH US.
TRUST ME. IF YOU KNOW WHO MY BOSS IS...

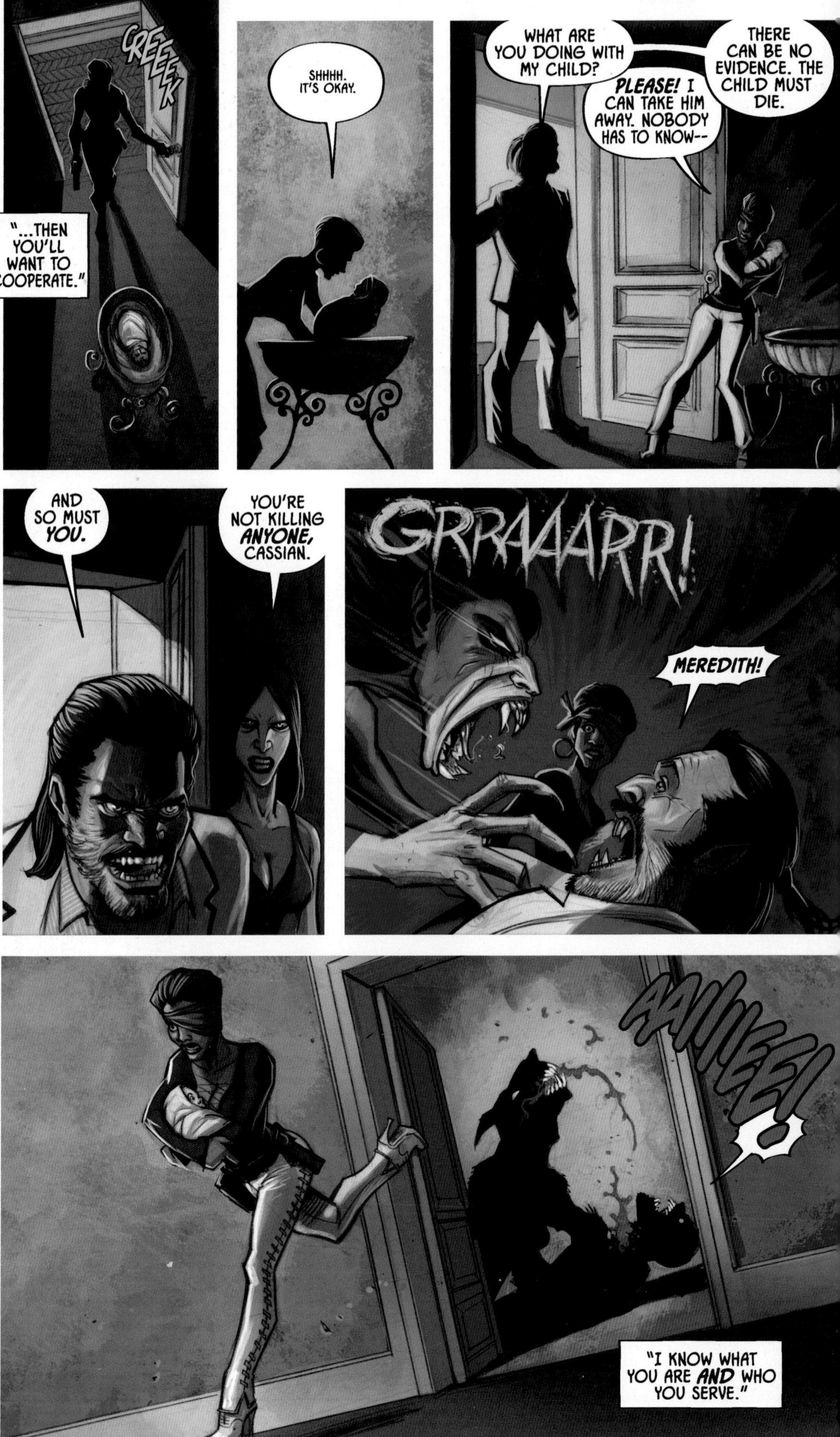
CREEEK
"...THEN YOU'LL WANT TO COOPERATE."
SHHHH. IT'S OKAY.
WHAT ARE YOU DOING WITH MY CHILD?
THERE CAN BE NO EVIDENCE. THE CHILD MUST DIE.
PLEASE! I CAN TAKE HIM AWAY. NOBODY HAS TO KNOW--
AND SO MUST YOU.
YOU'RE NOT KILLING ANYONE, CASSIAN.
GRRAAARR!
MEREDITH!
AAIIIEEE!
"I KNOW WHAT YOU ARE AND WHO YOU SERVE."

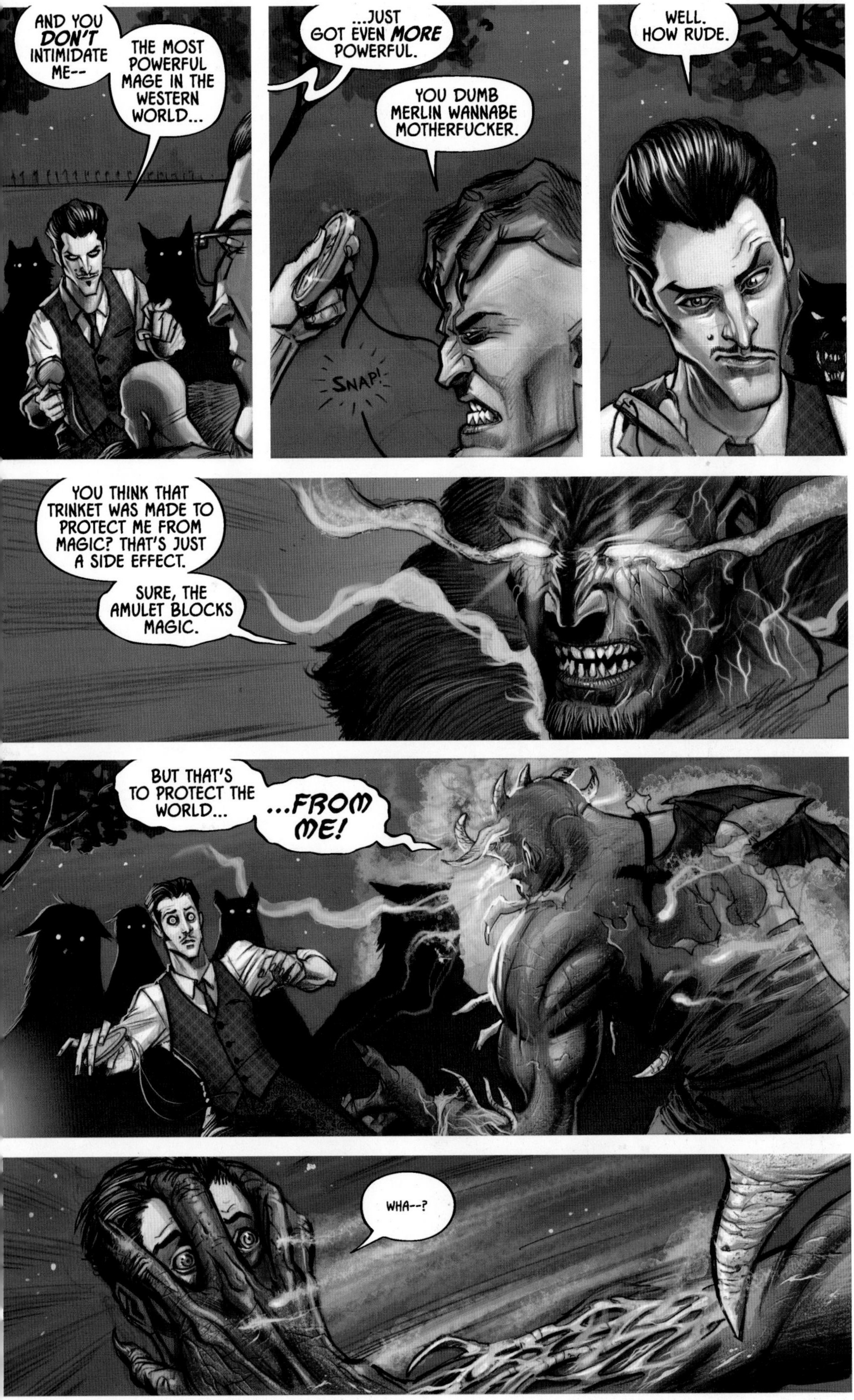
AND YOU *DON'T* INTIMIDATE ME--
THE MOST POWERFUL MAGE IN THE WESTERN WORLD...
...JUST GOT EVEN *MORE* POWERFUL.
YOU DUMB MERLIN WANNABE MOTHERFUCKER.
SNAP!
WELL. HOW RUDE.
YOU THINK THAT TRINKET WAS MADE TO PROTECT ME FROM MAGIC? THAT'S JUST A SIDE EFFECT.
SURE, THE AMULET BLOCKS MAGIC.
BUT THAT'S TO PROTECT THE WORLD...
...FROM ME!
WHA--?

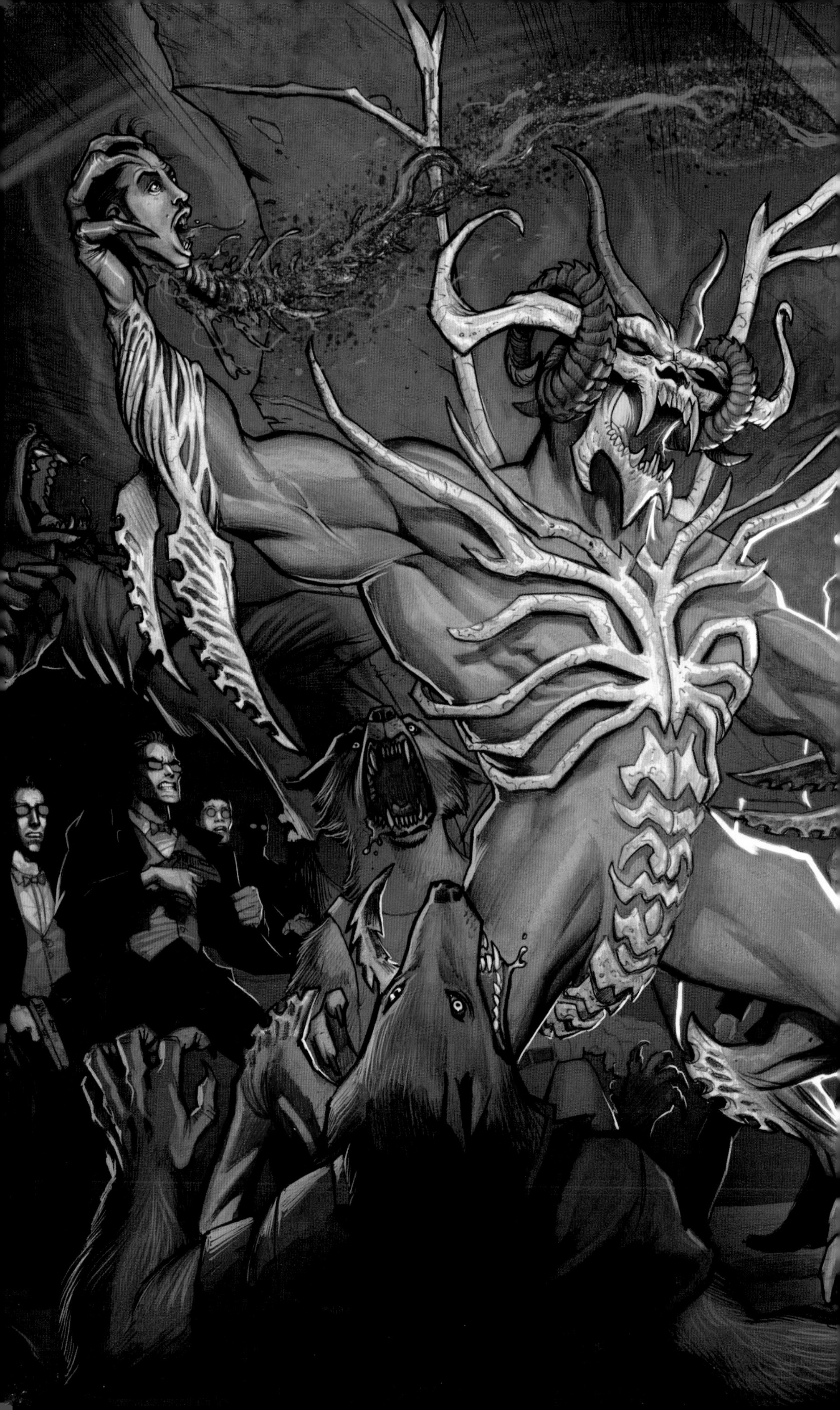

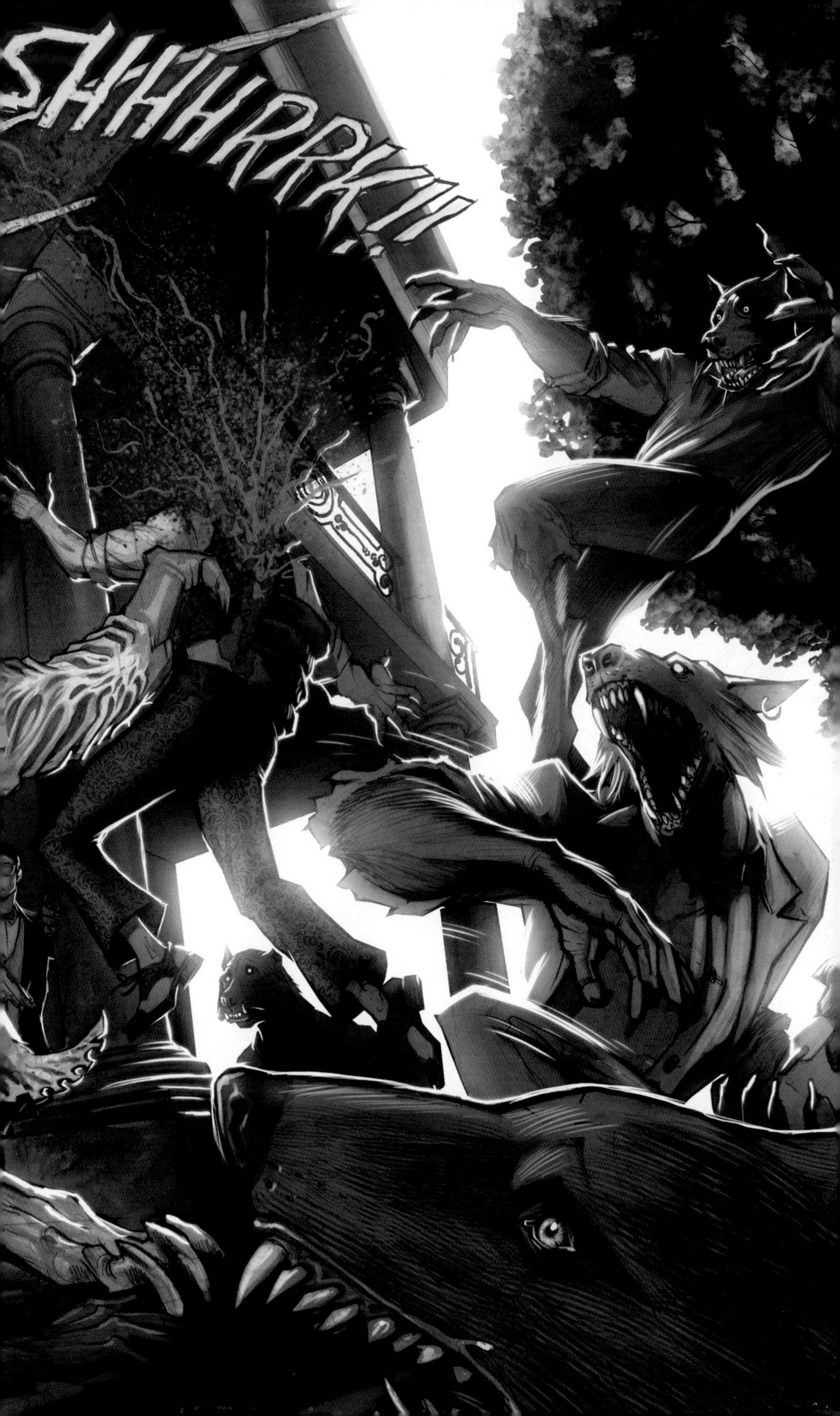
SHHHRRK!!!

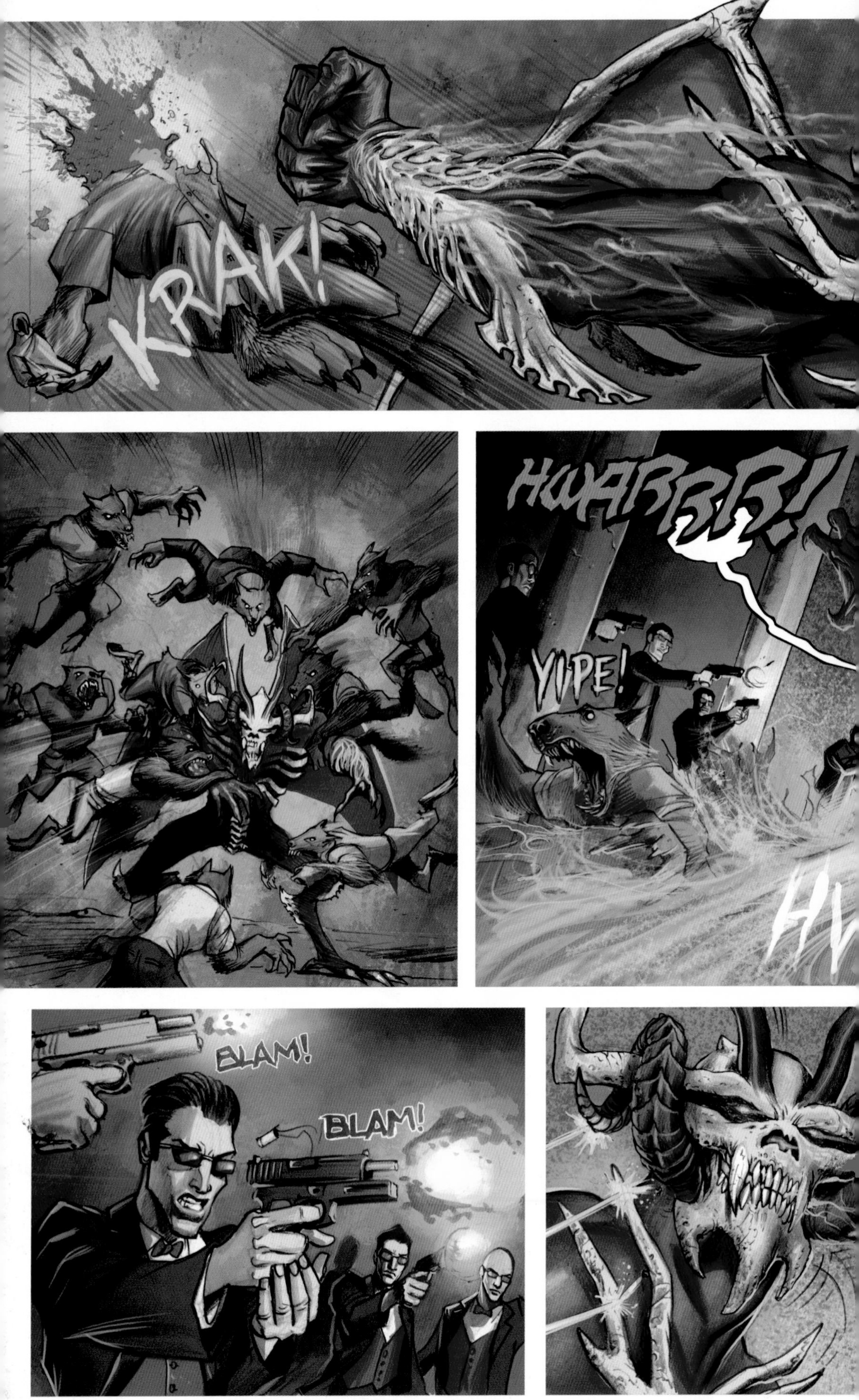
KRAK!
HWARRR!
YIPE!
BLAM!
BLAM!

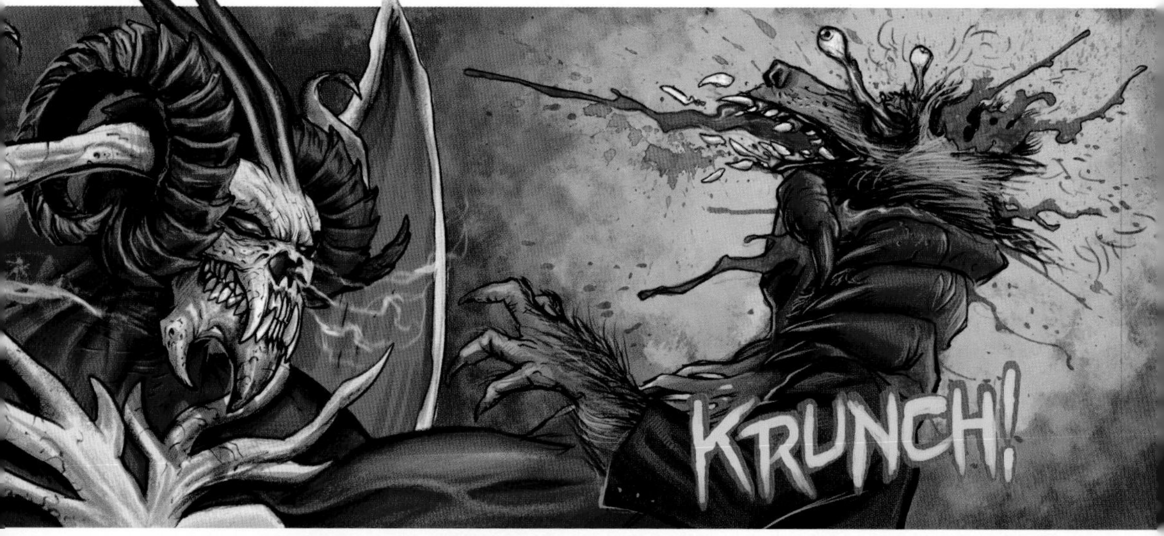
KRUNCH!

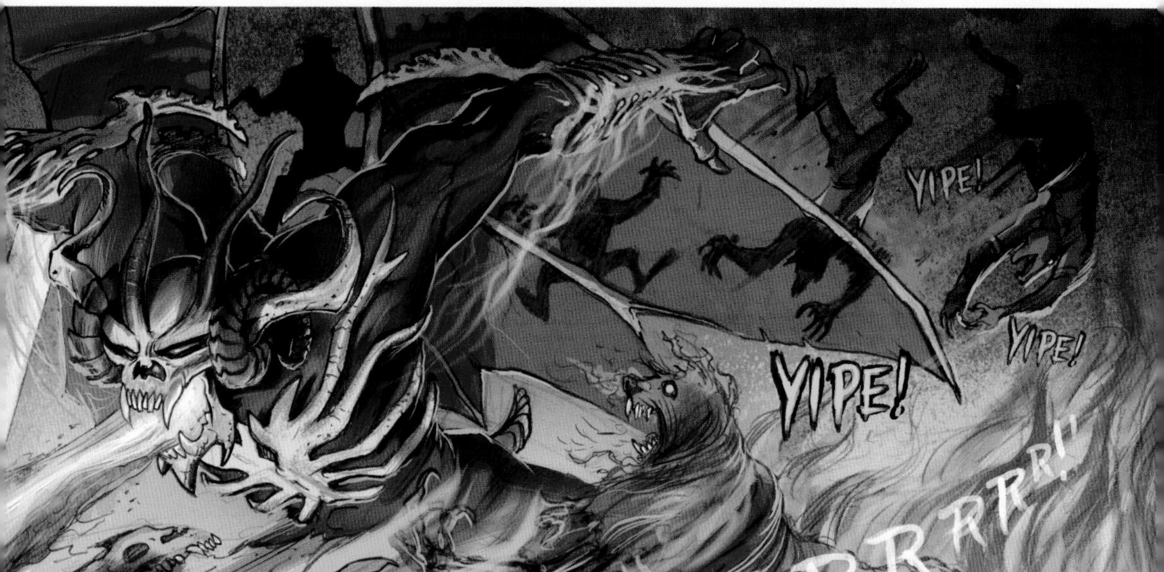
YIPE!
YIPE!
YIPE!
WAAAARRRRRRRRRRR!!

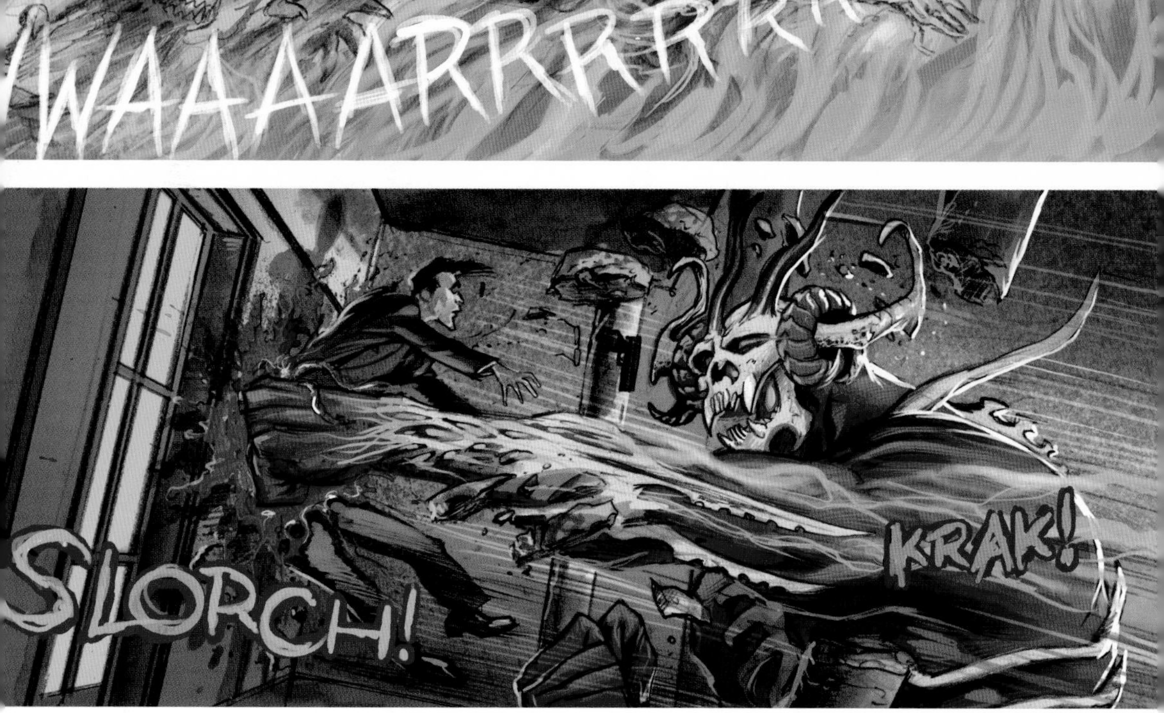
SLORCH!
KRAK!

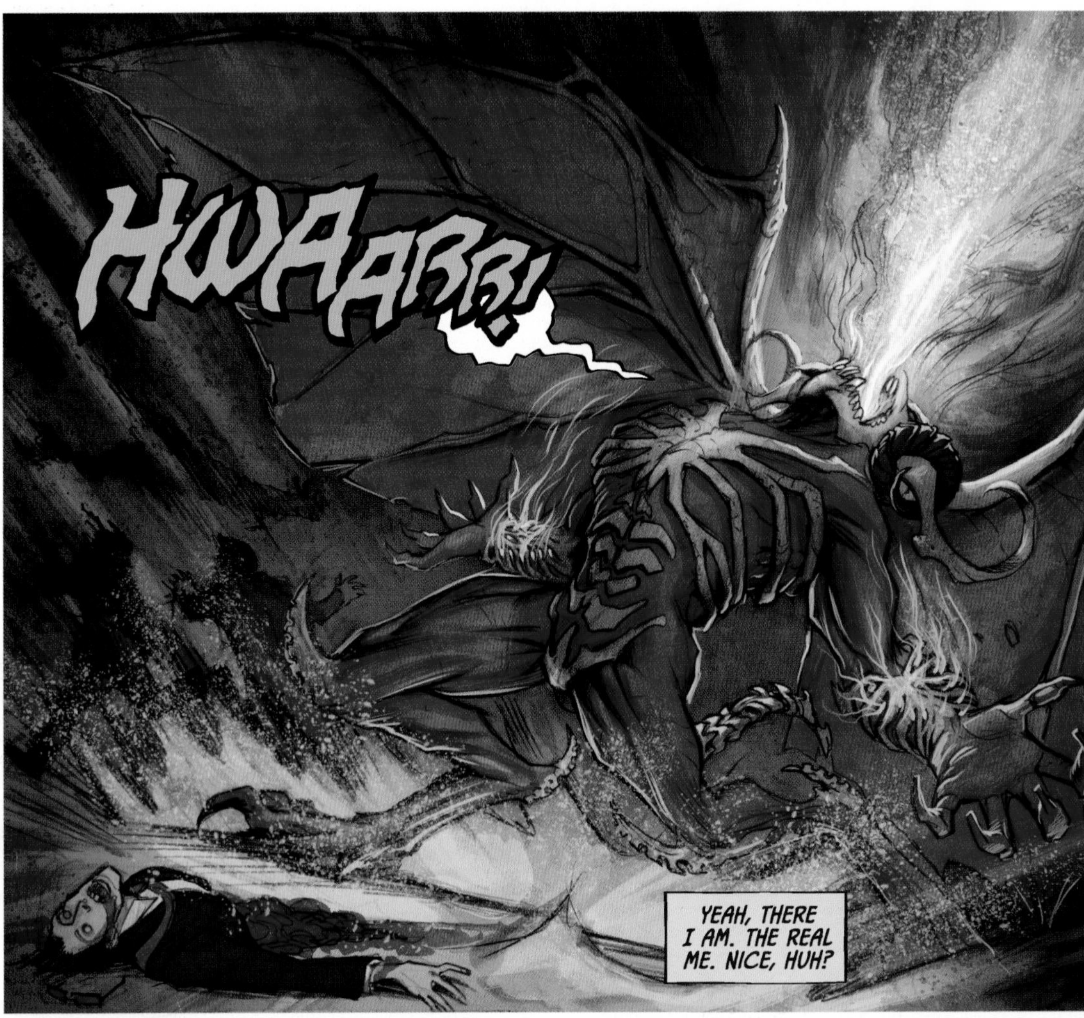
HWAARR!
YEAH, THERE I AM. THE REAL ME. NICE, HUH?

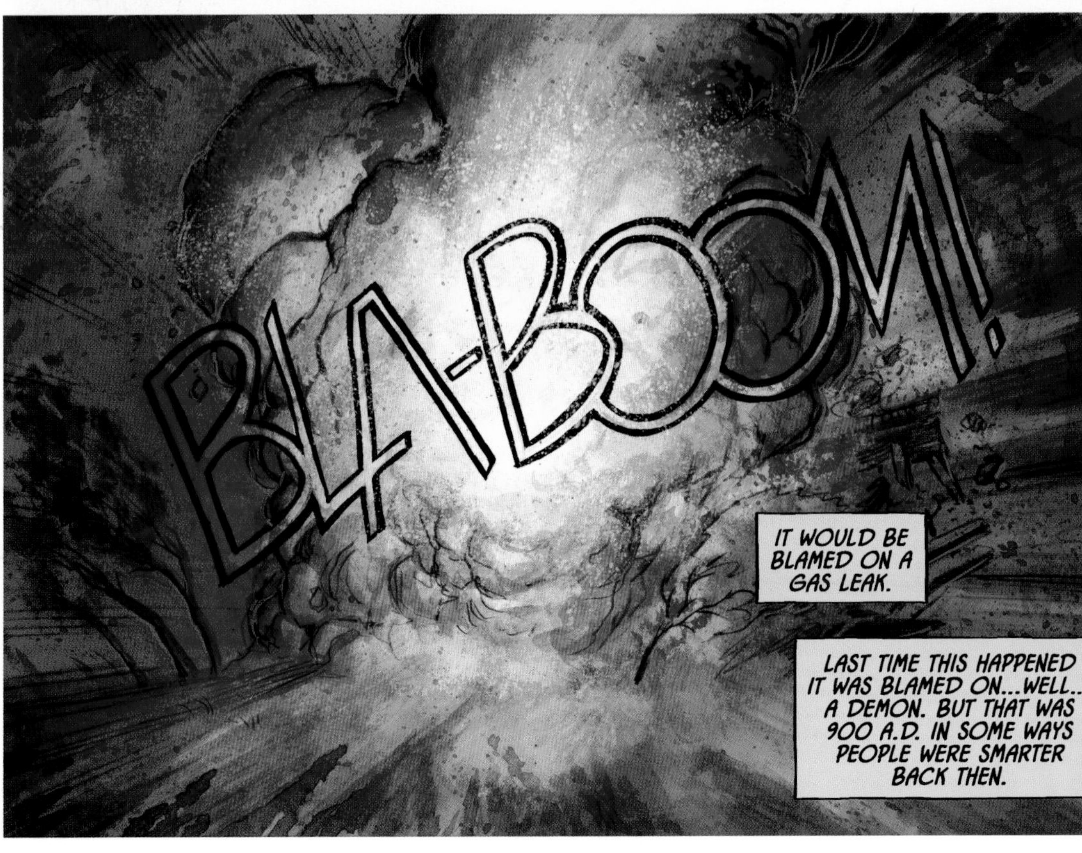
BLA-BOOM!
IT WOULD BE BLAMED ON A GAS LEAK.
LAST TIME THIS HAPPENED IT WAS BLAMED ON...WELL... A DEMON. BUT THAT WAS 900 A.D. IN SOME WAYS PEOPLE WERE SMARTER BACK THEN.

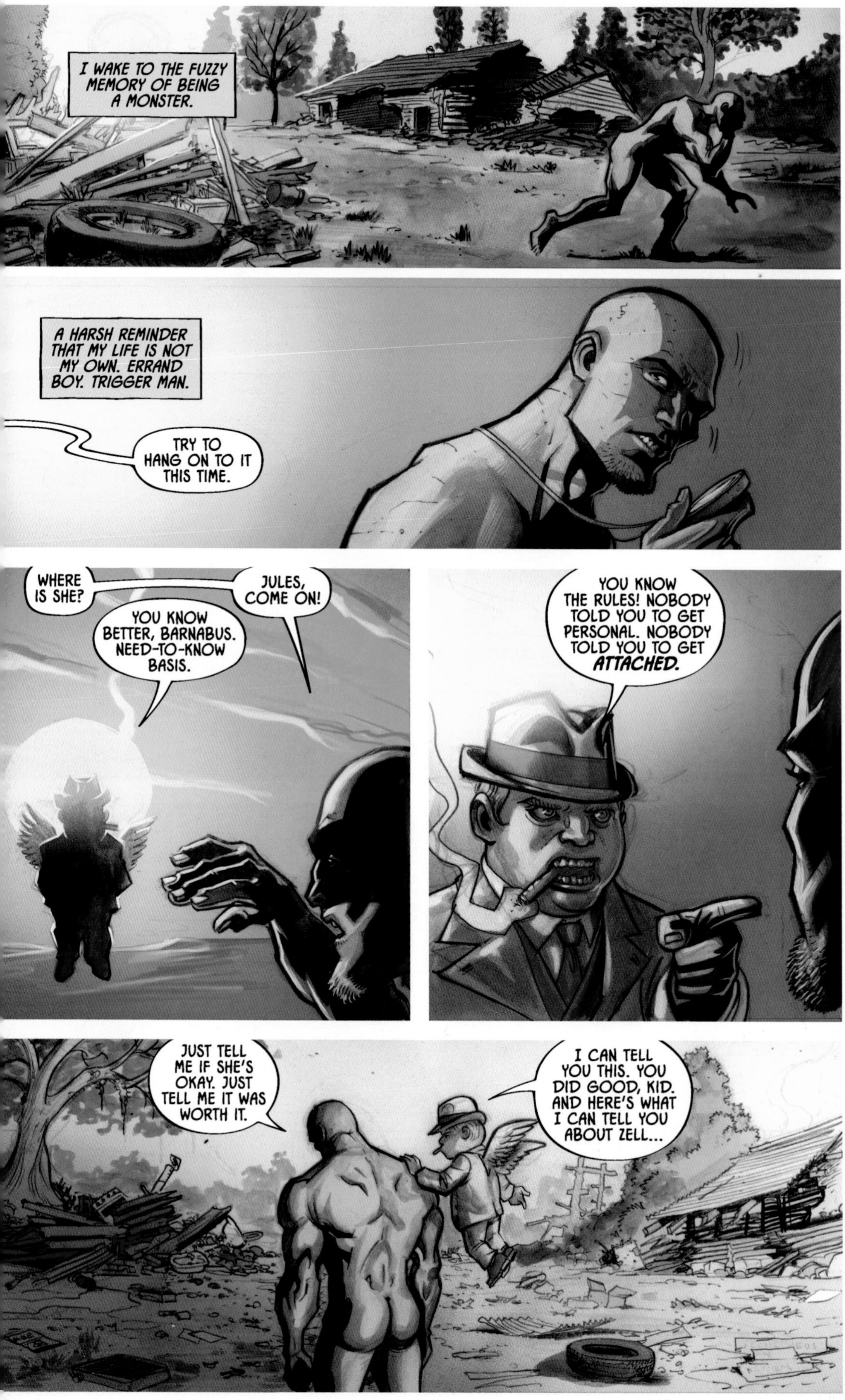
I WAKE TO THE FUZZY MEMORY OF BEING A MONSTER.
A HARSH REMINDER THAT MY LIFE IS NOT MY OWN. ERRAND BOY. TRIGGER MAN.
TRY TO HANG ON TO IT THIS TIME.
WHERE IS SHE?
JULES, COME ON!
YOU KNOW BETTER, BARNABUS. NEED-TO-KNOW BASIS.
YOU KNOW THE RULES! NOBODY TOLD YOU TO GET PERSONAL. NOBODY TOLD YOU TO GET ATTACHED.
JUST TELL ME IF SHE'S OKAY. JUST TELL ME IT WAS WORTH IT.
I CAN TELL YOU THIS. YOU DID GOOD, KID. AND HERE'S WHAT I CAN TELL YOU ABOUT ZELL...

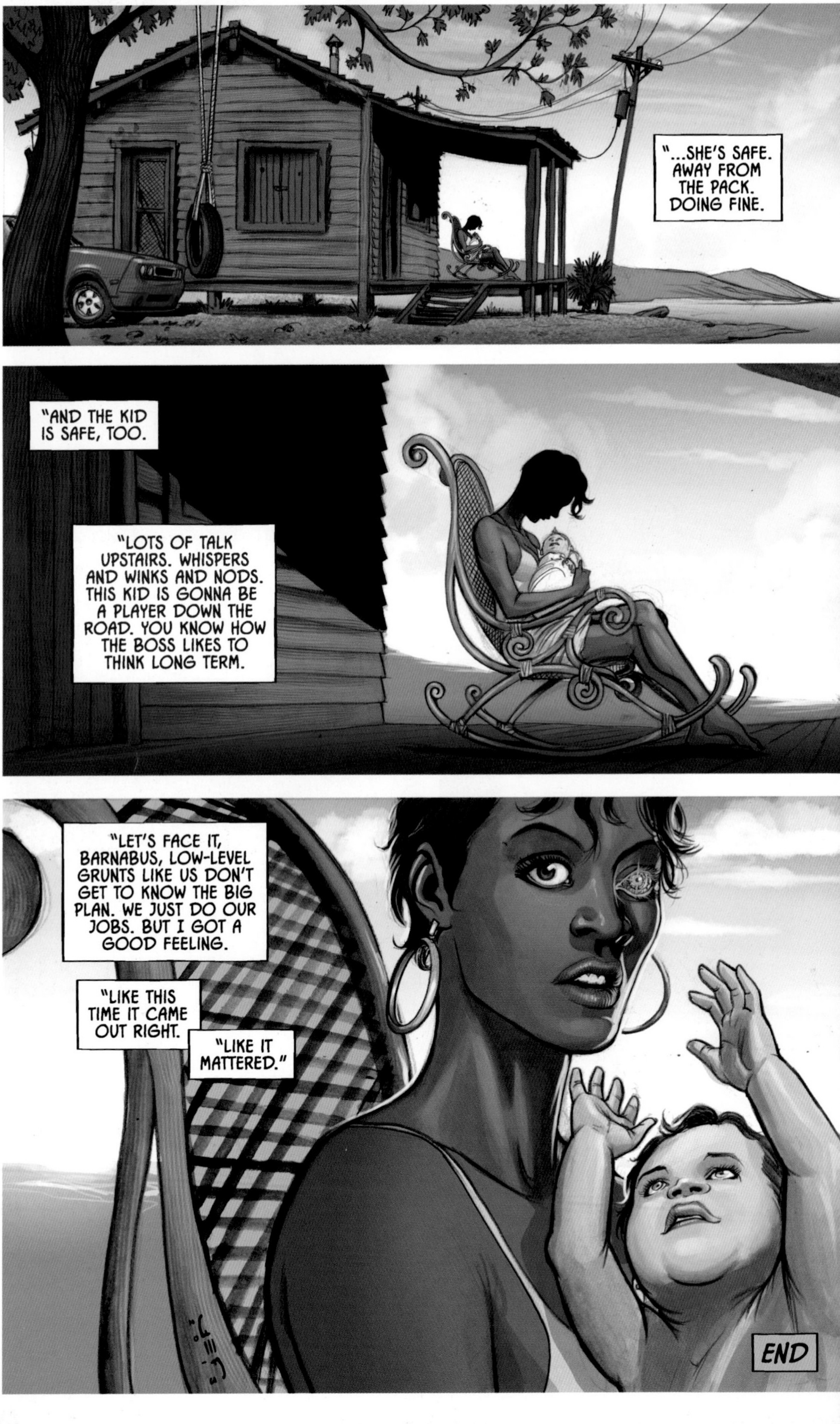
"...SHE'S SAFE. AWAY FROM THE PACK. DOING FINE.
"AND THE KID IS SAFE, TOO.
"LOTS OF TALK UPSTAIRS. WHISPERS AND WINKS AND NODS. THIS KID IS GONNA BE A PLAYER DOWN THE ROAD. YOU KNOW HOW THE BOSS LIKES TO THINK LONG TERM.
"LET'S FACE IT, BARNABUS, LOW-LEVEL GRUNTS LIKE US DON'T GET TO KNOW THE BIG PLAN. WE JUST DO OUR JOBS. BUT I GOT A GOOD FEELING.
"LIKE THIS TIME IT CAME OUT RIGHT.
"LIKE IT MATTERED."
END

SKETCHBOOK
NOTES BY JUAN FERREYRA

When I came onboard the *Kiss Me, Satan!* roller coaster (it was called *Witch Hunt* at the time), the main character, Barnabus, was already designed, so there is not much to say there, but I was able to design all the rest of the characters.

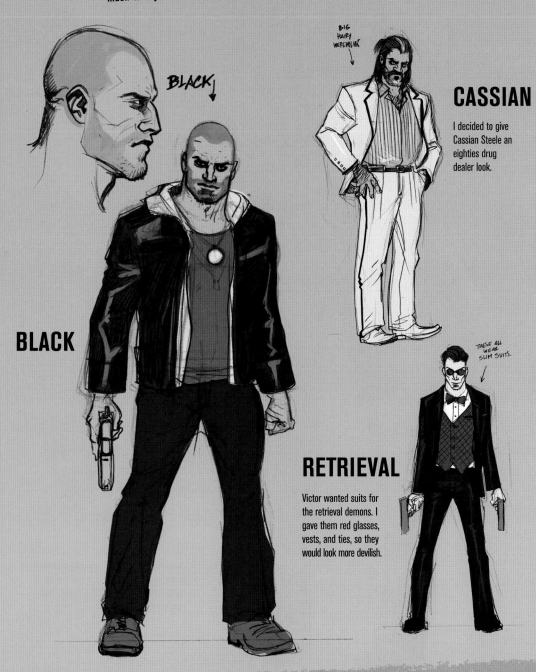

BLACK

BIG HAIRY WEREWOLF

CASSIAN

I decided to give Cassian Steele an eighties drug dealer look.

BLACK

THESE ALL WEAR SLIM SUITS.

RETRIEVAL

Victor wanted suits for the retrieval demons. I gave them red glasses, vests, and ties, so they would look more devilish.

DAX

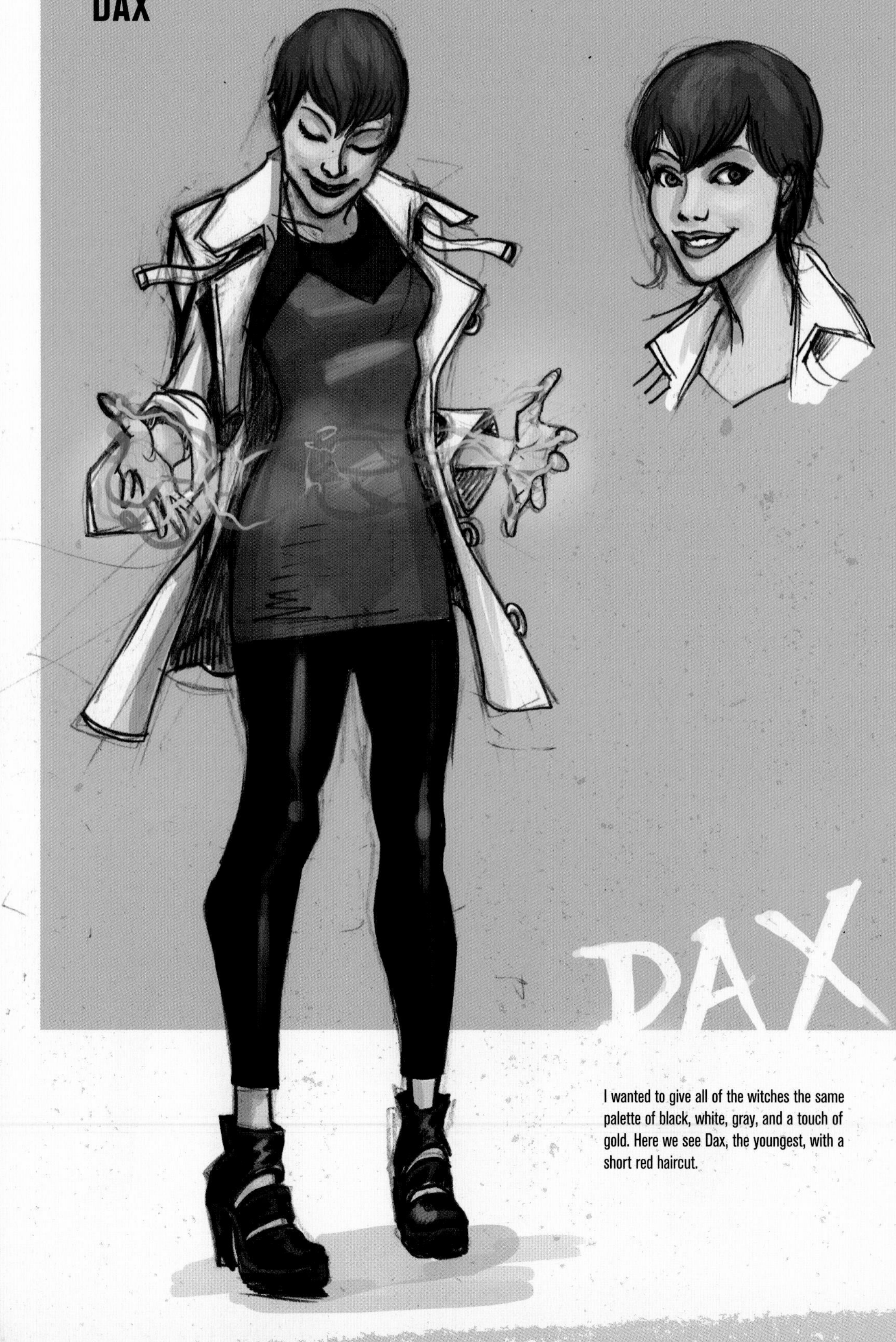
DAX

I wanted to give all of the witches the same palette of black, white, gray, and a touch of gold. Here we see Dax, the youngest, with a short red haircut.

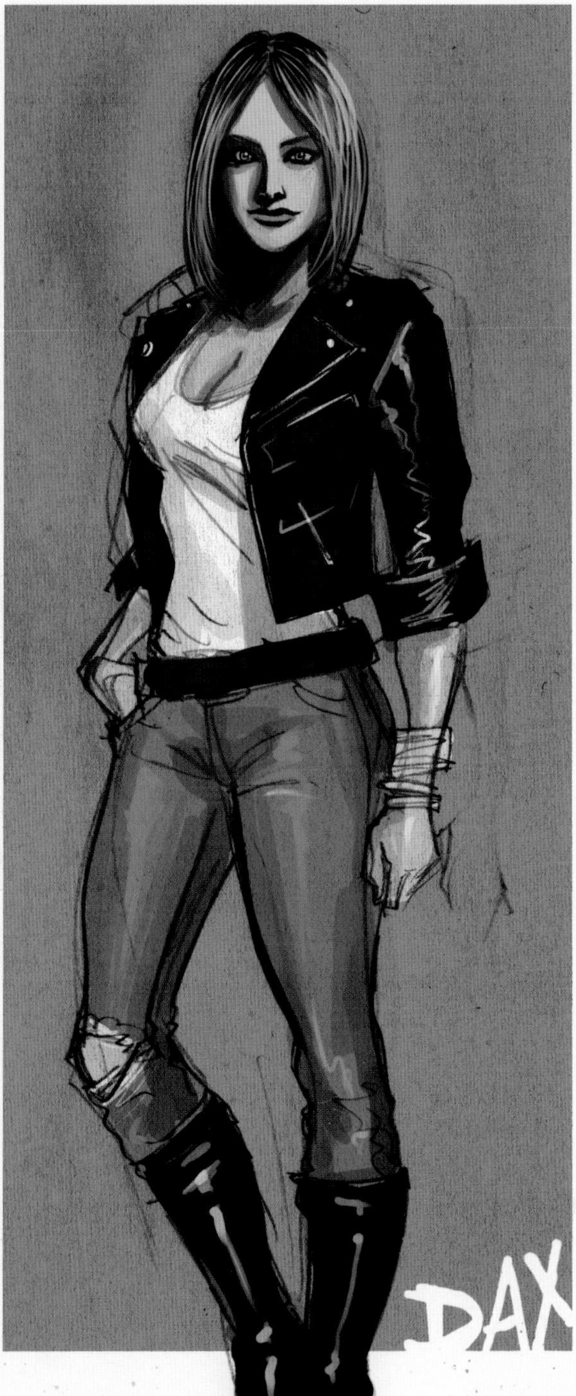
DAX

We can see the original Dax here, and she kinda sucked.

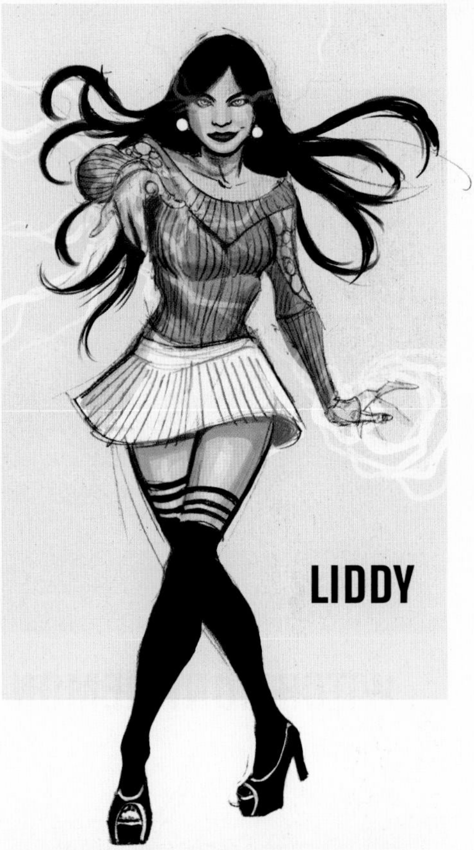
LIDDY

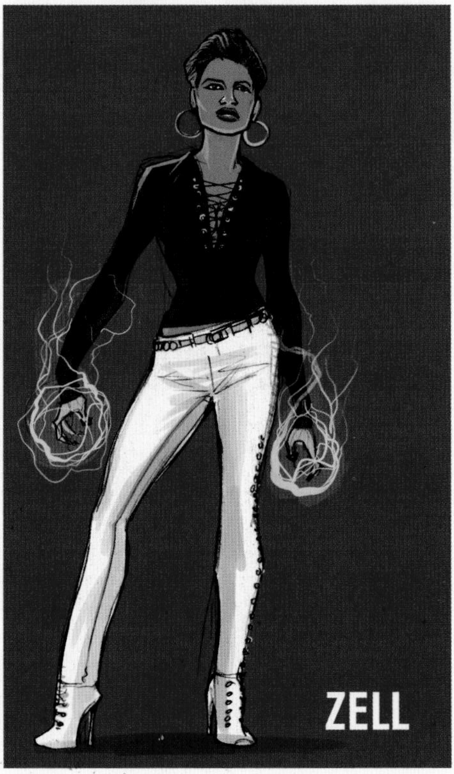
ZELL

Liddy and Zell have different haircuts than Dax, and they all have their own distinctive clothing styles.

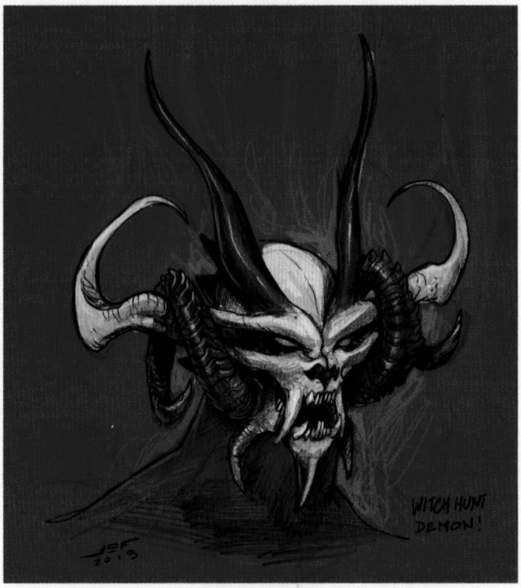
WITCH HUNT
DEMON!

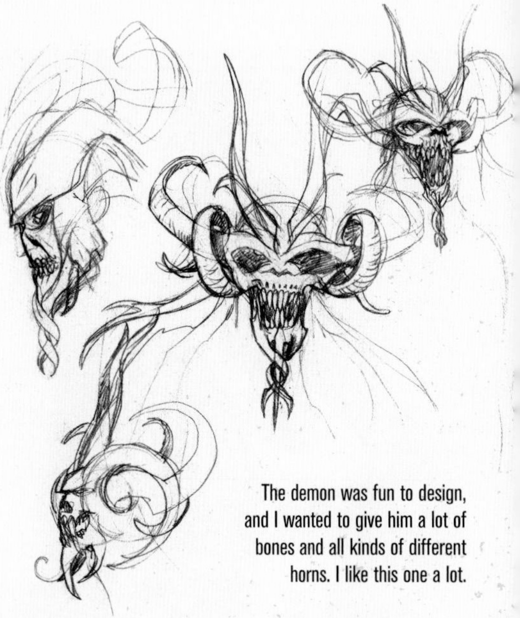

The demon was fun to design, and I wanted to give him a lot of bones and all kinds of different horns. I like this one a lot.

WITCH HUNT DEMON

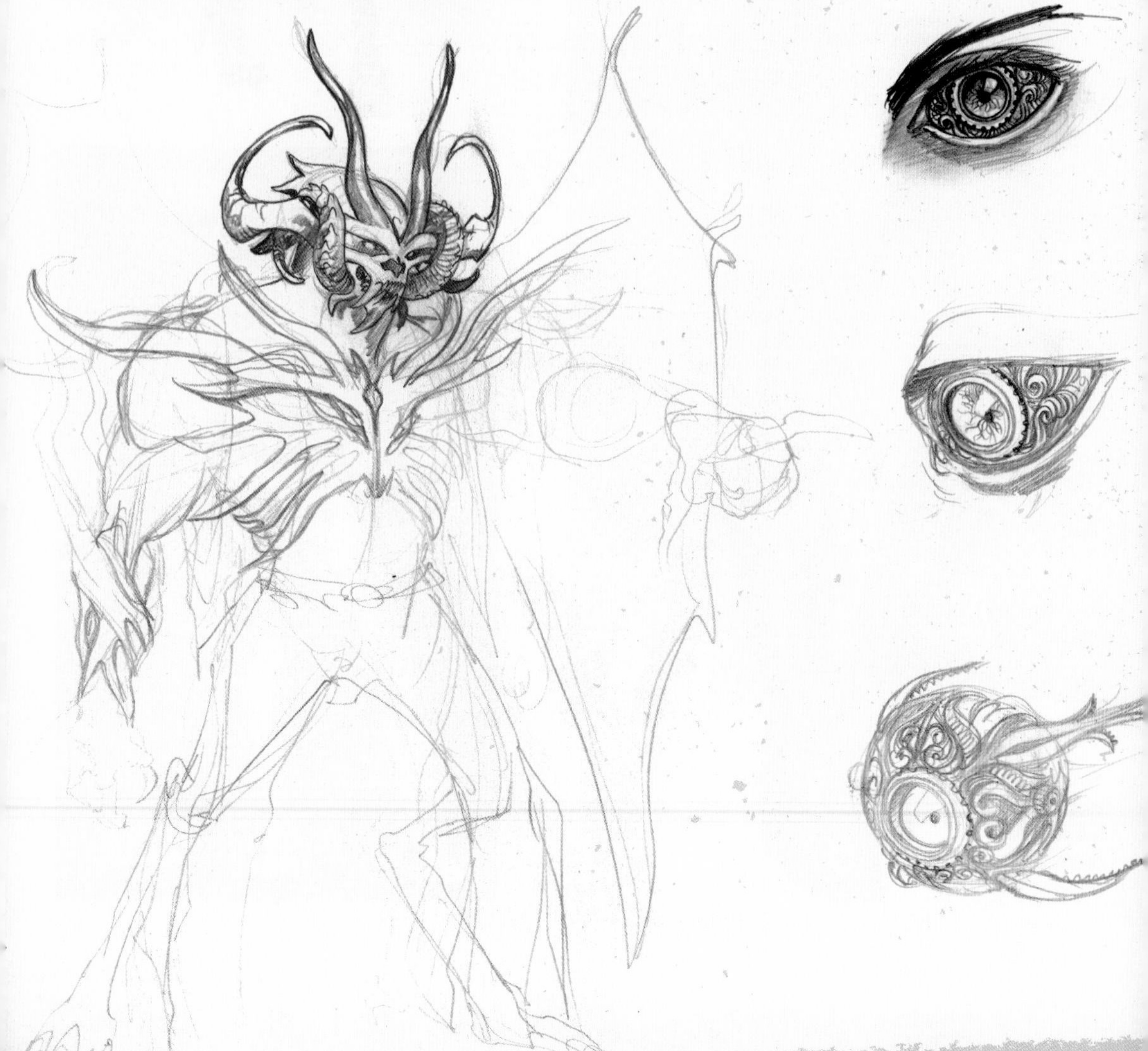

The Bone Wrangler was all Victor!

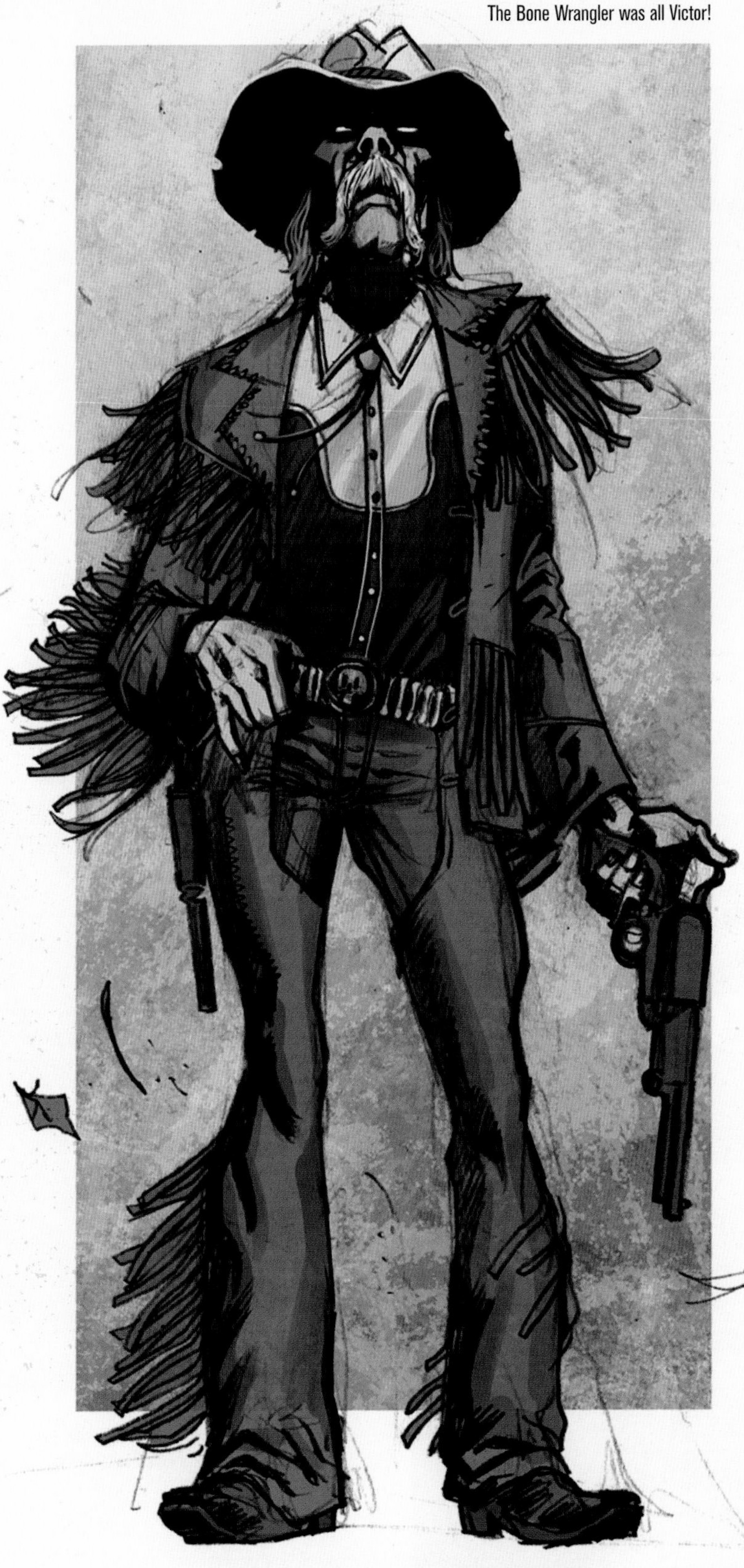

THE BONE WRANGLER

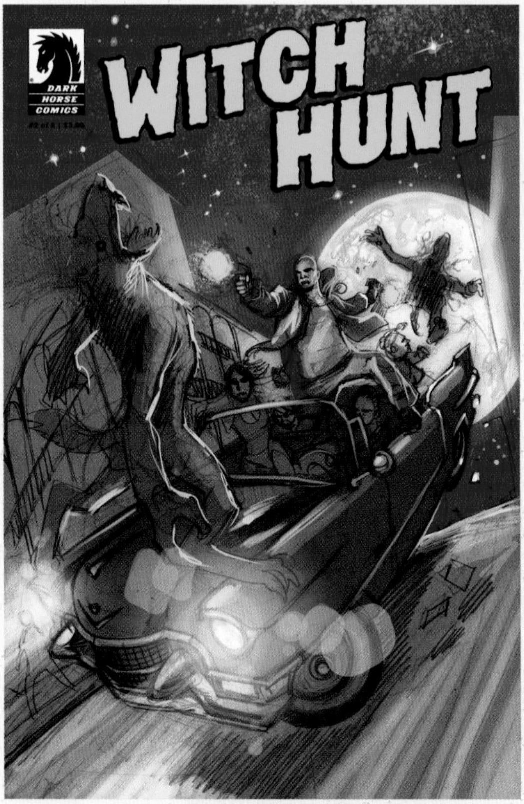
DARK HORSE COMICS
WITCH HUNT

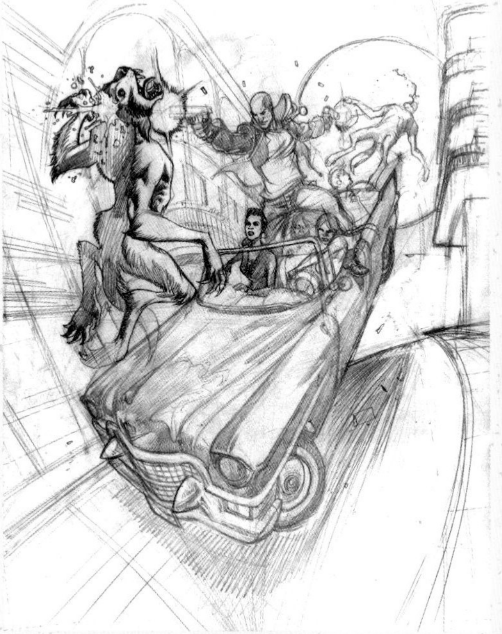

Some cover sketches and the pencils to the final cover I did. I liked the cover sketch of the reflection of the characters on the werewolf eye.

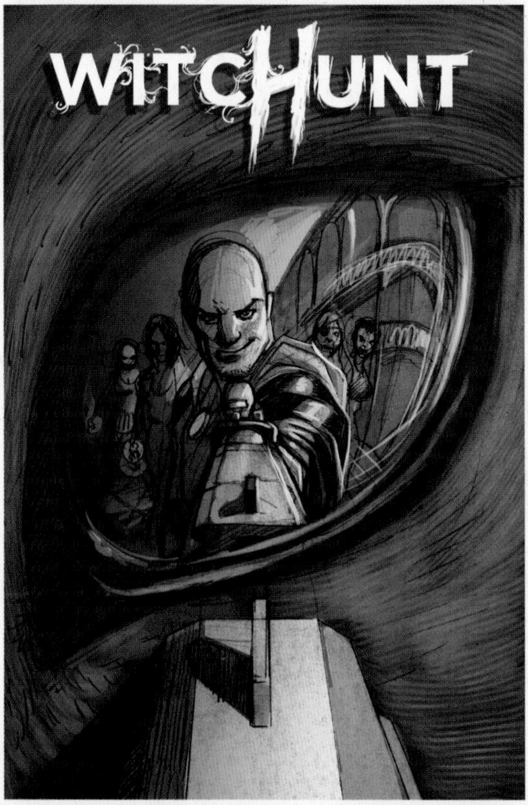
WITCHUNT

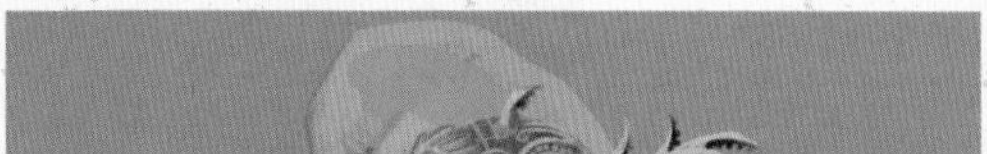

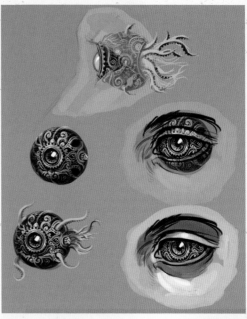

Designing the Eye of Fates was also really fun. I wanted a steampunk-meets-Cthulhu look.

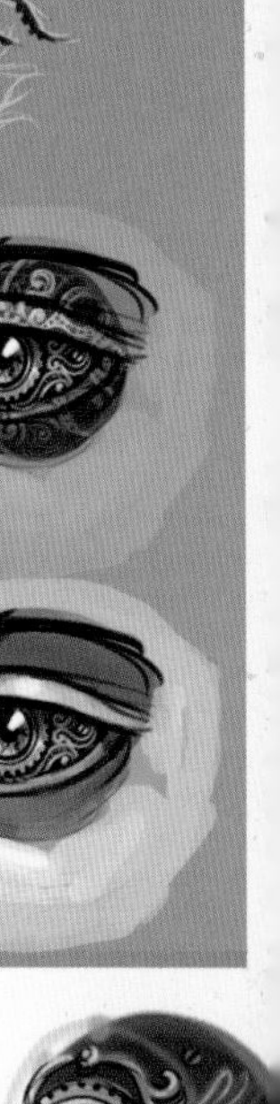

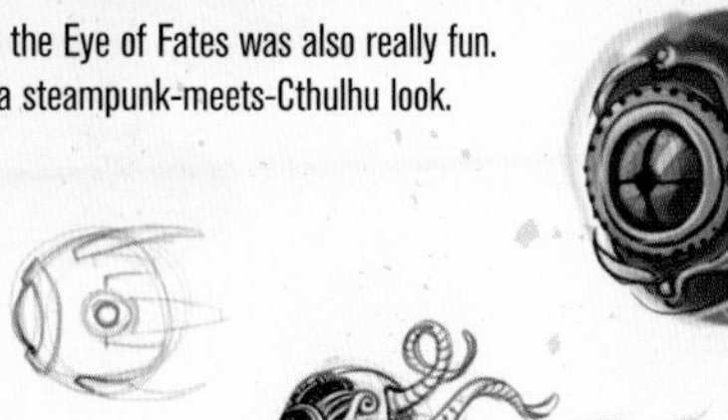

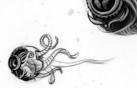

The inks to my variant cover for #1.

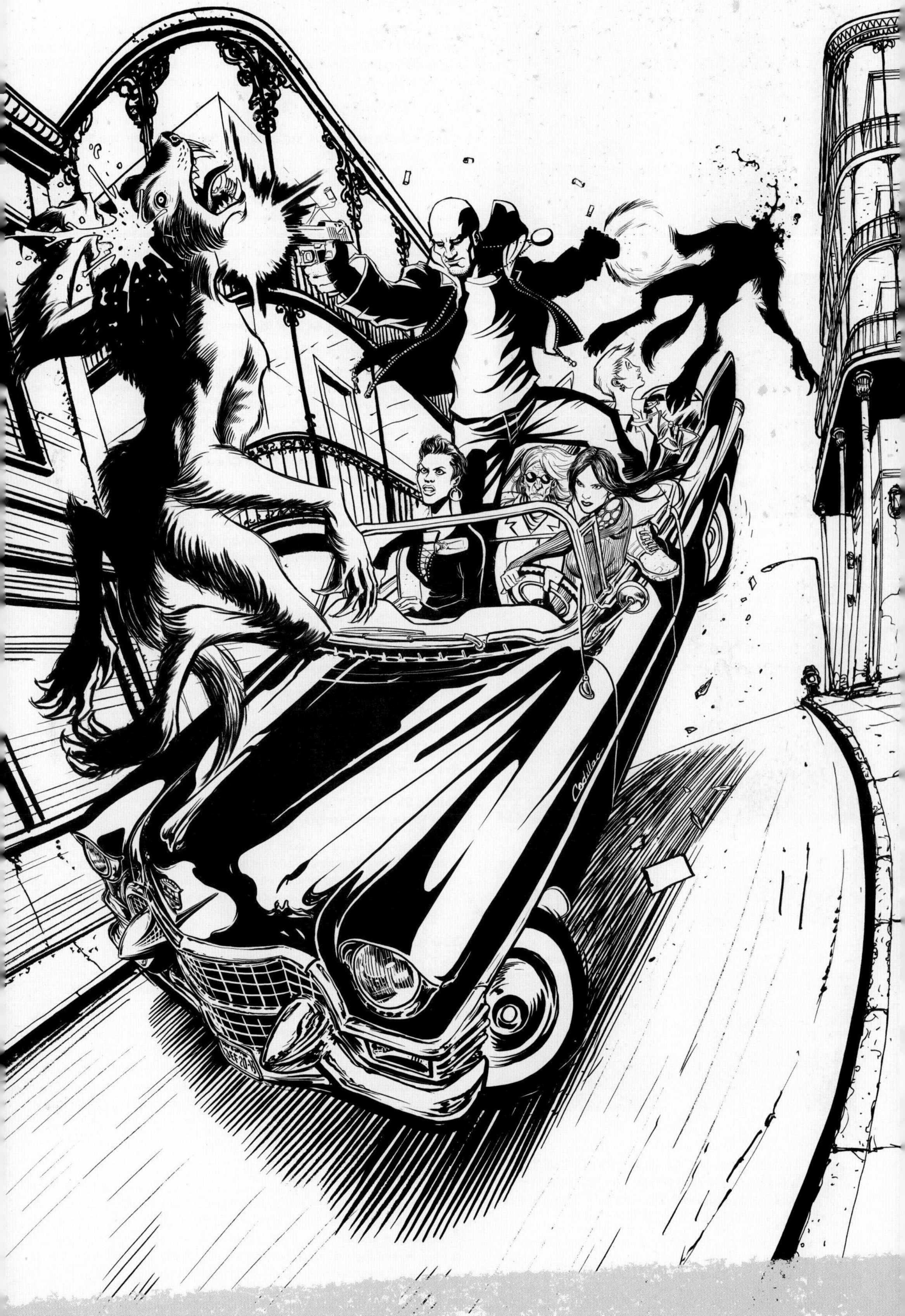
Cadillac

More works from VICTOR GISCHLER and JUAN FERREYRA

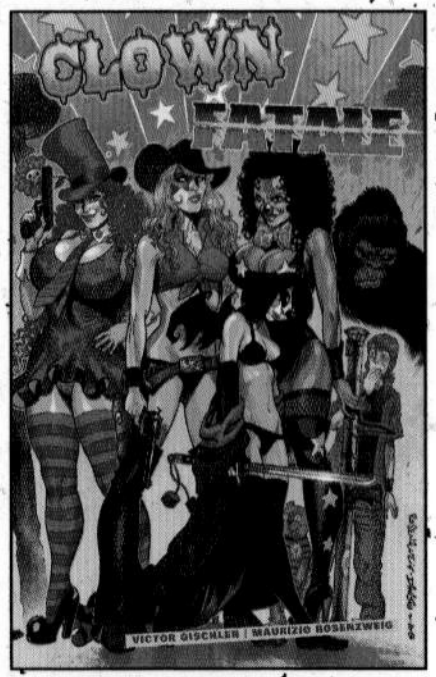
CLOWN FATALE
VICTOR GISCHLER | MAURIZIO ROSENZWEIG

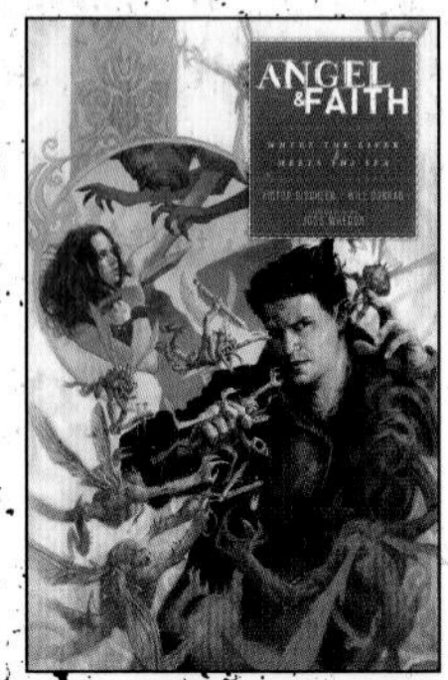
ANGEL & FAITH

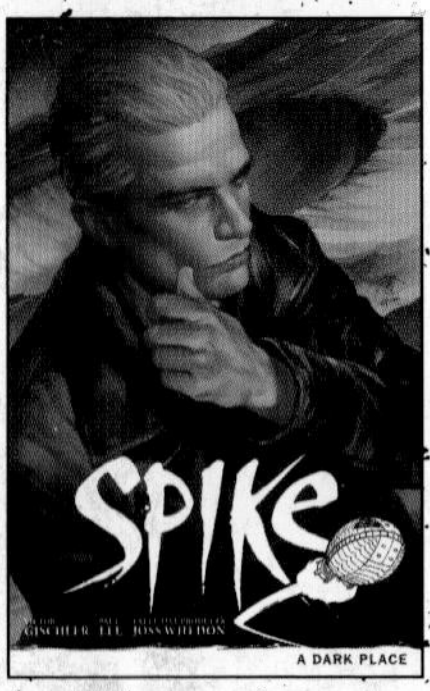
SPIKE
A DARK PLACE

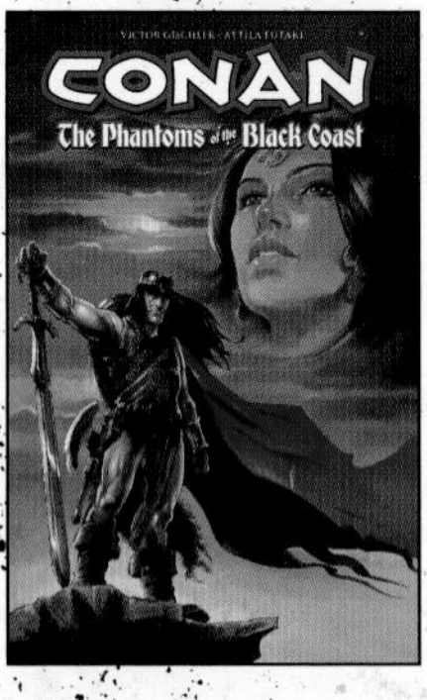
CONAN
The Phantoms of the Black Coast

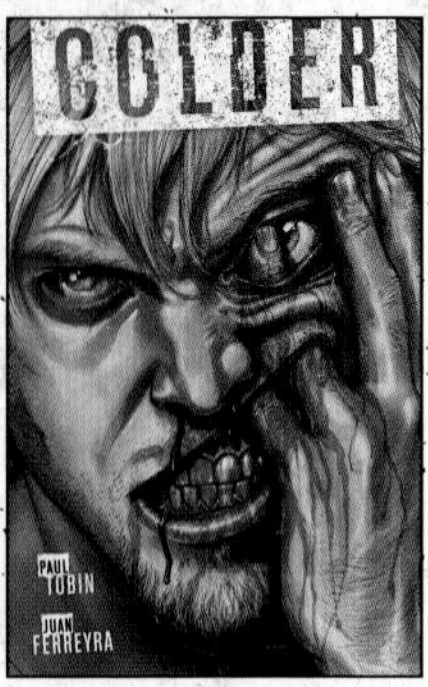
COLDER
PAUL TOBIN
JUAN FERREYRA

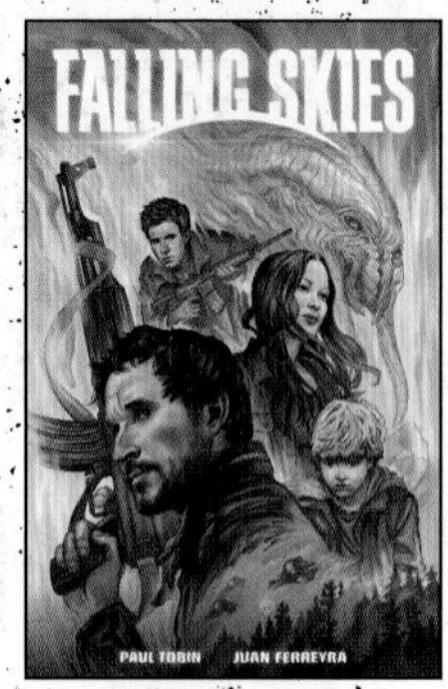
FALLING SKIES
PAUL TOBIN JUAN FERREYRA

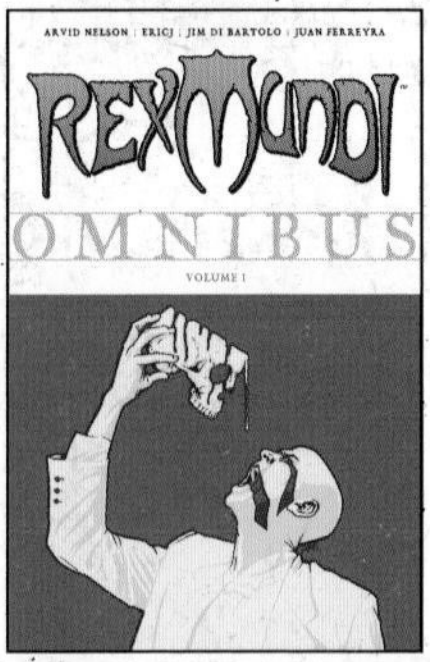
ARVID NELSON | ERICJ | JIM DI BARTOLO | JUAN FERREYRA
REX MUNDI
OMNIBUS
VOLUME 1

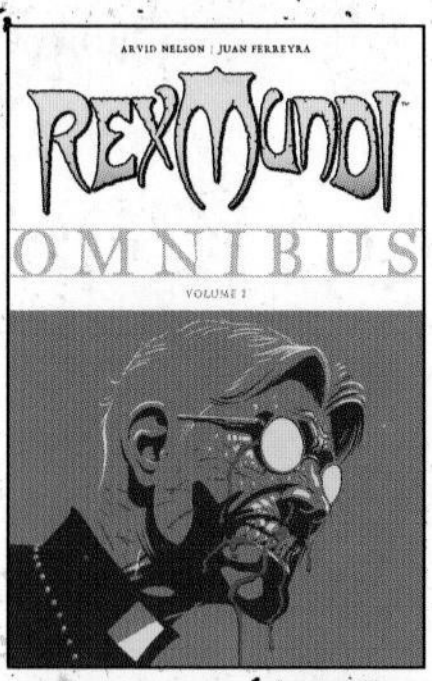
ARVID NELSON | JUAN FERREYRA
REX MUNDI
OMNIBUS
VOLUME 2

Clown Fatale TPB
Victor Gischler, Maurizio Rosenzweig

When four down-on-their-luck, sexy clowns are mistaken for contract killers, the pandemonium begins! To prove themselves in the high-profile world of contract killing and big bucks, the girls are going to need to paint their faces and head to war—with the real killers. Can the femmes fatales stand toe to toe?

$17.99 • ISBN 978-1-61655-434-7

Angel & Faith Season 10 Vol. 1: Where the River Meets the Sea TPB
Victor Gischler, Will Conrad

Angel's work is never done. Last time he averted an apocalypse, part of London turned into a chaotic stew of supernatural forces. Who better to watch over it than Angel himself? Or so he thinks—until he finds himself going down a really wrong road . . . Meanwhile, Faith begins a new chapter in her life—slaying the undead with Buffy, and then going corporate when a juicy offer tempts her . . .

$18.99 • ISBN 978-1-61655-503-0

Spike: A Dark Place TPB
Victor Gischler, Paul Lee, Cliff Richards

Fresh from his latest attempt to get Buffy to act on her feelings for him, Spike has fled to the dark side of the moon. His trip leads him to a group of dangerous demons and a rude awakening from his reverie, which in turn leads him on an unexpected adventure to . . . Sunnydale!

$17.99 • ISBN 978-1-61655-109-4

Conan: The Phantoms of the Black Coast TPB
Victor Gischler, Attila Futaki

King Conan is haunted by the ghost of his first—and some say greatest—love. If he is to ever know peace again, he must put her spirit to rest. Who is the mysterious sorceress Conan enlists to aid him in his quest, even as she secretly plots against him? And can the barbarian survive the danger-filled journey across the never-ending ocean, back to the forbidding temple on the coast, where his lost love met her end?

$19.99 • ISBN 978-1-61655-244-2

Colder TPB
Paul Tobin, Juan Ferreyra

Declan Thomas, an ex-inmate of an insane asylum that was destroyed in a fire, has the strange ability to step inside a person's madness—and sometimes cure it. He hopes to one day cure his own, but time is running out, as a demonic predator pursues him.

$17.99 • ISBN 978-1-61655-136-0

Falling Skies TPB
Paul Tobin, Juan Ferreyra

In the heart of Boston, following the devastating events of an alien invasion, history professor Tom Mason and his sons meet up with the Second Mass, a militia group determined to wipe out the aliens. But with the militia's supplies running low, Tom must locate an old friend to equip him and his team in order to ensure the survival of the human race!

$9.99 • ISBN 978-1-59582-737-1

Rex Mundi Omnibus Vol. 1 TPB
Arvid Nelson, Juan Ferreyra, EricJ, Jim Di Bartolo, Brian Churilla

Paris, 1933. Europe is still in the grip of feudalism, sorcerers stalk the streets at night, and secret societies vie for power. When a medieval scroll disappears from a Paris church, Dr. Julien Saunière begins uncovering a series of horrific ritual murders connected to the Catholic Church. His investigation turns into a one-man quest to uncover the deepest secrets of Christianity, a trail of conspiracy that extends all the way to the walls of Jerusalem during the First Crusade.

$24.99 • ISBN 978-1-59582-963-4

Rex Mundi Omnibus Vol. 2 TPB
Arvid Nelson, Juan Ferreyra

Dr. Julien Saunière's quest to catch his friend's murderer concludes with the discovery of a secret society dedicated to protecting the mystery of the Holy Grail. Now in pursuit of the Grail, Julien has been betrayed by his lover and hunted by the Inquisition, and witnessed slaughters and miracles in a wild mountain valley owned by the power-mad Duke of Lorraine.

$24.99 • ISBN 978-1-61655-068-4

DARK HORSE BOOKS

AVAILABLE AT YOUR LOCAL COMICS SHOP OR BOOKSTORE!
To find a comics shop in your area, call 1-888-266-4226.
For more information or to order direct visit DarkHorse.com or call 1-800-862-0052 Mon.-Fri. 9 AM to 5 PM